Forth Programmer's Handbook

Edward K. Conklin
Elizabeth D. Rather
and the technical staff of FORTH, Inc.

FORTH, Inc.

Software products and services since 1973
www.forth.com

First edition, September 1997
Second edition, August 1998
Third edition, August 2007
Latest revision, October 2010

ISBN 1-4196-7549-4

FORTH, Inc.
Los Angeles, California
www.forth.com

Contents

List of Figures

List of Tables

Preface to the Third Edition

It's hard to believe it's been nearly ten years since the release of the Second Edition of this book. I find that, although the language itself has changed relatively little, there have been vast improvements in Forth programming tools and in the collective experience of Forth programmers.

The advent of ANS Forth in 1994 freed Forth from supporting certain implementation strategies and from assumptions about cell size: its predecessor, FORTH-83, mandated an indirect-threaded implementation (see Section 1.1.7) with a 16-bit cell size. Following are just a few of the innovations that have followed:

- By the mid-1990s the majority of implementations were for 32-bit platforms and today several 64-bit Forths are available, at Sun Microsystems and other places.
- Compiler technology has vastly improved, with several sophisticated optimizing compilers available that deliver extremely efficient code, in both size and performance.
- Programming tools have improved, further enhancing the interactive and incremental programming strategy that has been a hallmark of Forth since the beginning. In particular, Windows-based development systems take full advantage of the features of this popular OS to provide programmer convenience as well as access to the vast libraries of DLLs and other facilities found on PCs.
- Cross-compilers have flourished, and now support most popular microprocessors and microcontrollers. Modern Forth cross-compilers use their powerful PC hosts to support compilers and optimization strategies that rival more conventional C/C++ tool chains, while delivering almost the same level of interactive support as resident Forths.
- OOP extensions have been developed for several popular Forth implementations. Unfortunately, these have not been standardized and vary significantly, so we have not included them here (see the documentation for virtually any popular Forth system). However, the widespread use of OOP techniques and terminology has enabled us to clarify the discussion of Forth defining words considerably.

I want to particularly acknowledge Leon Wagner and Ron Oliver for valuable input on this book, and Rick Van Norman, the "father" of SwiftForth which is the basis of most of the current systems at FORTH, Inc. Also particular thanks to a dedicated set of reviewers who have offered many valuable comments and suggestions on drafts of this book: Fred Carter, David Haas, Byron Jeff, Stan Katz, Simon Matthews, Morten Steien, Daniel Wright, and Mike Zdancewicz. Finally, many thanks to Marlin Ouverson, our longtime editor and webmaster, who contributed the cover of this as well as the previous edition, not to mention help with many other aspects.

Cheers,

Elizabeth D. Rather

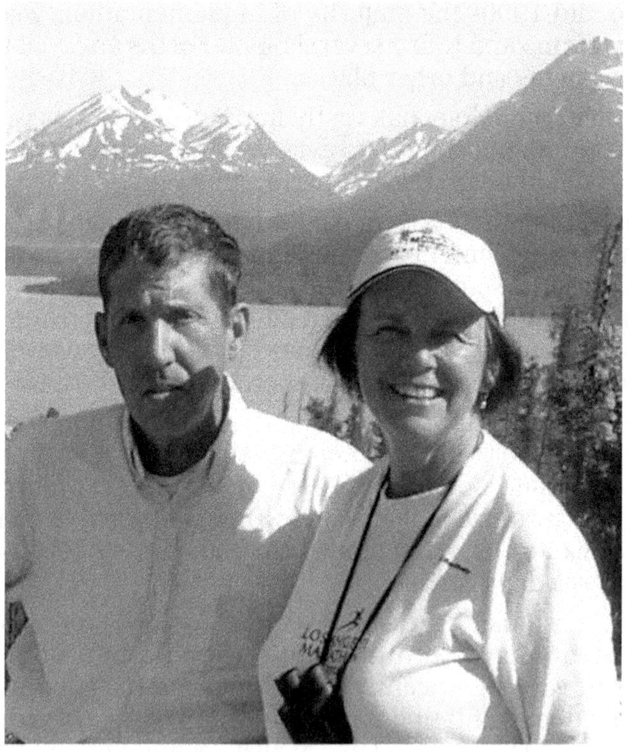

Authors Edward K. Conklin and Elizabeth D. Rather (2007)

Welcome!

About the Forth Programming Language

The Forth programming language was originally developed in the early 1970s by Charles H. Moore at the National Radio Astronomy Observatory. Forth was used at several NRAO installations for controlling radio telescopes and associated scientific instruments, as well as for high-speed data acquisition and graphical analysis.

Forth's popularity expanded considerably in the 1980s, with the advent of PCs and widespread use of microprocessors and microcontrollers in embedded systems. Early implementations were very simple, befitting the limited nature of the platforms on which they ran. As time passed, however, Forth technology advanced dramatically, as did implementations of other languages. An ANSI Standard for Forth was passed in 1994. Many modern Forths feature sophisticated optimizing compilers, fast multitasking executives, and powerful development systems.

Today Forth is used worldwide by people seeking maximum flexibility and efficiency in a wide variety of applications. Versions are available for all popular operating systems, as well as for most microcontrollers used in embedded applications. Befitting its origins, Forth continues to be widely used in scientific, industrial control, and data acquisition systems. One of the most widespread Forth applications is Open Firmware, a standardized boot firmware system originally developed at Sun Microsystems and used in many workstations and servers today.

About This Book

The *Forth Programmer's Handbook* provides a detailed technical reference for programmers and engineers developing software using Standard Forth *(ANSI X3.215:1994*, the standard adopted in 1994 and reaffirmed in 1999*;* equivalent to *ISO/IEC 15145:1997*) provided by FORTH, Inc. or other vendors. It features Standard Forth and many extensions commonly in use; some information in this book is taken directly from the official standard document.

This book assumes the reader has general knowledge of programming principles and practices, and general familiarity with computer hardware and software systems.

How to Use This Book

Each section of this book documents a single subject, and many are followed by a glossary containing pertinent Forth words and their descriptions. Each Forth word is shown with its stack effects and with the Standard Forth word list in which it appears, if any. Some words are included which are not part of Standard Forth; these are indicated by the phrase "Common usage." Sections in this book often conclude with references to related topics or other resources.

Appendix D provides an index of each Forth word that appears in these glossaries, including its stack effect, the page on which its description may be found, and the Standard Forth word list, if any, in which it appears.

Typographic Conventions

In this manual, typefaces are used as follows:

- This typeface is used for text, with *italic* used for some symbolic notation and for the first appearance of *new terms*;
- Executable Forth commands and source code are shown in a monospaced bold type, e.g., **`PAD 20 ACCEPT`**.
- Parameters that are described indirectly instead of explicitly are shown in distinctive plain type and inside brackets, e.g., `<addr>` `<len>` **`ACCEPT`**. When these parameters are discussed in text, they usually are shown in *italic*.
- Non-executable text strings such as error messages are shown in plain type without brackets, e.g., **`Page Fault`**.

Reference Materials

The following reference materials may be of use to the reader of this manual.

- *Forth Application Techniques* (introductory tutorial).
- American National Standard for Information Systems Programming Languages — Forth (ANSI X3.215:1994)
- *ISO/IEC 15145:1997 Information technology — Programming languages — Forth* (the content of this standard is identical to ANSI X3.215:1994)
- Additional publications are listed in Appendix A: "Bibliography" on page 229, with other sources of information about Forth.

How to Proceed

If you are not already familiar with Forth, we encourage you to begin by reading the *Introduction* and *Forth Fundamentals* chapters carefully, writing simple programs using an ANS Forth system of your choice. Use this book for technical details about your system and to assist you as you move on to more ambitious programming challenges.

Good luck!

1. Introduction

This *Forth Programmer's Handbook* provides a reference source for the most common features of the integrated software development systems based on the Forth programming language. We assume at least an elementary knowledge of programming, including any high-level language or assembler. If you are new to Forth, we encourage you to begin by reading *this chapter and the next* carefully, writing simple programs using an ANS Forth system of your choice.

This book is primarily intended to describe how a programmer can use Forth to solve problems. This is a rather different goal from explaining how Forth works, but it is a practical necessity for the new user of a Forth system. This manual is also organized to serve experienced programmers who need to check some point quickly.

We highly recommend that you spend time examining the Forth source code supplied with your system, along with its documentation. Forth was designed to be highly readable, and the source code offers many examples of good usage and programming practice.

This manual does not attempt to cover all Forth commands. Indeed, no book can do that—Forth is an extensible system, and no two implementations need or use identical components. What we can do is provide a detailed exposition of the most valuable and most commonly used features and facilities of the fundamental system from which your application begins.

FORTH, Inc. provides development environments for a growing number of computer systems and embedded microprocessors. Because hardware is unique for each computer, it is not feasible for this document to cover every feature of every system supported. The *Forth Programmer's Handbook* presents features common to Standard Forth and to the most common extensions found in all FORTH, Inc. systems. When discussing hardware-specific features, particularly dictionary structure, high-level object format, database management, and device drivers, an idealized model of a Forth system is used. Separate product documentation provides implementation details and descriptions of features specific to that system.

1.1 Forth Language Features

This section highlights special considerations arising from the actual implementation of a system. More detailed technical discussions of subjects covered here will be found in later sections of this book, especially Section 2. Appendix B, *Glossary & Notation* provides supplementary definitions of many of the terms used in this manual, as well as a detailed description of the notation conventions.

1.1.1 Definitions of Terms

Forth allows any kind of ASCII string (except one containing spaces) to be a valid name, and this introduces some ambiguities in references. For instance, Forth calls subroutines *words*, but *word* could also mean an addressable unit of memory. To resolve this, we use the following conventions:

- A Forth execution procedure is called a *definition*. A *word* is the name of such a definition.
- The word length of the processor is always referred to as a *cell*. This is also the size of an address and the size of a single item on Forth's stacks.
- Eight bits is called a *byte*. On a 32-bit or larger processor, a 16-bit item may be called a *16-bit cell* or *half-cell*.

A more extensive glossary of terms may be found in Appendix B.1.

1.1.2 Dictionary

The dictionary contains all the executable routines (or *words*) that make up a Forth system. *System routines* are entries predefined in the dictionary that become available when the system is booted. *Electives* are optionally compiled after booting. *User-defined words* are entries the user adds.

The basic form of the most common type of word definition is:

```
: <name>  <words to be executed> ;
```

...where **:** constructs a new definition called *name*, which is terminated by **;**. When *name* is referenced, the words in the body of the definition name will be executed. There are other kinds of words in Forth: words defined in assembler code, words that function as data objects, etc. All have dictionary entries with a similar structure and are managed by the same internal rules. The various kinds of definitions are discussed in Section 6.2.

Regardless of the kind of definition it is, each word is basically the same: an executable function with a defined behavior. This is true even of things that seem analogous to data objects in other languages and things that look like punctuation. There is no punctuation in Forth, and no syntax, just executable words.

The dictionary is the fundamental mechanism by which Forth allocates memory and performs *symbol table* operations. Because the dictionary serves so many purposes, it's important that you understand how to use it.

The dictionary is a linked list of variable-length entries, each of which is a Forth word and its definition. In most implementations, the dictionary grows toward high memory; the discussion in this section will assume it does. Each dictionary entry points to the entry that logically precedes it (see Figure 1).

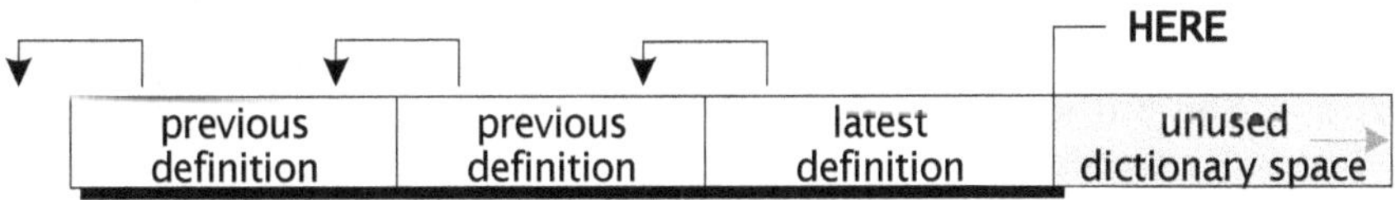

Figure 1. Dictionary entry links

Dictionary entries are not necessarily contiguous. For example, in cross-compilers used to construct programs for embedded systems, the searchable portion of the dictionary (name, link, and a pointer to the content—see Figure 2) may reside in a host computer, and the actual content may reside in a target image being constructed in the host computer's memory for later downloading or for burning into flash or PROM.

The dictionary is searched by sequentially matching names in source text against names compiled in the dictionary. On some systems, the search is speeded by providing more than one chain of definitions, with entries linked in logical sequences that do not necessarily reflect their physical locations. The Forth *text interpreter* selects one of these chains to search; the selection mechanism is implementation dependent and may include two or more chains in a programmer-controlled order (see Section 6.6). The search follows the selected chain until a match is found or the end of the chain is reached. Because the latest definition will be found first, this organization permits words to be redefined, a technique that is frequently useful.

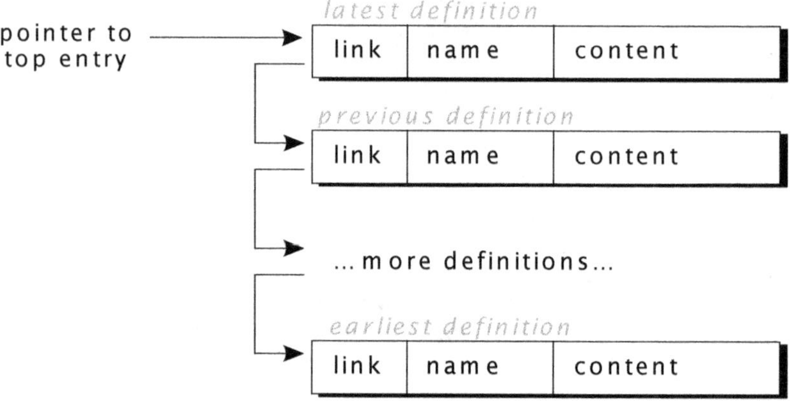

Figure 2. Logical structure of the Forth dictionary

The Standard Forth term for one of these chains is *word list.* A word list is a subset of the dictionary containing words for some special purpose. Several word lists usually are present in a system and they are normally available to all users on a re-entrant basis.

The essential structure of dictionary entries is the same for all words and is diagrammed in Figure 2. The *link cell* contains the location of the preceding entry. Searches start at the recent end of the dictionary and work backwards to the older end. By this process, the most recent definition of a word is always found. In a developed application, where the user is dealing with the highest level of the program, this process optimizes search time.

The *name field* in a dictionary entry contains the count of characters in the full name, followed by some number of characters in the name. The count (and, thus, the longest allowable name length) usually is limited to 31 characters. On most systems, any characters other than space, backspace (BS or DEL), and carriage return (CR) can be used as part of a name field. However, Standard Forth advises that you can only depend on being able to use displayable graphic characters.

Some systems are case sensitive and others are not; see your product documentation for details. To avoid problems and to maximize the transportability of code, the names of the words provided in a standard system are defined in upper-case letters and should always be referred to in upper-case letters when using them in subsequent definitions. When defining and using new names, it is important to be consistent: always refer to a name using exactly the same case(s) in which it was defined. Also, in systems that are case sensitive, avoid creating names that differ *only* in their use of case; such code will not be transportable to a case-insensitive system.

Although fields in a dictionary entry are arranged differently in each implementation to optimize dictionary searches, Figure 3 shows a general model with the fields grouped into a *head* and a *body*. The head contains features that enable a definition to be found in the dictionary, while the body contains information that makes it executable or enables it to carry data.

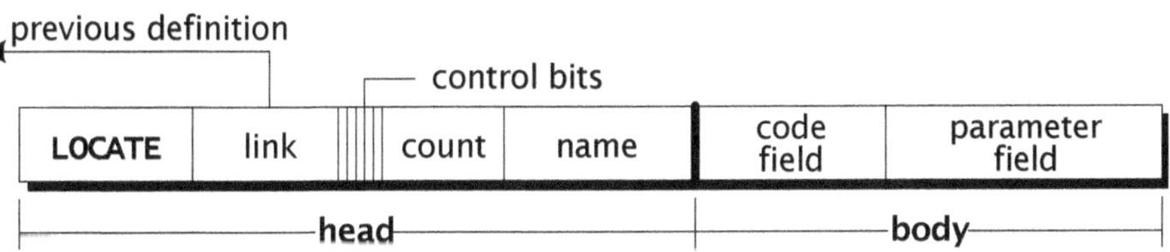

Figure 3. Structural details of a typical dictionary entry

The head will always include a *link field* and a *name field.* There may also be a *locate field* containing information about where this word is defined in source code. In addition, there are usually several *control bits*[1] to control the type and use of the definition. Because the longest name field in some implementations has 31 characters, thus requiring only five bits to express its count, the control bits are often found in the byte containing the count.

The most important control bit is the *precedence bit.* A word whose precedence bit is set executes at compile time. The precedence bit is

1. Not all implementations use control bits for these purposes; here we describe a common implementation strategy.

set by the word **IMMEDIATE**. The precedence bit is used for a few special words, such as compiler directives, but it is zero for most words.

Another common control bit is the *smudge bit.* A word whose smudge bit is set is invisible to a dictionary search. This bit is set by the compiler when starting to compile a high-level **:** (colon) definition, to prevent unintentional recursive references. It is reset by the word **;** (semicolon) that ends the definition.

The body will usually include a *code field.* The code field will contain either a pointer to the run-time code to be executed when this definition is invoked, or in some implementations the code itself. There is often a *parameter field* of variable length, containing references to data needed when this definition executes. Data objects such as variables keep their data in their parameter fields.

On cross-compilers used for developing programs for embedded systems, the head may exist only on the host, with a pointer to the actual executable portion being constructed in the target image. The *data space* portion of the body need not be contiguous with the code field; on Harvard architecture parts, for example, *code space* may be in ROM or flash, and data space in RAM.

References

Code field addresses, Section 6.2.2
Creating dictionary entries, Section 6.2.1
Word lists, Section 6.6

1.1.3 Data Stack

Every Forth system contains at least one *data stack.* In a multitasked system, each task may have its own data stack. The stack is a cell-wide, push-down LIFO *(last-in, first-out)* list; its purpose is to contain numeric operands for Forth commands. Commands commonly expect their input parameters on this stack and leave their output results there. The stack's size is indefinite. Usually it is located at a relatively high memory address and grows downward towards areas allocated for other purposes; see your product documentation for your system's particular layout. The data stack rarely grows deeper than just a few entries in a well-written application.

When numbers are *pushed* onto or *popped* off the stack, the remaining numbers are not moved. Instead, a pointer is adjusted to indicate the last used cell in a static memory array. On most implementations, the top-of-stack pointer is kept in a register.

Stacks typically extend toward low memory for reasons of implementation efficiency, but this is by no means required or universally true. On implementations in which the stack grows toward low memory, a push operation involves decrementing the stack pointer, while a pop involves incrementing it.

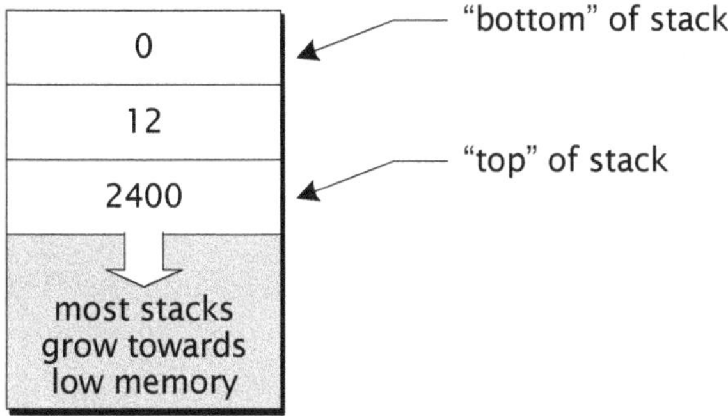

Figure 4. Items on the data stack

A number encountered by the text interpreter will be converted to binary and pushed onto the stack. Forth *data objects* (such as those defined by **VARIABLE** and **CONSTANT**) push their addresses or values onto the stack. Thus, the stack provides a medium of communication not only between routines but between a person and the computer. You may, for example, place numbers or addresses on the stack and then type words which act on them to produce a desired result. For example, typing:

```
12 2400 * 45 / .
```

...(a) pushes the number 12 on the stack; (b) pushes 2400 above it (see Figure 4); (c) executes the multiply routine ***** which replaces both numbers by their product; (d) pushes 45 on the stack; (e) executes the divide routine **/** which replaces the product and the 45 withs the quotient; and (f) executes the output routine **.** ("dot"), which removes and displays the top stack item (the quotient). All numbers put on the stack have been removed, leaving the stack as it was before typing 12.

The standard Forth dictionary provides words for simple manipulation of single- and double-length operands on the stack: **SWAP**, **DUP**, **DROP**, **2SWAP**, etc. (covered in detail in Section 2.1).

The push-down stack simplifies the internal structure of Forth and produces naturally re-entrant routines. Passing parameters via the stack means fewer variables must be named, reducing the amount of memory required for named variables (as well as reducing the programmer's associated housekeeping).

A pointer to the top (i.e., the latest entry) of the user's stack is maintained by the system. There is also a pointer to the "bottom" of the stack, so that stack-empty or underflow conditions can be detected, and to aid in clearing the stack if an abort condition is detected.

Most Forth systems check for stack underflow only after executing (or attempting to execute) a word from the *input stream* (see Figure 5). Underflows that occur in the process of execution will not be detected immediately when they occur, but only when the text interpreter is ready to parse the input stream again.

The usual result of a detected stack underflow is the message:

```
Stack empty
```

...followed by a system abort.

References

Stack manipulation, Section 2.1
System abort routines, Section 5.3
Data types in stack notation, Section B.2
Stack operations, Section 2.1

1.1.4 Return Stack

Every Forth system also has a *return stack*. In a multitasked system, each task has its own return stack. Like the data stack, the return stack is a cell-wide LIFO list. It is used for system functions, but may also be accessed directly by an application program. It commonly serves the following purposes:

- It holds return addresses for nested definitions.
- It holds loop parameters.
- It may be used by the system for other temporary purposes; consult your system documentation.

Because the return stack has multiple uses, care must be exercised to avoid conflicts when accessing it directly.

There are no commands for directly manipulating the return stack, except those for moving one or two parameters between the data stack and the return stack.

The maximum size of the return stack for each task is specified at the time the task is defined, and remains fixed during operation; a typical size is 128 cells.

References

Loading, Sections 5.5.1, C.2
Loop parameters, Section 4.5
Data stack, Section 1.1.3
Transfers between stacks, Section 2.1.3

1.1.5 Text Interpreter

The text interpreter processes the input stream, which may contain:

- the commands users type (often called the *command line*);
- source code stored on disk;
- a string whose address and length are supplied to the word **EVALUATE**.

The operator's keyboard is the default input stream source. The keyboard handler will accept characters into a text buffer called the *terminal input buffer* until a user event occurs, such as a Return or Enter keypress, function keypress, etc. Most implementations provide keyboard editing of the line before the Return or Enter keypress. When the Return or Enter keypress is detected, the text interpreter will process the text in the buffer. Interpretation from source code on disk is buffered separately in an implementation-dependent fashion.

Another name for the place text resides while the text interpreter processes it is the *parse area*, because the process involves parsing the text in the input stream looking for words separated by spaces.

The text interpreter repeats the following steps until the parse area is exhausted or an error has occurred:

1. Starting at the beginning of the parse area, skip leading spaces and extract a word from the input string using the space character (ASCII 32) as a delimiter. Set the interpreter pointer to point to the first character beyond the delimiter. If there was no delimiter (end of input buffer was reached), set the interpreter pointer to the end of the parse area, to complete the operation. If the text is coming from a text file, the interpreter will treat any non-graphic characters as "whitespace" (equivalent to a space character).
2. Search the dictionary for a definition name matching the input word (including case sensitivity, if applicable). If a matching definition is found, perform its *interpretation behavior* (if currently in interpretation mode) or *compilation behavior* (if currently in compiling mode). Then check for stack underflow and, if there has been no error, return to step (1); if there was a stack underflow, abort.
3. If a definition name matching the input word is not found, attempt to convert the word to a binary number (see next section). If this is successful, place the number on the data stack (if currently in interpretation mode); or, if in compilation mode, compile code that, when executed, will place this number on the data stack (see the definition of **LITERAL**). Then return to step 1.
4. If neither the dictionary search nor the number conversion is successful, abort.

For example, typing:

```
PAD 100 DUMP
```

...causes the word **PAD** to be interpreted from the text input buffer. It will be found in the dictionary and executed, returning the address of a scratch area (described in Section 3.1.2) to be pushed on the stack. Then the string 100 is converted to a number that is pushed on the stack, and **DUMP** is found in the dictionary and executed. The result is to display 100 bytes of memory starting at the location given by **PAD**.

INCLUDE and **INCLUDE-FILE** temporarily re-direct the interpreter to process source code from text files (Section 5.5). For this, the prior position in the input stream is saved, and is restored after the file is completely processed. If an **INCLUDE** command is found in a file being processed, the pointers to that input stream are saved and restored, so the **INCLUDE**s are nested.

When the text interpreter executes a defining word (e.g., **CREATE**, **VARIABLE**, or **:**), a definition is compiled into the dictionary.

A flow diagram for the interpreting process is shown in Figure 5.

The commands **SAVE-INPUT** and **RESTORE-INPUT** are available if you wish to manually direct the text interpreter to a different area. These are not required around standard words that redirect the interpreter, such as **INCLUDE-FILE**, and **EVALUATE**.

References

Text files for program source, Section 5.5
System abort routines, Section 5.3
Text interpreter words, Section 6.1
Disk blocks, Appendix C

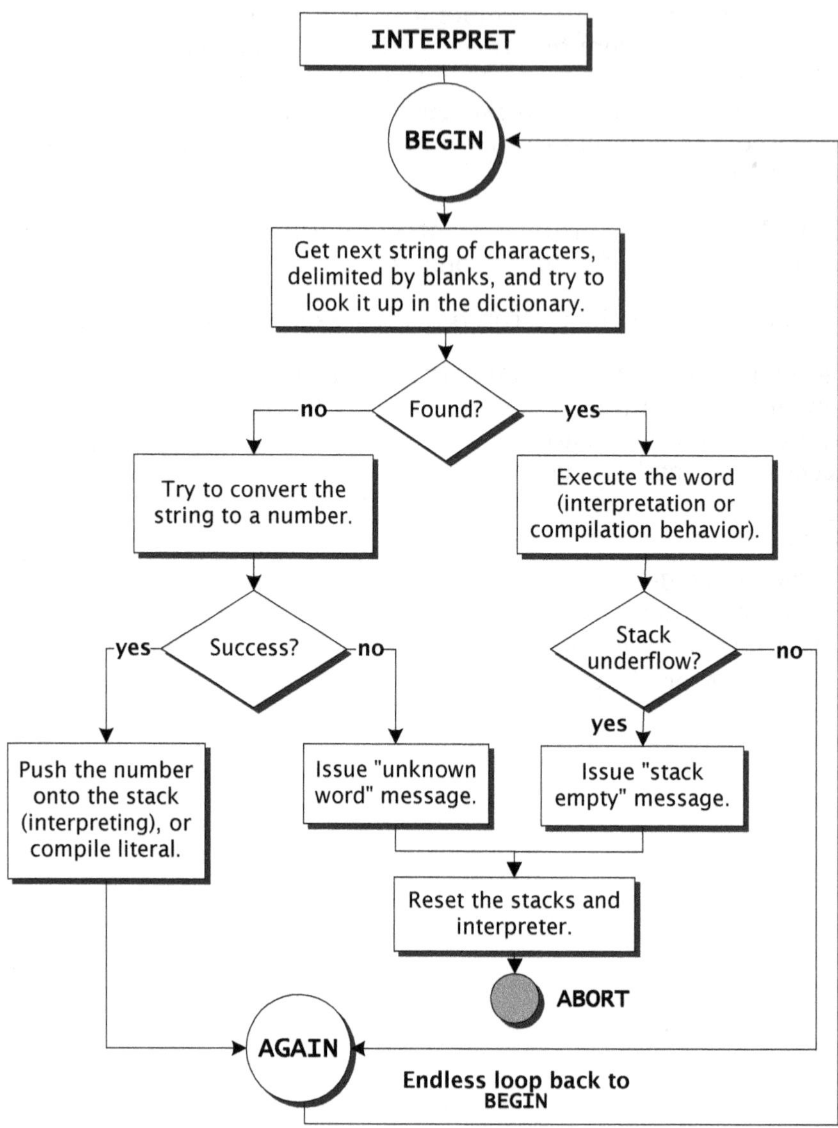

Figure 5. Flow diagram of the text interpreter

1.1.6 Numeric Input

If the text interpreter fails to find a word in the dictionary, it will attempt to convert it into a binary integer that will be pushed onto the stack. If there is no punctuation (except for an optional leading minus sign), a string of valid numerals is converted to a single-cell number, regardless of length. If a string of valid numerals is terminated by a decimal point, the text interpreter will convert it to a double-cell (double-precision) number regardless of length. A double-precision number will occupy two data stack cells, with the high order part on top.

On eight-bit and 16-bit systems, a single-precision integer is 16 bits wide and a double-precision integer is 32 bits wide. On 32-bit systems, these widths are 32 and 64 bits, respectively. On systems with optional floating-point routines, valid numeric strings containing an **E** or **e** (for *exponent*) will be converted as floating-point numbers occupying one floating-point stack location (see Section 5.8 in this book and your product documentation for details).

Table 1: Integer precision and CPU data width

CPU Data Width	Forth Single-Precision Integer	Forth Double-Precision Integer
8 bits	**16 bits**	**32 bits**
16 bits	**16 bits**	**32 bits**
32 bits	**32 bits**	**64 bits**

All Standard Forth systems will interpret a number with a trailing period as a double-precision integer, but some, including those from FORTH, Inc., will interpret any number containing embedded punctuation (see below) in any position as a double-precision integer. Single-precision numbers are recognized by their lack of special punctuation. Conversions operate on character strings of the following format:

```
[ - ] dddd [ punctuation ] dddd … delimiter
```

…where **dddd** is one or more valid digits according to the current base or radix in effect for the user. The content of the user variable **BASE** is always used as the radix. All numeric strings must be ended by a blank or the end of the input stream. If another character is encountered—i.e., a character which is neither a valid digit in the current base, nor punctuation, nor a whitespace character (see glossary)—an abort will occur. There must be no spaces within a number, because a space is a delimiter.

On systems allowing embedded punctuation, the characters shown in Table 2 may appear in a number. A leading minus sign, if present, must immediately precede the first digit or punctuation character.

Table 2: Valid numeric punctuation characters

Character	Description
,	comma
.	period
+	plus
-	hyphen, may appear anywhere except to the immediate left of the most-significant digit
/	slash
:	colon

All punctuation characters are functionally equivalent, including the period *(decimal point)*. The punctuation performs no function other than to set a flag that indicates its presence. Multiple punctuation characters may be contained in a single number; the following character strings both convert to the same double-precision integer 123456:

```
1234.56
12,345.6
```

On some systems, a punctuation character also causes the digits that follow it to be counted, with the count available to subsequent number-conversion words. Immediately after a number conversion, on many systems, the count of digits to the right of the rightmost punctuation is found in the address given by **DPL**.

Glossary

BASE (– a-addr) Core

Return *a-addr*, the address of a cell containing the current number conversion radix. The radix is a value between 2 and 36, inclusive. It is used for both input and output conversion.

DECIMAL (–) Core

Sets **BASE** such that numbers will be converted using a radix of 10.

HEX (–) Core Ext

Sets **BASE** such that numbers will be converted using a radix of 16.

References

Use of the text interpreter for number input, Section 3.6.1
Floating point input, Section 5.8.2

1.1.7 Two-stack Virtual Machine

A running Forth system presents to the programmer a *virtual machine* (VM), like a processor. It has two push-down stacks, code and data space, an Arithmetic Logic Unit (ALU) that executes instructions, and several registers. Previous sections briefly discuss the stacks and some aspects of memory use in Forth; this section describes some features of the virtual machine as a processor.

A number of approaches to implementing the Forth VM have been developed over the years. Each has features that optimize the VM for the physical CPU on which it runs, for its intended use, or for some combination of these. Here we discuss the most common implementation strategies.

The function of the Forth VM, like that of most processors, is to execute instructions. Two of the VM's registers are used to manage the stacks. Others control execution in various ways. Various implementations name and use these registers differently; for purposes of discussion in this book, we use the names in Table 3.

Table 3: Registers in the Forth virtual machine

Name	Mnemonic	Description
S	data *S*tack pointer	Pointer to the current top of the data stack.
R	*R*eturn stack pointer	Pointer to the current top of the return stack.
I	Instruction pointer	Pointer to the next instruction (definition) to be executed; controls execution flow.

Table 3: Registers in the Forth virtual machine *(continued)*

Name	Mnemonic	Description
W	*W*ord pointer	Pointer to the current definition being executed; used to get access to the parameter field of the definition.
U	*U*ser pointer	In multitasked implementations, a pointer to the currently executing task.

A standard Forth high-level, or *colon*, definition consists fundamentally of a name followed by references to previously defined words. When such a definition is invoked by a call to its name, the run-time code needs to manage the sequential execution of the words comprising the body of the definition. Exactly how this is done depends on the particular system and the method it uses to implement the Forth virtual machine. The implementation strategy affects how definitions are structured and how they are executed; see the relevant documentation for your system. There are several possibilities:

- *Indirect-threaded code.* This was the original design and is still the most common method. Pointers to previously defined words are compiled into the executing word's parameter field. The code field of the executing word contains a pointer to machine code for an *address interpreter* that sequentially executes those definitions by performing indirect jumps through register **I**, which is used to keep its place. When a definition calls another high-level definition, the current **I** is pushed onto the return stack; when the called definition finishes, the saved **I** is popped off the return stack. This process is analogous to subroutine calls, and **I** in this model is analogous to a physical processor's instruction pointer.
- *Direct-threaded code.* In this model, the code field contains the actual machine code for the address interpreter, instead of a pointer to it. This is somewhat faster but requires more memory for some classes of words. For this reason, it has been most prevalent on 32-bit systems.
- *Subroutine-threaded code.* In this model, for each referenced definition in the executing word, the compiler places an in-line, jump-to-subroutine instruction with the destination address. This is an enabling technique to allow progression to native code generation. In this model, the underlying processor's instruction pointer is used as Forth's **I** (which usually is not a named register in such implementations).

- *Native code generation.* Going one step beyond subroutine-threaded code, this technique generates in-line machine instructions for simple primitives, such as +, and uses jumps to other high-level routines. Many native code implementations also apply optimizing strategies to the generated code. The result can run much faster, at the cost of compiler complexity. A side-effect of this technique is that it may not be possible to reconstruct the source code from the compiled instructions.
- *Token threading.* This technique compiles references to other words by using a token, such as an index into a table, which is more compact than an absolute address. Token threading was a key element in the original implementation of MacForth and has been used in a number of other specialized Forth systems. In other respects, such an implementation resembles an indirect-threaded model.

References

:, Section 6.2.2
Compiling words and literals, Section 6.3

1.2 Forth Operating System Features

Early Forth implementations ran in a fully *standalone mode*, in which Forth provided all drivers for the hardware attached to the system. More recently, most versions of Forth run in a *co-resident mode*, with a host operating system such as Windows or a variant of Unix. Standalone implementations are still used in embedded systems, however.

In co-resident implementations, the drivers that supply I/O services for peripherals such as disks and printers do so by issuing calls to the host system. Although co-resident systems are typically slower than standalone versions, they offer full file compatibility with the host OS and usually are more flexible with respect to hardware configuration, in that they automatically have access to all devices supported by the OS.

Co-resident versions of Forth usually offer all the system-level features of native systems plus added commands for interacting with the host OS. The latter are documented in the system's product documentation.

1.2.1 Disk I/O

Disk I/O is handled by Forth systems in different ways, depending on the system environment. Co-resident Forth systems access disk using a file-based system, as described in Section 5.5. Files may contain program source or data, and are compatible with the host OS. Source files may be edited by any programmer's editor, although some Forths also provide an editor.

Standalone systems that include a disk drive typically use standard *blocks* of 1024 bytes. This fixed block size applies both to Forth source program text and to data used by Forth programs. This standard format allows I/O—using different media with different physical sector or record sizes, or even on different operating systems—via a standard block handler. Block-based Forths are rare today, but several are still available. Some systems achieve a hybrid approach by mapping blocks into host OS files; this provides a measure of source code portability between the two types of systems. Blocks are discussed further in Appendix C. Also see your product documentation for details.

The majority of Forth implementations today are purely file based, so we will assume this strategy for the balance of this book.

1.2.2 Multitasking

Since the early 1970s, standalone Forth systems have commonly offered the ability to control multiple asynchronous tasks, either *background tasks* or *terminal tasks* that provide independent user interfaces. A small set of commands controls the multitasking facility. The number of tasks in the system usually is limited only by memory size. Because Forth definitions are naturally re-entrant, tasks rarely require much memory.

A terminal task has associated hardware that allows it to support a user interface (perform text input and output). Each terminal task has a partition that contains its stacks, private (or *user*) variable area, and a scratch **PAD** (for text strings).

A background task has a much smaller area, with only enough space for its stacks. There is no terminal associated with it, and it cannot perform text I/O. The routines the background task executes are in a shared area or in the dictionary of one of the terminal tasks.

The use in Forth of stacks for parameter passing facilitates multitasking, because it enables most words to be inherently re-entrant. Providing a unique set of stacks for each task enables words to be re-entrant, concurrently executable by multiple tasks.

A standalone Forth normally runs with interrupts enabled. Interrupt vectors transfer control directly to code that services the interrupting device, without system intervention or overhead. The interrupt code is responsible for saving and restoring any registers it changes.

Interrupt code (actual assembler code) is responsible for performing time-critical actions such as reading a value from an analog device and storing it in a temporary location. The interrupt routine may also notify the task responsible for the device, although some (notably clock interrupts) are self-contained. Notification may take many forms, ranging from incrementing a counter, to "awakening" the task by storing in the task's status area a pointer to code that will cause the task to become active the next time the task is available. Many interrupt handlers do nothing else.

Any processing that is not time-critical can be done by a task running a high-level Forth routine. In effect, the time-critical aspect of servicing an interrupt is decoupled from the more logically complex aspects of dealing with the consequences of the event signalled by the interrupt. Thus, it is guaranteed that interrupts will be serviced promptly, without having to wait for task scheduling, yet as a programmer you have the convenience of using high-level Forth (executed by the responding task) for the main logic of the application.

Co-resident Forths also commonly offer multitasking capabilities consistent with the OS under which they run. Consult your product documentation for details.

References

PAD, Section 3.1.2
Terminal I/O, Section 5.3

1.3 The Forth Assembler

Most Forth systems contain an assembler for the CPU on which the system runs. Although it offers most of the same capabilities of other assemblers, its integration into the Forth environment means it may not use the same notation as assemblers supplied by the computer's manufacturer.

A Forth assembler produces *exactly the same code* as a conventional assembler, which means the assembled code runs at full machine speed, but may do it somewhat differently. The differences are in *notation* and *procedure*, and are described in the following sections.

1.3.1 Notational Differences

Notational differences occur for two reasons:

1. To take advantage of Forth's stack and natural post-fix notation to simplify the assembler and improve flexibility.
2. To produce an assembler that generates immediately executable code, thus facilitating interactive programming and debugging.

Code words in Forth have the form:

```
CODE <name>    <instructions> END-CODE
```

This defines a new word *name*, which is linked in the dictionary like all other words. And like other words, it is immediately executable. It will expect arguments on the data stack and leave its results there. The only difference is that its behavior is defined in terms of instructions which will be assembled to machine code.

Forth assemblers use the manufacturer's instruction mnemonics whenever possible. Occasionally, there are differences, for example, to resolve awkward name conflicts. Any differences should be explained in your Forth product documentation.

Most assemblers encourage a four-column source format, with one instruction per line; this allows space for labels, opcodes, addressing operands, and remarks. But in some Forth assemblers, the opcode itself is a Forth command that assembles the instruction according to addressing operands passed on the stack. This leads to a format in which addressing operands and mode specifiers *precede* the opcode.

Some Forth assemblers support structured programming in the same way high-level Forth does. In these assemblers, arbitrary branching to labelled locations is discouraged; on the other hand, structures such as **BEGIN** … **UNTIL** and **IF** … **ELSE** … **THEN** are available in the assembler, implemented as macros that assemble appropriate conditional and unconditional branches.

1.3.2 Procedural Differences

The Forth assembler is normally resident at all times. This means a programmer can assemble code at any time, either from source on disk or from the command line. Regardless of where the code comes from, the assembled version will be the same.

In conventional programming, assemblers leave their object code in a file, which a linker must integrate with code in files from high-level language compilers (if any) before the resultant program can be loaded into memory for testing. But the resident Forth assembler assembles its code directly into memory in executable form, thus avoiding this cumbersome procedure.

The Forth assembler is used to write short words that function just like words written in high-level Forth; that is, when their names are invoked, it will be executed. Like other Forth words, code words normally expect their arguments on the stack and leave their results there. Within a code definition, one may refer to defined constants (to get a value), variables (to get an address), or other defined data types. Code words may be called from high-level definitions, just as other Forth words are, but cannot themselves call high-level definitions except on subroutine-threaded or machine code implementations. Consult your product documentation for details.

A Forth system runs on a virtual machine. For optimum performance, some of its virtual registers are permanently assigned to actual hardware registers. The product documentation for each Forth system documents the register assignments for that CPU. Some registers may be designated as *scratch*, meaning they can be used within a code routine without saving or restoring their contents. Because the scratch registers are sufficient for most Forth code routines, there is less need to save and restore registers than in conventional programming. But registers containing Forth pointers must be used carefully. Forth system registers are given names that make references to them in code easy and readable. In co-resident systems, Forth code routines may need to save and restore Forth registers when calling host operating system services.

Consult your product documentation for details of your assembler.

1.4 Documentation and Programmer Aids

In Forth, as in all other languages, the primary responsibility for producing readable code lies with the programmer. Forth supports the programmer's efforts to produce easily managed code by providing aids to internal documentation. In addition to these, we recommend that each Forth programming group adopt uniform editorial and naming standards and conventions. Sample standards adopted by some groups are offered in Section 8. Although readability is rather subjective, a set of standards that all members of a group adhere to will improve their ability to share code and to support one another.

1.4.1 Comments

Comments embedded in Forth source are enclosed in parentheses. For example:

```
( This is a comment)
```

The word `(` must have a space after it, so that it can be recognized and executed as a command (to begin the comment). A space is not needed before the closing right parenthesis delimiter. The `\` (backslash) character is used to indicate that the entire remainder of the current line of source is a comment.

The word `.(` (note the preceding dot) is like `(` but begins a comment that will be displayed when it is encountered. If it occurs inside a definition, the text will be displayed when the definition is compiled, not when it is executed. It is commonly used in source code to indicate progress in compilation, e.g.:

```
.( Begin application compilation)
```

Forth comments are most often used to give a picture of a word's stack arguments and results; for example, a high-level definition of the Forth word **=** is:

```
: = ( n n -- flag )   - 0= ;
```

The dashes in the comment separate a word's arguments (on the left) from its results. By convention, certain letters have specific, common meanings:

Table 4: Common stack notation

Symbol	Data type	Size on stack
n	Signed number	1 cell
u	Unsigned number	1 cell
flag	Flag (boolean)[a]	1 cell
addr	Address	1 cell
d	Signed double number	2 cells
ud	Unsigned double number	2 cells

a. A single-cell Boolean value (zero is false, non-zero is true; a "well-formed flag" has all bits set for true).

Thus, in the example above, the word **=** expects two single-cell integers and returns a truth flag.

On some systems, addresses must be aligned on cell boundaries for cell fetches. The stack notation *addr* is sometimes further specified as a character-aligned address (*c-addr*) or cell-aligned address (*a-addr*). A character-aligned address is on a byte boundary, which on most systems is equivalent to saying there is no particular alignment. The notation *addr* indicates no alignment is implied.

Defining words, which have separate interpretive and run-time behaviors, should have comments[1] for both behaviors:

```
: CONSTANT ( n -- )   CREATE ,
   DOES> ( -- n )   @ ;
```

Glossaries in this book that feature defining words show an entry for

1. The **DOES>** part of this type of definition starts with the address of the instance on the stack, but it's conventional to omit this from the stack comment as the calling routine is not expected to provide it.

the word's defining behavior and an entry for the instance behavior of words defined by it, i.e., what an instance will do when executed.

Most implementations also have a way to denote multi-line comments that may include parentheses, however this has not been standardized. Consult your product documentation or look at the source provided with your system.

References

Stack notation, Section 2.1.1

Data types in stack notation, Section B.2

Defining words, Section 2.3.1

Glossary

((–) Core, File

Begin a comment. Stop compilation or interpretation and parse the characters that follow, looking for a right parenthesis **)** which closes the comment.

.((–) Core Ext

Like **(**, but begin a comment that will be sent to the display device when it is encountered. Terminated by a right parenthesis **)**.

**** (–) Block Ext, Core Ext

Begin a comment that includes the entire remainder of the current line of source code. No closing delimiter is needed.

1.4.2 Locating Command Source[1]

After code has been compiled from source files, the **LOCATE** command can display the source code for a command. For example:

```
LOCATE /STRING
```

...starts the editor, opens the correct source block or file, and positions the cursor at the start of the definition of **/STRING**:

```
: /STRING ( c-addr1 len1 n -- c-addr2 len2)
   OVER MIN >R  SWAP R@ +  SWAP R> - ;
```

1. This facility is common, but not standardized, and may not be implemented on all systems.

Glossary

LOCATE <name> (–) Common usage
If *name* is the name of a definition compiled from source code, display the source code for *name*. On some systems, the phrase **VIEW** *name* performs a similar function.

1.4.3 Cross-references[1]

This tool finds all the places a word is used. The syntax is:

```
WHERE <name>
```

It gives the first line of the definition of the word *name*, followed by each line of source code in the currently compiled program that contains *name*.

If the same name has been redefined, **WHERE** gives the references for each definition separately. The shortcut:

```
WH <name>
```

...does the same thing.

This command is not the same as a source search, because it is based on the code you currently have compiled and are debugging. This means you will be spared instances of *name* in files you aren't using.

Glossary

WH <name> (–) Common usage
Short synonym for **WHERE**, defined for typing convenience.

WHERE <name> (–) Common usage
Display all the places in the currently compiled program where *name* has been used, showing any re-definitions separately.

1. This facility is common, but not standardized, and may not be implemented on all systems.

1.4.4 Decompiler and Disassembler[1]

The disassembler/decompiler is used to reconstruct readable source code from **CODE** and **:** (colon) definitions. This is useful as a cross check, whenever a new definition fails to work as expected.

The command **SEE** *name* decompiles and/or disassembles both **CODE** commands and colon definitions. On indirect, direct, and subroutine-threaded implementations, **SEE** can reconstruct the high-level definition from which the running version was compiled. On native code systems, this is not possible; use **LOCATE** (Section 1.4.2) to view the source.

For example, one source definition for **/STRING** is:

```
: /STRING ( c-addr1 len1 n -- c-addr2 len2)
   >R  SWAP R@ +  SWAP R> - ;
```

...but if you decompile it (on a FORTH, Inc. 68000 cross-compiler, for example, which is an optimized native code generator), you get:

```
SEE /STRING
08BE   A6 )+ A7 -) MOV                    2F1E
08C0   SWAP BSR                           6100FB72
08C4   A7 ) A6 -) MOV                     2D17
08C6   A6 )+ D0 MOV                       201E
08C8   D0 A6 ) ADD                        D196
08CA   SWAP BSR                           6100FB68
08CE   A7 )+ A6 -) MOV                    2D1F
08D0   A6 )+ D0 MOV                       201E
08D2   D0 A6 ) SUB                        9196
08D4   RTS                                4E75 ok
```

This example clearly shows the combination of in-line code and subroutine calls in this implementation.

An alternative approach is to start disassembly or decompilation at some address. This is useful for decompiling headless code, such as code preceded only by a **LABEL**. The command to disassemble a **CODE** definition, given an address *addr*, is:

```
<addr> DASM
```

1. This facility is common, but not standardized, and may not be implemented on all systems.

The word `.'` is becoming increasingly popular in this debugging context, though it is not in Standard Forth nor in all systems. It attempts to identify the definition in which an address occurs. For example, given **/STRING** above, you could type:

```
HEX 8C6 .'
```

...and get:

```
/STRING +08  ok
```

...indicating that the location $8C6 was eight bytes into the definition of **/STRING**.

Glossary

SEE <name> (–) Tools
Reconstruct the source code for *name*, using a decompiler for high-level definitions or a disassembler for code definitions.

DASM (addr –) Common usage
Begin disassembly at the address *addr* on top of the stack. The disassembler stops when it encounters an unconditional transfer of control outside the range of the definition, such as returns from interrupt or from subroutines, branches, and jumps. Subroutine calls are excluded, as control is assumed to return to the location following the call.

.' (addr –) Common usage
Display the name of the nearest definition before *addr*, and the offset of *addr* from the beginning of that definition. "dot-tick"

1.5 Interactive Programming—An Example

The Forth language was designed from first principles to support an interactive development style. By developing a very simple application in this section, we will show how this style translates into practice.

The general process of developing a program in Forth is consistent with the recommended development practices of *top-down design* and *bottom-up coding and testing*. However, Forth adds another element: extreme modularity. You don't write page after page of code and then try to figure out why it doesn't work; instead, you write a few very brief definitions and exercise them one by one.

Suppose we are designing a washing machine. The highest-level definition might be:

```
: WASHER   WASH SPIN RINSE SPIN ;
```

The colon indicates that a new word is being defined; following it is the name of that new word, **WASHER**. The remainder are previously defined words that comprise this definition. Finally, the definition is terminated by a semi-colon.

```
\ Port addresses
HEX
7000 CONSTANT MOTOR3     7002 CONSTANT VALVE
7004 CONSTANT FAUCETS    7006 CONSTANT DETERGENT
7008 CONSTANT TIMER      700A CONSTANT CLUTCH
7010 CONSTANT LEVEL
DECIMAL

\ Basic commands
: ON ( port -- )     -1 SWAP OUTPUT ;
: OFF ( port -- )   0 SWAP OUTPUT ;
: SECONDS ( n -- )   1000 * MS ;
: MINUTES ( n -- )   60 * SECONDS ;

\ Machine functions
: ADD ( port -- )   DUP ON  10 SECONDS  OFF ;
: TILL-FULL ( -- )   BEGIN  LEVEL INPUT  UNTIL ;
: DRAIN ( -- )   VALVE ON  3 MINUTES  VALVE OFF ;
: AGITATE ( -- )   MOTOR ON  10 MINUTES  MOTOR OFF ;
: SPIN ( -- )   CLUTCH ON  MOTOR ON  5 MINUTES
   MOTOR OFF  CLUTCH OFF ;
: FILL ( -- )   FAUCETS ON  TILL-FULL  FAUCETS OFF ;

\ Sequencing
: WASH ( -- )   FILL  DETERGENT ADD  AGITATE  DRAIN ;
: RINSE ( -- )   FILL  AGITATE  DRAIN ;
: WASHER ( -- )   WASH  SPIN  RINSE  SPIN ;
```

Figure 6. Example of a control program that runs a washing machine

Typically, we design the highest-level routines first. This approach leads to conceptually correct solutions with a minimum of effort. In

Forth, words must be compiled before they can be referenced. Thus, a listing begins with the most primitive definitions and ends with the highest-level words. If the higher-level words are entered first, lower-level routines are added above them in the listing.

Figure 6 shows a complete listing of the washing machine example. Comments follow parentheses (to a delimiting right-parenthesis) or backslashes. In this example, the first few lines define named constants, with hex values representing hardware port addresses. The remaining definitions define, in sequence, the application words that perform the work.

The code in this example is nearly self-documenting; the few comments show parameters being passed to certain words. Forth allows as many comments as desired, with no penalty in object code size or performance.

When reading,

```
: WASHER ( -- )   WASH  SPIN  RINSE  SPIN ;
```

...it is obvious what **RINSE** does. To determine *how* it does it, you read:

```
: RINSE ( -- )   FILL  AGITATE  DRAIN ;
```

When you wonder how **FILL** works, you find:

```
: FILL ( -- )   FAUCETS ON  TILL-FULL   FAUCETS OFF ;
```

Reading further, one finds that **FAUCETS** is simply a constant which returns the address of the port that controls the faucet, while **ON** is a simple word that turns on the bits at that address.

Even from this simple example, it may be clear that Forth is not so much a language as a tool for building application-oriented command sets. The definition of **WASHER** is based not on low-level Forth words, but on washing-machine words like **SPIN** and **RINSE**.

Because Forth is extensible, Forth programmers write collections of words that apply to the problem at hand. The power of Forth, which is simple and universal to begin with, grows rapidly as words are defined in terms of previously defined words. Each successive, newer word becomes more powerful and more specific. The final program becomes as readable as you wish to make it.

When developing this program, you would follow your top-down logic, as described above. But when the time comes to test it, you see the real convenience of Forth's interactivity.

If your hardware is available, your first step would be to see if it works. Even without the code in Figure 6, you could read and write the hardware registers by typing phrases such as:

```
HEX 7010 INPUT .
```

This would read the water-level register at 7010_H and display its value. And you could type:

```
-1 7002 OUTPUT    0 7002 OUTPUT
```

...to see if the valve opens and closes.

If the hardware is unavailable, you might temporarily re-define the words **MOTOR**, etc., as variables you can read and write, and so test the rest of the logic.

You can **INCLUDE** your file of source (as described in Section 5.5), whereupon all its definitions are available for testing. You can further exercise your I/O by typing phrases such as:

MOTOR ON or **MOTOR OFF**

...to see what happens. Then you can exercise your low-level words, such as:

```
DETERGENT ADD
```

...and so on, until your highest-level words are tested.

As you work, you can use any of the additional programmer aids described in Section 2.1.4. You can also easily change your code and re-load it. But your main ally is the intrinsically interactive nature of Forth itself.

References

Disk and file layout and design, Section 8.1

Stack notation conventions, Section 2.1, Table 16, and Section B.2

Number base, Sections 1.1.6, 3.6

Numeric output (the word **.**), Section 3.6.2

Programmer conveniences, Section 2.1.4

2. Forth Fundamentals

This section defines the major elements of the Forth language. These words are grouped into categories. Except where noted as deriving from "common usage," all words are found in, and comply with, the American National Standard for the Forth language (ANSI X3.215:1994, equivalent to *ISO/IEC 15145:1997)*, commonly referred to here as *Standard Forth*. Appendix B, "Glossary & Notation" on page 233 provides definitions of many of the terms used in this section, as well as a detailed description of the notation conventions.

2.1 Stack Operations

Forth is based on an architecture incorporating push-down stacks (last-in, first-out lists). The *data stack* is used primarily for passing parameters between procedures. The *return stack* is used primarily for system functions, such as storing procedure return addresses, loop parameters, etc. Because the data stack is the one most directly used by programmers, references to "the stack" should be interpreted as referring to the data stack. Where we refer to the return stack, we explicitly say so.

Stack operators work on data that are on one or more of the stacks. The words defined in this section are principally tools you can use to manipulate stack items directly (to duplicate items, change their order, etc.). Many other Forth words also result in modification of the stack, and are described in the sections of this manual that deal with their primary functions. In addition to the stack operators discussed in this manual, stack manipulation words that relate to assembly language are covered in your Forth system's documentation.

2.1.1 Stack Notation

Stack parameters used as input to and output from a procedure are described using the notation:

```
( before - after )
```

Operations that use the stack usually require that a certain number of items be present on the stack, and then leave another number of items on the stack as results. Most operations remove their operands, leaving only the results. To document an operation's effect on the number and type of items on the stack, each word has a *stack notation.*

Individual stack items are depicted using the notation in Table 16, Section B.2. Any other, special notation will be explained when it is used. Where several arguments are of the same type, and clarity demands that they be distinguished, numeric subscripts are used.

If you type several numbers on a line, the rightmost will end up on top of the stack. As a result, we show multiple stack arguments with the top element to the right. In rare cases when alternate conditions may exist, they are separated by a vertical bar (|), meaning "or." For example, the notation *(— n_1 | n_2 n_3)* indicates a word that may leave either one or two stack items; and *(— addr | 0)* indicates that the procedure takes no input and returns either a valid address or zero.

Please remember that the items shown in a word's stack notation are relative to the top of the stack and do not affect any stack items that may be below the lowest stack item referenced by the operation. For example, *(x_1 x_2 — x_3)* describes an operation that uses the top two stack items and leaves a different, one-item result. Therefore, if the stack initially contained three items, execution would result in a stack of two items, with the bottom item unchanged and the top item derived as a result of the operation.

Some procedures have stack effects both when they are compiled and when they are executed. The stack effects shown in this manual refer to the execution-time behavior unless specifically noted, because this is usually the behavior of most interest to a programmer.

Where an operation is described that uses more than one stack, the data stack behavior is shown by S: and the return stack behavior by R:. When no confusion is possible, the S: is omitted.

With the addition of the floating-point stack (see Section 5.8), it becomes necessary to document its contents, as well. Floating-point stack comments follow the data stack comments, and are indicated by F:. If a command does not affect the floating-point stack, only the data stack comments are shown, and vice versa. If neither stack is affected, a null data stack comment is shown.

For example:

```
: SF@   ( a-addr  — ) ( F:  — r )
```

...indicates that a cell-aligned address (*a-addr*) is removed from the data stack, and a floating-point number (*r*) which was fetched from that address is pushed on the floating-point stack by the execution of **SF@**.

```
: F.    ( F: r  — )
```

...indicates that there are no data stack arguments, and that a floating-point number is removed from the floating-point stack by the execution of **F.**.

A more complete table of stack comment notation is given in Section B.2.

References

Data stack, Section 1.1.3
Data types in stack notation, Section B.2

2.1.2 Data Stack Manipulation

This category of stack operations contains words which manipulate the contents of the data stack without performing arithmetic, logical, or memory reference operations.

2.1.2.1 Single-item operators

The words in the glossary below manipulate one or more single items on the data stack.

Glossary

?DUP (x — 0 | x x) Core
Conditionally duplicate the top item on the stack if its value is non-zero. "question-dup"

Logically equivalent to: **DUP IF DUP THEN**

DEPTH (— +n) Core
Return the number of single-cell values that were on the stack before

this word executed. **DEPTH** will return 2 for each double-precision integer on the stack.

DROP (x –) Core

Remove the top entry from the stack.

DUP (x – x x) Core

Duplicate the top entry on the stack.

NIP (x_1 x_2 – x_2) Core Ext

Drop the second item on the stack, leaving the top unchanged.

OVER (x_1 x_2 – x_1 x_2 x_1) Core

Place a copy of x_1 on top of the stack.

PICK (+n – x) Core Ext

Place a copy of the *n*th stack entry on top of the stack. The zeroth item is the top of the stack; i.e., **0 PICK** is equivalent to **DUP** and **1 PICK** is equivalent to **OVER**.

ROT (x_1 x_2 x_3 – x_2 x_3 x_1) Core

Rotate the top three items on the stack.

SWAP (x_1 x_2 – x_2 x_1) Core

Exchange the top two items on the stack.

TUCK (x_1 x_2 – x_2 x_1 x_2) Core Ext

Place a copy of the top stack item below the second stack item.

2.1.2.2 Two-item operators

In the following glossary, the naming convention uses the prefix "2" to indicate that the word is dealing with one or more *pairs* of stack items. The prefix itself has no special meaning to Forth (a name is just a name), but naming conventions such as this are helpful to humans. The **2...** operators always maintain the order of items within the pair. They do not assume any particular relationship between members of the pair: they could be the high and low parts of a double-length number, an address and length of a string, or any other two items.

Glossary

2DROP (x_1 x_2 –) Core

Remove the top pair of cells from the stack. The cell values may or may not be related. "two-drop"

2DUP (x_1 x_2 – x_1 x_2 x_1 x_2) Core

Duplicate the top cell pair. "two-dup"

2OVER (x_1 x_2 x_3 x_4 – x_1 x_2 x_3 x_4 x_1 x_2) Core

Copy cell pair x_1 x_2 to the top of the stack. "two-over"

2ROT (x_1 x_2 x_3 x_4 x_5 x_6 – x_3 x_4 x_5 x_6 x_1 x_2) Double ext

Rotate the top three cell pairs on the stack, bringing cell pair x_1 x_2 to the top of the stack. "two-rote"

2SWAP (x_1 x_2 x_3 x_4 – x_3 x_4 x_1 x_2) Core

Exchange the top two cell pairs. "two-swap"

2.1.3 Return Stack Manipulation

The *return stack* is so named because it is used by the Forth virtual machine (VM) to keep track of where Forth words will return when they have finished executing. When a high-level Forth word invokes a previously defined Forth word, the address of the next word to be executed is pushed onto the return stack; it will be popped off the return stack when the called word is finished, so execution can resume where it left off.

The return stack is a convenient place to keep values temporarily, but it must be cleared before an executing word reaches the end of the current definition, or the virtual machine will return to the "address" on the return stack. The words **>R**, **R@**, and **R>** move an item from the data stack to the return stack, fetch to the data stack a copy of the top of the return stack, and remove an item from the return stack and push it onto the data stack. Careful use of these operators can simplify stack handling when you have more than two or three items to deal with.

If you use the return stack for temporary storage, you must be aware that this is also a system resource, and obey the following restrictions:

- Your program must not access values on the return stack (using **R@**, **R>**, **2R@**, or **2R>**) that it did not place there using **>R** or **2>R**.
- When inside a **DO** loop (see Section 4.5), your program must not access values placed on the return stack *before* the loop was entered.
- All values placed on the return stack *within* a **DO** loop must be removed before **I**, **J**, **LOOP**, **+LOOP**, **UNLOOP**, or **LEAVE** is executed.
- All values placed on the return stack within a definition must be removed before the end of that definition or before **EXIT** is executed.

The glossary below documents operations that involve both the return stack and the data stack.

Glossary

2>R (S: x_1 x_2 –) (R: – x_1 x_2) Core Ext

Pop the top two cells from the data stack and push them onto the return stack. "two-to-R"

2R> (S: – x_1 x_2) (R: x_1 x_2 –) Core Ext

Pop the top two cells from the return stack and push them onto the data stack. **2R>** is the inverse of **2>R**. "two-R-from"

2R@ (S: – x_1 x_2) (R: x_1 x_2 – x_1 x_2) Core Ext

Push a copy of the top two return stack cells onto the data stack. "two-R-fetch"

>R (S: x –) (R: – x) Core

Remove the item on top of the data stack and put it on the return stack. "to-R"

R> (S: – x) (R: x –) Core

Remove the item on the top of the return stack and put it on the data stack. "R-from"

R@ (S: – x) (R: x – x) Core

Place a copy of the item on top of the return stack onto the data stack. "R-fetch"

References

Finite (counting) **LOOP**s, (**DO**), Section 4.5
EXECUTE, Section 5.1

2.1.4 Programmer Conveniences

The words in this section are intended as programming aids. They may be used interpretively at the keyboard or inside definitions.

Glossary

.S (–) Tools
Display the contents of the data stack using the current base (e.g., decimal, octal, hex, binary). Stack contents remain unchanged. "dot-S"

? (a-addr –) Tools
Fetch the contents of the given address and display the result according to the current base. "question"

Equivalent to the phrase: **@ .**

DUMP (addr +n –) Tools
Display the contents of a memory region of length *+n* starting at *addr*:

```
<addr> <+n> DUMP
```

Output is formatted with the address on the left and up to eight values on a line. On some systems this word's output is always in hex; on others, it may be in the current base. Two cells are removed from the stack.

ENVIRONMENT? (c-addr u – false | i*x true) Core
This word is used to inquire about the values of system parameters and the existence of options. See Section 5.2 for a full description. "environment-query"

WORDS (–) Tools
List all the definition names in the first word list of the search order.

References

Environmental interrogation, Section 5.2
Search orders, Section 6.6.1

2.2 Arithmetic and Logical Operations

Forth offers a comprehensive set of commands for performing arithmetic and logical functions. The functions in a standard system are optimized for integer arithmetic, because not all processors have hardware floating-point capability and software floating point is too slow for most real-time applications. All Forth systems provide words to perform fast, precise, scaled-integer computations; many provide fixed-point fraction computations, as well. On systems with hardware floating-point capability, many implementations include an optional, complete set of floating-point operations, including an assembler. See Section 5.8 in this manual and the product documentation for these systems for details.

2.2.1 Arithmetic and Shift Operators

In order to achieve maximum performance, each version of Forth implements most arithmetic primitives to use the internal behavior of that particular processor's hardware multiply and divide instructions. Therefore, to find out at the bit level what these primitives do, you should consult either the manufacturer's hardware description or the implementation's detailed description of these functions.

In particular, signed integer division where only one operand (either dividend or divisor) is negative and there is a remainder may produce different, but equally valid, results on different implementations. The two possibilities are *floored* and *symmetric* division[1]. In floored division, the remainder carries the sign of the divisor and the quotient is rounded to its arithmetic floor (towards negative infinity). In symmetric division, the remainder carries the sign of the dividend and the quotient is rounded towards zero, or truncated. For example, dividing -10 by 7 can give a quotient of -2 and remainder of 4 (floored), or a quotient of -1 and remainder of -3 (symmetric).

Most hardware multiply and divide instructions are symmetric, so floored division operations are likely to be slower. However, some applications (such as graphics) require floored division in order to get a continuous function through zero. Consult your system's documentation to learn its behavior.

1. One reference about this topic is *The Logic of Computer Arithmetic* by Ivan Flores, Prentice Hall, 1963.

The following general guidelines may help you use these arithmetic operators:

- The order of arguments to order-dependent operators (e.g., - and /) is such that, if the operator were moved to an infix position, it would algebraically describe the result. Some examples:

Table 5: Order of arguments, Forth postfix vs. infix

Forth	Algebraic
a b -	a - b
a b /	a / b
a b c */	a * b / c

- All arithmetic words starting with the letter U are unsigned; others are normally signed. The exception to this rule is that, on most systems, M*/ requires a positive divisor.

These operators perform arithmetic and logical functions on numbers that are on the stack. In general, the operands are removed (popped) from the stack and the results are left on the stack.

Glossary

Single-Precision Operations

***** (n_1 n_2 – n_3) Core

Multiply n_1 by n_2 leaving the product n_3. "star"

***/** (n_1 n_2 n_3 – n_4) Core

Multiply n_1 by n_2, producing an intermediate double-cell result *d*. Divide *d* by n_3, giving the single-cell quotient n_4. "star-slash"

***/MOD** (n_1 n_2 n_3 – n_4 n_5) Core

Multiply n_1 by n_2, producing intermediate double-cell result *d*. Divide *d* by n_3, giving single-cell remainder n_4 and single-cell quotient n_5. "star-slash-mod"

+ (n_1 n_2 – n_3) Core

Add n_1 to n_2, leaving the sum n_3. "plus"

- (n_1 n_2 – n_3) Core

Subtract n_2 from n_1, leaving the difference n_3. "minus"

/ (n_1 n_2 – n_3) Core

Divide n_1 by n_2, leaving the quotient n_3. See the discussion at the beginning of this section about floored and symmetric division. "slash"

/MOD (n_1 n_2 – n_3 n_4) Core

Divide n_1 by n_2, leaving the remainder n_3 and the quotient n_4. "slash-mod"

1+ (n_1 – n_2) Core

Add one to n_1, leaving n_2. "one-plus"

1- (n_1 – n_2) Core

Subtract one from n_1, leaving n_2. "one-minus"

2+ (n_1 – n_2) Common usage

Add two to n_1, leaving n_2. "two-plus"

2- (n_1 – n_2) Common usage

Subtract two from n_1, leaving n_2. "two-minus"

2* (x_1 – x_2) Core

Return x_2, the result of shifting x_1 one bit toward the most-significant bit, filling the least-significant bit with zero (same as **1 LSHIFT**). "two-star"

2/ (x_1 – x_2) Core

Return x_2, the result of shifting x_1 one bit towards the least-significant bit, leaving the most-significant bit unchanged. "two-slash"

LSHIFT (x_1 u – x_2) Core

Perform a logical left shift of *u* places on x_1, giving x_2. Fill the vacated least-significant bits with zeroes. "L-shift"

MOD (n_1 n_2 – n_3) Core

Divide n_1 by n_2, giving the remainder n_3.

RSHIFT (x_1 u – x_2) Core

Perform a logical right shift of *u* places on x_1, giving x_2. Fill the vacated most-significant bits with zeroes. "R-shift"

Double-precision Operations

In this group of words, we see another naming convention: the "D" prefix identifies words that work with double-length integers. These are always represented as two stack items with the high-order (most significant) part in the higher stack position and the low-order (least significant) part beneath.

D+ (d_1 d_2 – d_3) Double

Add d_1 to d_2, leaving the sum d_3. "D-plus"

D- (d_1 d_2 – d_3) Double

Subtract d_2 from d_1, leaving the difference d_3. "D-minus"

D2* (d_1 – d_2) Double

Return d_2, the result of shifting d_1 one bit toward the most-significant bit and filling the least-significant bit with zero. "D-two-star"

D2/ (d_1 – d_2) Double

Return xd_2, the result of shifting d_1 one bit towards the least-significant bit and leaving the most-significant bit unchanged. "D-two-slash"

Mixed-precision Operations

The "M" prefix in this group identifies mixed-precision operators, involving at least one double-length integer and at least one single-length integer. Take special note of the order in which they appear on the stack!

D>S (d – n) Double

Convert double-precision number *d* to its single-precision equivalent *n*. Results are undefined if *d* is outside the range of a signed single-cell number. "D-to-S"

FM/MOD (d n_1 – n_2 n_3) Core

Divide *d* by n_1, using floored division, giving quotient n_3 and remainder n_2. All arguments are signed. This word and **SM/REM** will produce different results on the same data when exactly one argument is negative and there is a remainder. "F-M-slash-mod"

M* (n_1 n_2 – d) Core

Multiply n_1 by n_2, leaving the double-precision result *d*. "M-star"

M*/ (d_1 n_1 $+n_2$ – d_2) Double

Multiply d_1 by n_1, producing a triple-cell intermediate result *t*. Divide *t* by the positive number n_2, giving the double-cell quotient d_2. If double-precision multiplication or division only is needed, this word may be used with either n_1 or n_2 set equal to 1. "M-star-slash"

M+ (d_1 n – d_2) Double

Add *n* to d_1, leaving the sum d_2. "M-plus"

M- (d_1 n – d_2) Common usage

Subtract *n* from d_1, leaving the difference d_2. "M-minus"

M/ (d n_1 – n_2) Common usage

Divide *d* by n_1, leaving the single-precision quotient n_2. This word does not perform an overflow check. "M-slash"

S>D (n – d) Core

Convert a single-precision number *n* to its double-precision equivalent *d* with the same numerical value. "S-to-D"

SM/REM (d n_1 – n_2 n_3) Core

Divide *d* by n_1, using symmetric division, giving quotient n_3 and remainder n_2. All arguments are signed. This word and **FM/MOD** will produce different results on the same data when exactly one argument is negative and there is a remainder. "S-M-slash-rem"

UM/MOD (ud u_1 – u_2 u_3) Core

Divide *ud* by u_1, leaving remainder u_2 and quotient u_3. This operation is called **UM/MOD** because it assumes the arguments are unsigned and it produces unsigned results. Compare with **SM/REM** and **FM/MOD**. "U-M-slash-mod"

UM* (u_1 u_2 – ud) Core

Multiply u_1 by u_2, leaving the double-precision result *ud*. All values and arithmetic are unsigned. "U-M-star"

2.2.2 Logical Operations

As in the case of arithmetic operations, Forth's implementation of logical and relational operations optimizes for speed and simplicity. The words described in this section provide a rich, flexible set of logical operations.

Glossary

Single-Precision Logical Operations

ABS (n — +n) Core

Replace the top stack item with its absolute value.

AND (x_1 x_2 – x_3) Core

Return x_3, the bit-wise logical *and* of x_1 with x_2.

INVERT (x_1 – x_2) Core

Invert all bits of x_1, giving its logical inverse x_2.

MAX (n_1 n_2 – n_3) Core

Return n_3, the greater of n_1 and n_2.

MIN (n_1 n_2 – n_3) Core

Return n_3, the lesser of n_1 and n_2.

NEGATE (n - -n) Core

Change the sign of the top stack value; if the value was negative, it becomes positive. The phrase **NEGATE 1-** is equivalent to **INVERT** (one's complement of the input value).

OR (x_1 x_2 – x_3) Core

Return x_3, the bit-wise inclusive *or* of x_1 with x_2.

WITHIN (x_1 x_2 x_3 – flag) Core

Return *true* if x_1 is greater than or equal to x_2 and less than x_3. The values may all be either unsigned integers or signed integers, but must all be the same type.

XOR (x_1 x_2 – x_3) Core

Return x_3, the bit-wise exclusive *or* of x_1 with x_2. The phrase **-1 XOR** is equivalent to **INVERT** (one's complement of the input value).

Double-Precision Logical Operations

Once again, we see the "D" prefix in use to indicate double-precision integers.

DABS (d – +d) Double

Return the absolute value of a double-precision stack value. "D-abs"

DMAX (d_1 d_2 – d_3) Double

Return d_3, the larger of d_1 and d_2.

DMIN (d_1 d_2 – d_3) Double

Return d_3, the lesser of d_1 and d_2.

DNEGATE (d – -d) Double

Change the sign of a double-precision stack value. Analogous to **NEGATE**.

2.3 Memory and Data Storage

In other languages, you can't do anything without naming data. In Forth, you can do quite a lot. This is one of the big sources of efficiency in the language. But complex applications usually do require named data items and structures. Forth not only supports this, but also offers a unique level of flexibility in defining new kinds of data structures, which we discuss in Section 6.2.1.

This section describes the standard ways of making definitions whose purpose is to provide storage for data.

2.3.1 Defining Words

The word **:** (colon) is a defining word; that is, it makes a dictionary entry. In this and in later sections we encounter other defining words. Indeed, Section 6.2 documents how to make your own custom defining words.

Each defining word creates *instances* of its class of words. We may describe a defining word as having two "behaviors:" a *defining behavior* (when it creates a member of this class of words) and an *instance behavior* (shared by all words defined by this defining word). All members of a class—that is, constructed by the same defining word—share the same, characteristic defining and instance behaviors.

For example, the word **VARIABLE** defines a word associated with a single cell of data storage:

```
VARIABLE ITEM
```

...defines a word which, when invoked, returns the address of its data space.

The two behaviors of **VARIABLE** are as follows:

1. **VARIABLE**'s *defining behavior* (that is, what happens when **VARIABLE** is executed, as in creating the definition of **ITEM** above) creates a dictionary entry and allocates one cell of data space. This action is equivalent to the phrase:

   ```
   1 CELLS ALLOT
   ```

2. When it is executed, the *instance behavior* of a word defined by **VARIABLE** (such as **ITEM**) pushes the address of its data space onto the stack.

The two behaviors of **:** are:

1. Its *defining behavior* is to create a dictionary entry and associate it with the words that follow the name until a terminating **;** is encountered.
2. The *instance behavior* of words defined by **:** is to execute those words.

All Forth defining words are immediately followed by the *name* of the object being defined. All define permanent (static) global objects. These are independent definitions, just like colon definitions. Forth's data stack fills the role used by *local variables* in other languages. ANS Forth has a limited provision for local variables, but they are rarely used and are not recommended for beginners because their use tends to inhibit the development of good stack management skills.

In the following glossary, and in others featuring defining words, we show one entry for the word's defining behavior and another for the instance behavior of words defined by it, i.e., what an instance will do when executed.

2.3.2 Single Data Objects

There are two generic kinds of individual data objects, variables (named storage locations) and constants (named values). A third kind of data object has characteristics of both: it is a named value that can be changed (whereas constants cannot be changed).

2.3.2.1 Variables

A **VARIABLE** is a named memory location whose value may equally easily be fetched onto the stack or stored into.

The definition of a **VARIABLE** takes the form:

```
VARIABLE <name>
```

This constructs a definition for *name*, with one cell allotted for a value. A single-cell value may be stored into the parameter field of the definition. For example:

```
VARIABLE DATA
6 DATA !
```

...will store 6 in the parameter field of **DATA**.

When a **VARIABLE** is referenced by *name*, the address of its parameter field is pushed onto the stack. This address may be used with **@** or **!** to fetch or store, respectively, the variable's value.

Similarly, the word **2VARIABLE** defines a variable whose parameter field is two cells long. Such a variable may contain one double-precision number, a pair of single-precision numbers (such as *x,y* coordinates), or even two unrelated values. **2VARIABLE** differs from **VARIABLE** only in the number of bytes allotted. The operators **2@** and **2!** are used with this format.

On some eight-bit and 16-bit CPUs, such as those used in embedded systems in which data space is limited, **CVARIABLE** defines a variable that is one byte long. The operators **C@** and **C!** are used with this format. Note that **CVARIABLE** allots only one byte, so it leaves the data space pointer unaligned. If you are concerned about alignment, either group **CVARIABLE**s to leave the space aligned or use **ALIGN** afterwards.

In summary, to place the value of a variable on the stack, invoke its name and a fetch instruction. For example, you could type:

```
      <variable name> @
or    <2variable name> 2@
```

To store a value into a variable, invoke its name and a store instruction. For example:

```
        <value> <variable name> !
or      <value1> <value2> <variable name> 2!
```

In a read-only-memory environment, **VARIABLE** is re-defined to allot space in read/write memory rather than in *name*'s parameter field; in this case, the assigned read/write memory address is compiled into the parameter field. The run-time behavior of a variable in ROM is to return the contents of its ROM parameter field (like a constant does); that value is the address of the variable's data space in RAM.

Glossary

VARIABLE <name> (–) Core

Create a dictionary entry for *name* associated with one cell of data space.

> name (– a-addr)
> Return the address of the data space associated with name.

2VARIABLE <name> (–) Double

Create a dictionary entry for *name* associated with two cells of data space. "two-variable"

> name (– a-addr)
> Return the address of the first cell of the data space associated with *name*.

CVARIABLE <name> (–) Common usage

Create a dictionary entry for *name* associated with one character of data space. Typically found in smaller systems for embedded microcontrollers and other environments where it is advantageous to allocate variables only one character in size. "C-variable"

> name (– c-addr)
> Return the address associated with *name*.

References

@, **!**, **2@**, and **2!**, Section 2.3.4
ALIGN, Section 2.3.3

2.3.2.2 Constants and Values

The purpose of a **CONSTANT** is to provide a name for a value that is referenced often but never changed. There are both single- and double-precision versions. Figure 7 shows an example of a dictionary entry built by **CONSTANT**.

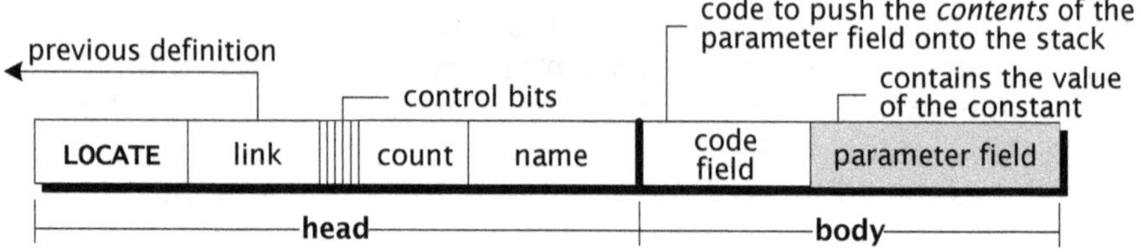

Figure 7. Dictionary entry built by CONSTANT

The syntax for defining constants is:

```
<value> CONSTANT <name>
```

For example, you may define:

```
1000 CONSTANT LIMIT
0 5000 2CONSTANT LIMITS
3141593. 2CONSTANT PI
```

When a **CONSTANT** is referenced by name, its value (not its address) is pushed onto the stack. Similarly, when a **2CONSTANT** is referenced, two stack items are pushed onto the stack. In the case where a **2CONSTANT** is used for two values (as in **LIMITS**, above), the values are placed on the stack in the order specified (e.g., 5000 on top, 0 below). In the case of a double-precision number, the high-order part of the number is on top of the stack.

The purpose of a **VALUE** is to provide a name for a single-precision value that is referenced often and may need to change. On systems with a mix of RAM and ROM, **VALUE**s are compiled into RAM. The procedure for defining values is to declare:

```
<initial value> VALUE <name>
```

For example, you may define:

```
1000 VALUE LIMIT
```

When a **VALUE** is referenced by *name*, its current value is pushed onto the stack. The word **TO** is used to change a value. The syntax is:

```
<new value> TO <name>
```

For example, you might type this:

```
1000 VALUE LIMIT   LIMIT .      500 TO LIMIT   LIMIT .
```

The first phrase creates a **VALUE** named **LIMIT** whose value when defined is 1000. The second phrase changes the value to 500.

VALUE combines the convenience of a **CONSTANT**—it returns its value without requiring an explicit **@**—with the writeability of a **VARIABLE**.

Glossary

CONSTANT <name> (x –) Core

Create a dictionary entry for *name* associated with the value *x*. Note: the value of a **CONSTANT** cannot be changed.

> name (– x)
> Return the value associated with *name*.

2CONSTANT <name> (x_1 x_2 –) Double

Create a dictionary entry for *name* associated with the two values x_1 and x_2. Note: the value of a **2CONSTANT** cannot be changed. "two-constant"

> name (– x_1 x_2)
> Return the values associated with *name*.

VALUE <name> (x –) Core Ext

Create a dictionary entry for *name* associated with one cell of data space initialized to *x*.

> name (– x)
> Return the value associated with *name*. (To change the **VALUE**, use **TO**.)

References

TO, used to change the value of a **VALUE**, Section 2.3.4

2.3.3 Arrays and Tables

CREATE is a generic defining word that provides a minimal defining behavior: construct the dictionary entry and associate it with the next available location in data space. It doesn't allocate any memory and, hence, should be followed by something that does. **ALLOT** will allocate a specified number of bytes of memory; the words **,** and **C,** place specified values in memory (one cell and one byte, respectively) and allocate the required amount of space for them.

CREATE is often used to mark the beginning of an array. The space for the rest of the array is reserved by incrementing the data space pointer with **ALLOT**, as in this example:

```
CREATE DATA  100 ALLOT
```

The example reserves a total of 100 bytes for an array named **DATA**. When **DATA** is used in a colon definition, the address of the first byte of **DATA** will be pushed on the stack by the instance behavior of **CREATE**. The array is not initialized. If you wish to set all the elements of the array to zero, you may use **ERASE**, as in the following example:

```
DATA  100 ERASE
```

When executing operations involving address calculations, use the words **CELL+**, **CELLS**, **CHAR+**, and **CHARS** as appropriate to convert logical values, rather than literal numbers, to bytes. For example, to increment an address by three cells on a 32-bit system, use **3 CELLS +**, not **12 +**; this makes the code portable to systems with other cell widths.

On the vast majority of platforms in use today, a character is exactly one byte in size, so the terms "character" and "byte" are equivalent and **1 CHARS** is equal to 1. On these systems, **CHARS** is usually a no-op and **CHAR+** is equivalent to **1+**. If you are confident the program you're writing will not be required to run on a platform where a character is other than one byte in size, you can omit these words. However, you should document the fact that you have made this assumption. If you wish to maintain compatibility with systems on which a character may occupy more than one byte (such as those using international character sets), use **CHARS** to convert characters to the equivalent number of bytes. The example above, for example, would be:

```
CREATE DATA  100 CHARS ALLOT
```

This book generally assumes that a character occupies one byte.

If you wish to allocate a number of cells, or to increment an address by a certain number of cells, you may use **CELLS**:

```
CREATE CELL-DATA  100 CELLS ALLOT
```

CELL-DATA returns the address of the beginning of this region, which is 400 bytes long on a 32-bit implementation or 200 bytes long on a 16-bit implementation. The next cell would be **CELL-DATA CELL+**, and subsequent cells would be **CELL-DATA** <n> **CELLS +**.

The word **,** ("comma") stores the top stack item into the next available dictionary location, and increments the data space pointer by one cell.

The most common use of **,** is to put values into a table whose starting address is defined by using **CREATE**; **CREATE** defines a word that behaves identically to **VARIABLE**, in that, when the new word is executed, its address is returned. **CREATE** differs from **VARIABLE** only in that it does not allot any space.

Consider this example:

```
CREATE TENS  1 , 10 , 100 , 1000 , 10000 ,
```

This establishes a table whose starting address is given by **TENS** and which contains powers of ten from zero through four. Indexing this table by a power of ten will give the appropriate value. A possible use might be:

```
: 10** ( n1 n2 -- n)  CELLS \ Convert n2 to a byte offset
   TENS +    \ Add offset to address
   @ * ;     \ Fetch value & multiply
```

Given a single-precision number n_1 on the stack, with a power of ten n_2 on top, **10**** will multiply the number by the power of ten to yield the product.

When a single byte of data is sufficient, **C,** performs for bytes the same function that **,** performs for cells. On processors that do not tolerate addresses that are not cell-aligned (e.g., 68000), uses of **C,** must be for strings of even cell length or some other action must be taken to re-align the data space pointer.

Even on processors that allow references to any byte address in data space, there may be an execution penalty for addresses that are not cell-aligned (the even addresses in a 16-bit system and the addresses divisible by four in a 32-bit system). Most dictionary entries, such as those created by a colon definition, contain only cell-sized items, so the data space pointer will stay aligned if is aligned to begin with. However, use of words such as **C,** or string-compiling words may result in subsequent unaligned addresses.

Two words facilitate alignment in such cases. **ALIGN** takes no stack arguments; when executed, it examines the data space pointer and, if it is not cell-aligned, reserves enough additional bytes to align it. **ALIGNED** takes an arbitrary address and returns the first aligned address that is greater than or equal to the given address.

Dictionary entries made by **CREATE** and by words that use **CREATE** are aligned. Data laid down by **,** are not automatically aligned, but cell-sized words that access data (such as **@**) may require alignment. Therefore, if you are mixing uses of **,** and **C,** you must manually perform the alignment, e.g.:

```
CREATE TEST 123 C, ALIGN 1234 ,
```

...so the phrase **TEST CELL+ @** will properly return **1234**.

The notation *a-addr* indicates an address that will be cell-aligned on platforms where this is required; the notation *c-addr* indicates character alignment (i.e., may be an odd or unaligned address).

Glossary

, (x –) Core

Reserve one cell of data space and store *x* in the cell. If the data-space pointer is aligned initially, it will be aligned after **,** executes. "comma"

ALIGN (–) Core

If the data-space pointer is not aligned, reserve enough space to align it.

ALIGNED (addr – a-addr) Core

Return *a-addr*, the first aligned address greater than or equal to *addr*.

ALLOT (u –) Core

Allocate *u* bytes of data space beginning at the next available location. Normally used immediately following **CREATE**.

BUFFER: <name> (n –) Common usage

Create a dictionary entry for *name* associated with *n* bytes of data space. "buffer colon"

> name (– addr)
>
> Return the address of the first byte of the data space associated with *name*.

C, (char –) Core
Reserve one byte of data space and store *char* in the byte. "C-comma"

CELL+ (a-addr$_1$ – a-addr$_2$) Core
Add the size in bytes of a cell to *a-addr$_1$*, giving *a-addr$_2$*. Equivalent to **2 +** on a 16-bit system and to **4 +** on a 32-bit system. "cell-plus"

CELLS (n$_1$ – n$_2$) Core
Return n_2, the size in bytes of n_1 cells.

CHAR+ (c-addr$_1$ – c-addr$_2$) Core
Add the size in bytes of a character to *c-addr$_1$*, giving *c-addr$_2$*. "care-plus"

CHARS (n$_1$ – n$_2$) Core
Return n_2, the size in bytes of n_1 characters. On many systems, this word is a no-op. "cares"

CREATE <name> (–) Core
Create a dictionary entry for *name* associated with the next available location in data space. Normally followed by one or more words that allocate data space, such as **ALLOT** or **,** (comma).

> name (– a-addr)
> Return the address associated with *name*.

2.3.4 Memory Stack Operations

Having defined words that return memory addresses, we now need to consider how to access memory. This category of operations allows you to reference memory by using addresses that are on the stack.

The words **@** and **!** (pronounced "fetch" and "store," respectively) are used to reference single cells. Each expects on the stack a memory address, such as that returned by an instance of **VARIABLE**.

@ expects an address on top of the stack. This address is replaced with the contents of the addressed cell. Similarly, **2@** and **C@** expect an address, which will be replaced by the two cells or one character, respectively, at that address. In the case of **C@**, its character will be placed in the low-order bits of the cell on top of the stack, with the higher order bits set to zero. **C@** does not "sign extend," i.e., it does not propagate the sign bit leftward into more-significant bit positions.

! expects an address on top of the stack and will replace its contents by the contents of the cell beneath it. Similarly, **2!** expects two cells beneath the address. **C!** expects one character in the low-order bits of the cell beneath the address; the high-order bits of this lower cell are ignored. The character is stored in the addressed location; the address and character cells are removed from the stack.

For example, the following phrase would fetch the first character in **PAD** to the top of the stack:

```
PAD C@
```

It is the programmer's responsibility to use the appropriate fetch and store operators for the size of the container being referenced. For example, storing a cell into a place defined by **CVARIABLE** will damage the adjacent bytes with unpredictable results.

Glossary

! `( x a-addr — )` Core
Store *x* in the cell at *a-addr*, removing both from the stack. "store"

+! `( n a-addr — )` Core
Add *n* to the contents of the cell at *a-addr* and store the result in the cell at *a-addr*, removing both from the stack. "plus-store"

2! (x_1 x_2 a-addr —) Core
Store the cell pair x_1 x_2 in the two cells beginning at *a-addr*, removing three cells from the stack. The order of the two cells in memory is the same as on the stack, usually meaning that the one in the top stack position (x_2) is in the lower memory address. "two-store"

2@ (a-addr — x_1 x_2) Core
Push the cell pair x_1 x_2 at *a-addr* onto the top of the stack. The combined action of **2!** and **2@** will always preserve the stack order of the cells. "two-fetch"

@ `( a-addr — x )` Core
Replace *a-addr* with the contents of the cell at *a-addr*. "fetch"

BLANK `( c-addr u — )` Core
Set a region of memory, at address *c-addr* and of length *u*, to ASCII blanks (hex 20). Two cells are removed from the stack.

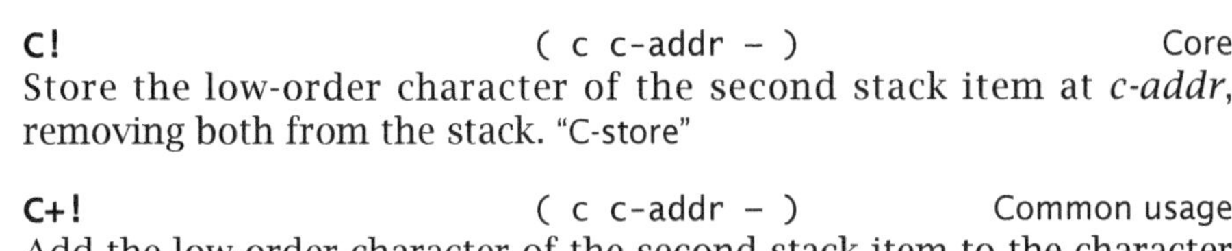

C! (c c-addr –) Core

Store the low-order character of the second stack item at *c-addr*, removing both from the stack. "C-store"

C+! (c c-addr –) Common usage

Add the low-order character of the second stack item to the character at *c-addr*, removing both from the stack. "C-plus store"

C@ (c-addr – c) Core

Replace *c-addr* with the contents of the character at *c-addr*. The character fetched is stored in the low-order character of the top stack item, with the remaining bits cleared to zero. "C-fetch"

ERASE (c-addr u –) Core Ext

Erase (set to zero) a region of memory, given its starting address *c-addr* and length *u*.

FILL (c-addr u b –) Core

Fill a region of memory, at address *c-addr* and of length *u*, with the least-significant byte of the top-of-stack item. Three cells are removed from the stack.

MOVE ($addr_1$ $addr_2$ u –) Core

Copy *u* bytes from a source starting at $addr_1$ to the destination starting at $addr_2$. After the transfer, the destination area at $addr_2$ contains exactly what the source area $addr_1$ did before the transfer, even if the address ranges overlap. See also **CMOVE** and **CMOVE>** for strings, Section 3.4.

TO <name> (x –) Core Ext

Store *x* in the data space associated with *name*. *name* must have been defined by **VALUE**.

References

Defining word **VALUE**, Section 2.3.1

2.3.5 Data Object and Memory Access Examples

This section presents some examples showing how data objects may be defined and accessed.

Example 1: A Variable

```
VARIABLE ITEM                      \ Defines a variable
100 ITEM !                         \ Sets its value to 100
: SEE-ITEM ( -- )    ITEM ? ;      \ Displays its value
```

Example 2: An array of characters or bytes

```
1000 CONSTANT SIZE                 \ Defines a constant
CREATE BYTE-ARRAY  SIZE ALLOT      \ Allocates SIZE bytes
BYTE-ARRAY SIZE DUMP               \ Displays its contents
```

Example 3: Two arrays of cell-wide items

```
CREATE DATA1 SIZE CELLS ALLOT      \ DATA1 is SIZE cells long
SIZE CELLS BUFFER: DATA2           \ Same size as DATA1
```

In these examples, the use of a constant for the array size improves readability. In Section 4.5 we also see this used to provide the upper limit (size parameter) for loops dealing with arrays. By defining such constant values you can avoid "magic numbers" (arbitrary literal values) in code. This makes your code more readable and more easily maintainable. If you need to change the size, you need do so in only one place and all other uses will automatically follow.

Example 4: Array of cells initialized to zeroes (nulls)

```
CREATE DATA  SIZE CELLS ALLOT  DATA SIZE CELLS ERASE
```

This defines **DATA**, which will return an address. Following the **ALLOT**, **DATA** returns the starting address of the array for **ERASE**, which will clear the region to zeroes.

Later sections describe accessing individual bytes or cells in an array.

References

CELLS, Section 2.3.3
Accessing elements of an array in a loop, Section 4.5

3. String Handling

This section covers a range of topics relating to character strings, both for text and for representing numbers.

Forth contains many words used to reference single characters (bytes) or character strings. Characters may be grouped and thought of as a string; this string can be operated on as a single variable.

A special set of string operations is devoted to converting numbers from characters to binary values on the stack, and vice-versa.

3.1 General String Topics

A standard working area is used to hold most character strings for processing. This area is referred to as **PAD**.

In addition to the words described here, other words may be used to reference character data in specific environments, e.g., database support. Such words are described in the product-specific manuals.

References

PAD, Section 3.1.2

3.1.1 Single Characters

It is frequently desirable to refer to the ASCII code for a character, for example, to specify a delimiter for a parsing operation. Forth provides two words for this purpose. They differ in that one is intended for use inside a definition, where it compiles a character as a literal; the other is intended to be used interpretively (i.e., in a command line or a source file outside a definition).

For example, if you type:

```
CHAR A
```

...you'll get the ASCII code for the capital letter A (65) on the stack.

However, inside a definition, you might write:

```
: ?DIGIT ( c -- t )   [CHAR] 0 [CHAR] 9 1+ WITHIN ;
```

...which returns true if the character supplied on the stack is a decimal digit. Specifying a character this way makes your code much more readable than plugging in the numeric ASCII code as a literal. And because **[CHAR]** compiles the ASCII code as a literal, there's no difference from other literals in either size or performance.

This strategy is only practical with visible graphic characters, however. If you're working with control codes, we recommend defining them as **CONSTANT**s, such as:

```
HEX 1B CONSTANT ESC DECIMAL
```

The constant **BL** returns the code for a blank or space ($20).

Glossary

CHAR <c> (– char) Core
Parse the word (normally a single character) following **CHAR** in the input stream. Put the ASCII value of the first character of this word on the stack. See **[CHAR]** for the function that compiles a character as a literal inside a definition. "care"

[CHAR] <c> (– char) Core
Inside a colon definition, parse the word (normally a single character) following **[CHAR]** in the input stream and compile the ASCII value of its first character as a literal. At run time, this character will be pushed on the stack. "bracket-care"

BL (– char) Core
Return the character for a blank or space ($20) on the stack.

3.1.2 Scratch Storage for Strings

PAD is a storage area of indefinite size (84 characters minimum) that is used to hold strings for intermediate processing. Each terminal task in a multitasked system contains a private **PAD** area. The word **PAD** places the address of the first byte in this area on the top of the stack.

The contents of the region addressed by **PAD** are under the complete control of the user. No words defined in a Standard Forth system or described in this manual place anything in this region, although changing data space allocations (e.g., by adding new words to the Forth dictionary) may change the address returned by **PAD.**

In cases where **PAD** is located relative to the top of the dictionary, the location of **PAD** changes whenever something is added to the dictionary. On implementations where data space is intermingled with the dictionary, the location of **PAD** will also be affected by adding data or data areas with **,** (comma), **C,** (c-comma), or **ALLOT** and by discarding definitions. Thus, information left in **PAD** before one of these operations may not be addressable after the operation (and may, in fact, be overwritten by a new definition).

Glossary

PAD (– addr) Core Ext

Return the address of a temporary storage area, usually used for processing strings. The area can hold at least 84 characters. It may be located relative to the top of the dictionary, in which case the address of **PAD** will vary as the dictionary is modified.

References

, and **C,**, Section 2.3.3
ALLOT, Section 2.3.3

3.1.3 Internal String Format

Many Forth words that store strings in memory use an internal format called a *counted string.* This format stores the length of the string (up to 255) in the first byte, as shown in Figure 8.

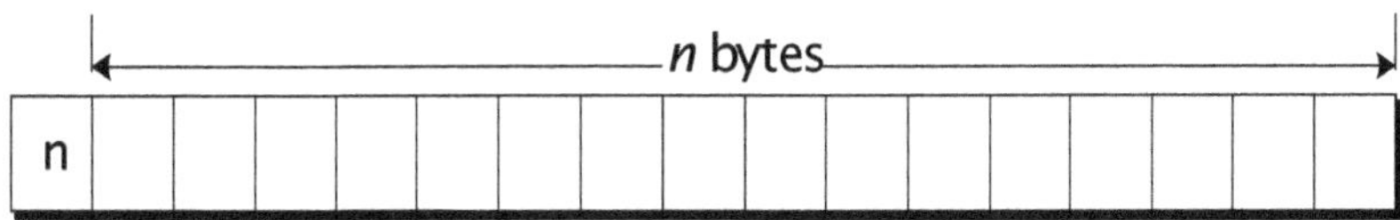

Figure 8. Format of a counted string

This format is more efficient than a *zero-terminated string* (a common format in C programming) because the count is stored when the string is acquired, and doesn't have to be repeatedly re-counted at run time.

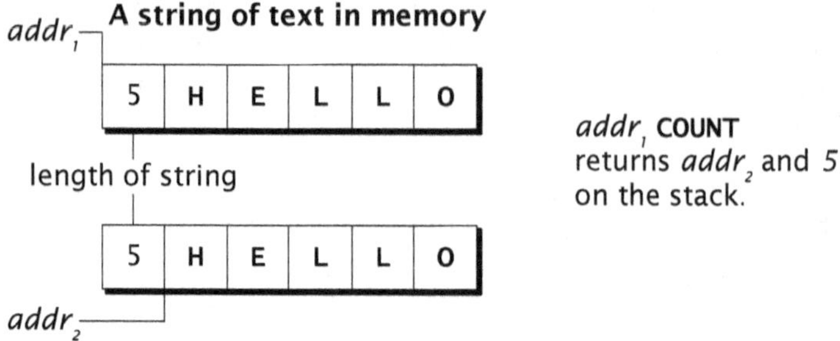

Figure 9. Use of COUNT

A word frequently used with counted strings is **COUNT**. **COUNT** takes as its parameter the address of a counted string. It returns the address of the string's first character and the length of the string, as shown in Figure 9.

COUNT's definition is equivalent to:

```
: COUNT ( addr1 -- addr2 u )   DUP 1+ SWAP C@ ;
```

Glossary

COUNT (c-addr1 – c-addr2 u) Core

Return the length *n* and address $c\text{-}addr_2$ of the text portion of a counted string beginning at $c\text{-}addr_1$.

3.2 Strings in Definitions

It is often desirable to have text messages included in definitions, e.g., to issue error messages, user prompts, or report headings. Forth provides several words that compile strings in definitions.

Of these words, the most generally useful is **S"** (pronounced "s-quote"). When used in a definition, **S"** compiles a string (delimited by a quotation mark), and stores it in the dictionary. When the word containing this string is executed, the address and length of the string are pushed on the stack. When used interpretively (i.e., not in a definition), it puts the string in a temporary location and leaves its address and length on the stack. You may then move the string to a permanent location, display it, or do anything else you might do with the string's address and length parameters.

Here is a word to search for a compiled string in a longer string whose address and count are on the stack:

```
: ?DUCK ( addr n -- flag)   S" duck"
   SEARCH  -ROT 2DROP ;
```

The phrase **-ROT 2DROP** discards the address and character count where the match (may have) occurred, leaving only the flag that reports the outcome.

In cases similar to the examples above, you might need to allow the test string to contain an arbitrary mixture of upper- and lower-case characters. If so, you should set or clear the appropriate bit in each byte of the test string, to standardize on all upper or all lower case, before making your comparison.

S" also may be executed interpretively to provide the address and count of a string outside of a definition. For example, **INCLUDED** (Section 5.5.3) loads a file, given the address and count of a string on the stack containing the filename and optional path information. Typical usage would be:

```
… S" <filename and path>" INCLUDED …
```

On many implementations, however, an interpreted **S"** uses a single buffer to hold the string. Therefore, successive uses of **S"** may overwrite the buffer from a previous use. If you're going to use the string immediately, as in the example above, that's no problem. If you want to save it for later use, move it to a more permanent location.

C" is a similar word that is used only inside colon definitions. It compiles a *counted string* (compiled with its count in the first byte, a common practice in Forth). At execution time, **C"** returns the address of the length byte. Therefore, it's common to use **COUNT** to fetch the address of the first byte of the string and the string's length.

For example, consider a word **?NO** that compares a data string—whose address and length are on the stack—to a string compiled as part of the definition of **?NO**, and returns *true* if they match:

```
: ?NO ( addr u -- flag)   C" no" COUNT COMPARE ;
```

?NO takes the address and length of an input string. When **?NO** is executed, **C"** will push the address of a compiled counted string on the stack. **COUNT** converts that address to a string address and length, leaving appropriate arguments for **COMPARE** to perform the comparison.

ABORT" is a generic error-handling word. It handles its input value as a truth flag: if it is non-zero, the string which follows will be displayed and a system abort will occur.

Finally, **."** simply displays its string.

Each of these words performs functions both when the definition in which it's used is compiled and when the definition is executed. At compile time for each, a reference to the execute-time function is compiled, followed by the string. At execute time the behavior differs among them: For **S"**, the address and length of the string will be pushed on the stack. For **C"**, the address of the counted string will be pushed on the stack. For **ABORT"**, the test will be performed. For both **."** and **ABORT"**, the string will be typed out. The stack notation for the words below refers to the execution-time behavior.

Glossary

S" `<string>"` `( – c-addr u )` Core, File

If interpreting, return the address and length of the following *string*, terminated by ", which is in a temporary buffer. If compiling (inside a colon definition), compile the string; at run time, the address and length of the string will be pushed on the stack. "S-quote"

C" `<string>"` `( – c-addr )` Core Ext

Similar to **S"** but only used inside colon definitions. **C"** compiles a counted string whose length is stored in the first byte. As with **S"**, the *string* is terminated by ". At run time, the address of the counted string will be pushed on the stack. "C-quote"

." `<string>"` `( – )` Core

Compile *string*, which will be typed when the word that contains it is executed. "dot-quote"

For example:

```
: GREETING ( -- )  ." Hi there" ;
```

References

Error handling, Section 5.3
Compiling strings, Section 6.3.4

3.3 Strings in Data Structures

In addition to compiling strings in definitions, you might want to compile a string in a data structure—for example, following **CREATE**. The word **,"** compiles a string up to a terminating **"** in the next available locations in data space. The string is compiled as a counted string (see Section 3.1.3), with its length in the first byte. Here's an example:

```
CREATE MARY ," Mary Brooks"
CREATE JOHN ," John Smith"
... more code ...
: GREETING ( addr -- )  ." Your instructor will be "
   COUNT TYPE ;
```

Usage:

```
MARY GREETING  Your instructor will be Mary Brooks.
```

Here the name **MARY** or **JOHN** provides the address of the counted string displayed by **GREETING**.

The name **,"** is intended to be consistent with **,** and **C,** which compile numbers in tables, as described in Section 2.3.3.

You must provide some way of getting the address of your string. In the examples above, **CREATE** is used to define a data structure whose content is the string. In this usage, it is not necessary to worry about address alignment (on platforms that require it), because **CREATE** will ensure that its data space pointer is aligned, as will other defining words. However, if you are using a more manual approach, such as:

```
HERE ," Mary"  HERE ," Brooks" 2CONSTANT NAME
```

...there is no guarantee these addresses will be aligned, and you may wish to use **ALIGN** before each **HERE**. Also note that the actual strings in this example are not contiguous because each is prefaced by its count byte and, if **ALIGN** is used, possibly by one or more alignment bytes.

Glossary

," <string>" (–) Common usage

Compile the following *string*, terminated by **"**. "comma-quote"

References

Address alignment, Section 2.3.3

3.4 String Management Operations

Forth contains several words used to reference strings, compare and adjust them, and move strings to different locations. Other words used to input or output character strings are discussed in Section 5.3.

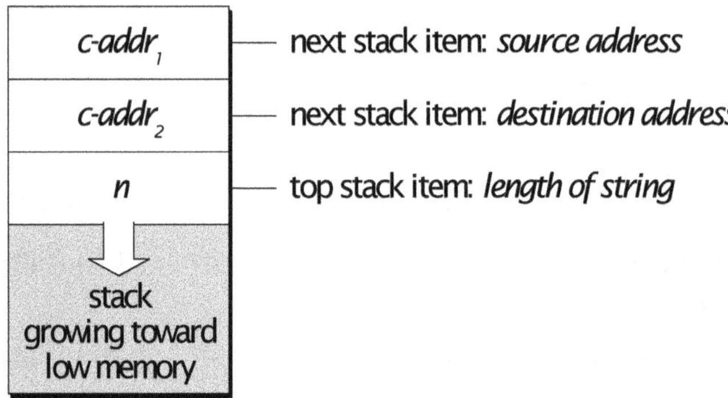

Figure 10. Format of arguments for most two-string operators

Most words that operate on one string expect the length of that string to be on top of the stack, with its address beneath it. Many words that operate on two separate strings expect three items on top of the stack in the format shown in Figure 10, in which one length count applies to both strings. The above format is used instead of two separate character counts.

The word **MOVE** (Section 2.3.4) is the general purpose string copy operator. **CMOVE** and **CMOVE>**, described in the glossary below, allow special handling if the string areas overlap. **MOVE** will detect overlap and handle the move so the original content of the source area is identical to the destination area after the move.

Two string move commands are diagrammed in Figure 11. This figure shows the difference in operation between **CMOVE** and **CMOVE>** and the effects of text movement. The strings overlap in both cases.

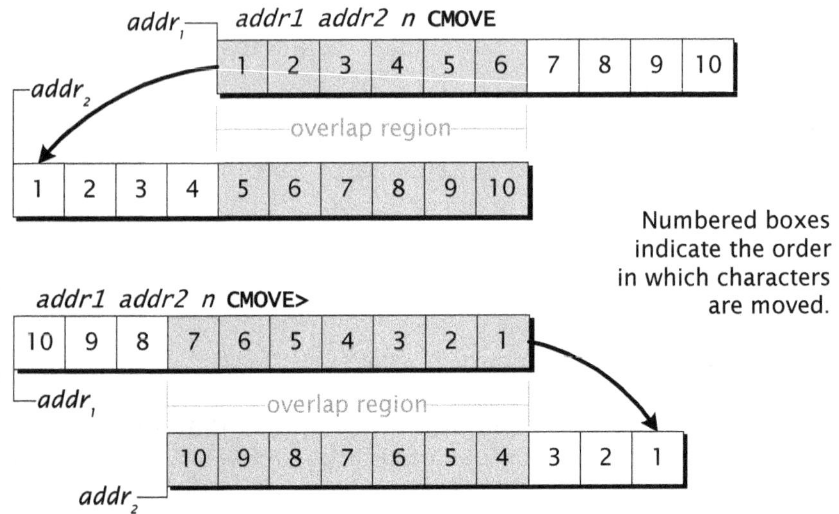

Figure 11. Actions of string copy operators

The behavior of **CMOVE** and **CMOVE>** can be exploited to "ripple" a particular bit pattern through a region of memory. Consider this sequence:

```
PAD 80 ERASE  HEX DEADBEEF PAD !  DECIMAL
PAD DUP 4 + 76 CMOVE
PAD 80 DUMP
```

CMOVE will copy each character to a position 4 bytes higher in memory, so the pattern **$DEADBEEF** will be replicated throughout the region. This trick is occasionally useful, for example in diagnostic procedures.

Glossary

-TRAILING (c-addr u_1 – c-addr u_2) String

Remove any trailing blanks in a string at address *c-addr* whose original length is u_1, and return adjusted string parameters. The same address is returned but with an adjusted length u_2 equal to u_1 less the number of spaces at the end of the string. If u_1 is zero, or if the entire string consists of blanks, u_2 is zero. "minus-trailing"

/STRING (c-$addr_1$ u_1 n – c-$addr_2$ u_2) String

Adjust the character string at *c-addr*$_1$ u_1 by *n* characters. Return the parameters *c-addr*$_2$ = *c-addr*$_1$ + *n*, and length $u_2 = u_1 - n$. "slash-string"

HERE (– addr) Core

Push the address of the next available location in data space onto the stack.

CMOVE (c-addr$_1$ c-addr$_2$ u –) String

Copy *u* characters from a source starting at address *c-addr$_1$* to the destination starting at *c-addr$_2$*. The copy proceeds character-by-character from *lower to higher* addresses. Three cells are removed from the stack. See also **MOVE**, Section 2.3.4. "C-move"

CMOVE> (c-addr$_1$ c-addr$_2$ u –) String

CMOVE> has the same arguments as **CMOVE** but the copy proceeds character-by-character from *higher to lower* addresses. **CMOVE>** is used for transferring from a data field to an overlapping data field in higher memory. Three cells are removed from the stack. See also **MOVE**, Section 2.3.4. "C-move-up"

References

Character string I/O, Section 5.3
Parsing strings, Section 6.1.5

3.5 Comparing Character Strings

Character-string comparisons operate on two separate character strings. This allows the two to be compared by use of the ASCII collating sequence.

The words in the following glossary are provided. Both of them compare strings, but they are intended for entirely different situations. **COMPARE** is intended for finding a match in a list or table, or in a sort or binary search operation when the collating order of non-matching strings is relevant. **SEARCH** is intended for finding a short string in a longer string, as in an editor's search function.

As an example of their use, you could compare a string whose address is returned by **NAME** with one temporarily stored at **PAD**, testing as follows:

```
PAD <length> DUP NAME SWAP COMPARE
```

For a more detailed example, consider the two strings in Figure 12.

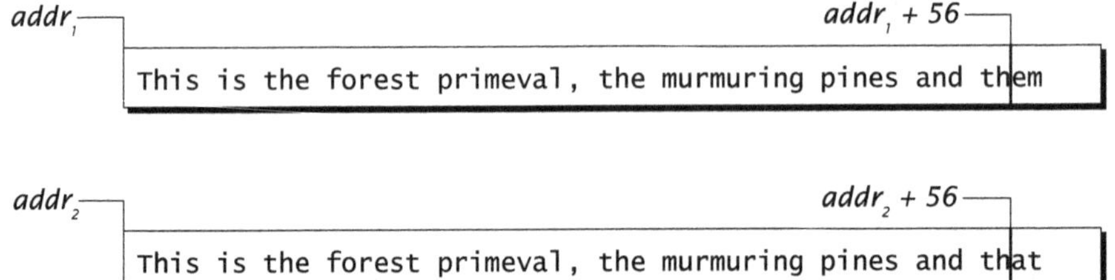

Figure 12. String comparison

Table 6 shows some comparisons and their results.

Table 6: String comparison examples

Phrase	Result	Remarks
<addr1> 55 <addr2> 55 **COMPARE**	0	Strings are equal
<addr1> 56 <addr2> 56 **COMPARE**	1	String at $addr_1$ is later in collating sequence
<addr1> 55 <addr2> 56 **COMPARE**	-1	String at $addr_1$ is shorter, hence earlier in collating sequence

SEARCH is generally used to find a short string in a longer string. It is used by the Forth editor. As an example of **SEARCH**, consider the strings in Figure 13.

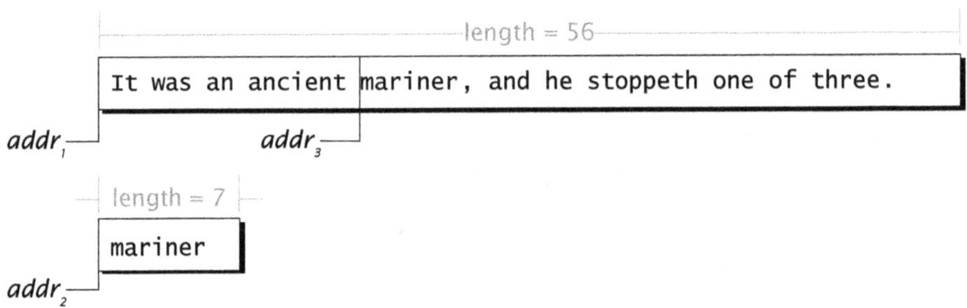

Figure 13. String search

```
<addr1> 56 <addr2> 7 SEARCH
```

...would return:

```
<addr3> 38 -1
```

...because there is a match starting at $addr_3$ with 38 characters left in the long string.

Glossary

COMPARE (c-addr$_1$ u$_1$ c-addr$_2$ u$_2$ – n) String
Compare the string specified by $c\text{-}addr_1$ u_1 to the string specified by $c\text{-}addr_2$ u_2 and return a result code *n*. The strings are compared character-by-character, beginning at the given addresses and continuing up to the length of the shorter string or until a difference is found. If the two strings are identical and of equal lengths, *n* is zero. If the two strings are identical up to the length of the shorter string, *n* is -1 if u_1 is less than u_2, and +1 otherwise. If the two strings are not identical up to the length of the shorter string, *n* is -1 if the first non-matching character in the string at $c\text{-}addr_1$ has a lesser numeric value than the corresponding character in the string at $c\text{-}addr_2$, and +1 otherwise.

SEARCH (c-addr$_1$ u$_1$ c-addr$_2$ u$_2$ – c-addr$_3$ u$_3$ flag) String
Search for a match of the string $c\text{-}addr_2$ u_2 in the string $c\text{-}addr_1$ u_1 (the latter is presumed to be longer). If a match is found, return *true* with the address $c\text{-}addr_3$ of the first matching character and the length u_3 of the remainder of the string. If no match is found, $c\text{-}addr_3 = c\text{-}addr_1$, $u_3 = u_1$, and *flag* is *false*.

References

PAD, Section 3.1.2

3.6 Number Conversions

The strings that comprise numeric values require special processing. This section discusses both input and output number conversions.

3.6.1 Input Number Conversion

Forth's text interpreter will automatically convert strings it encounters to numbers if they are not named words and if their characters contain only numeric digits from zero to **BASE**-1 plus optional special punctuation. Numbers converted in this fashion are pushed onto the data stack.

Wherever possible, design your applications to take advantage of Forth's interactive nature. Thus, a hypothetical word **SCANS** whose function is to perform some user-specified number of scans (an application function) should expect only its parameter on the stack. Then, to perform 100 scans, the user could type:

```
100 SCANS
```

Such usage is natural and convenient for the operator, and requires no special programming to handle the input parameter.

However, there are occasions in which normal Forth syntax is inadequate. Some examples include:

- Parsing a text string that comes from a source other than a terminal, such as magnetic tape.
- Entry of numbers that must be in double-precision but are not punctuated (i.e., zip codes).
- Entry of numbers that must follow, rather than precede, the command.
- Applications in which there is no user access to words in the dictionary.

Forth provides words to enable the user to handle numeric input in a variety of circumstances. This section describes these methods.

>NUMBER is the basic input number conversion routine. If it encounters any non-numeric digit during the conversion, it stops with a pointer to that character, rather than aborting. For this reason, **>NUMBER** is often used when a number is input by a program directly, without using the text interpreter.

>NUMBER expects a double-precision integer and the address and count of the input string. It leaves a double-precision integer (the result of the conversion), and an address and count. The initial address given to **>NUMBER** must point to the first (most-significant) digit of the string of numerals. The initial double-precision number is normally set to zero.

After **>NUMBER** stops, the address in the second stack item is the address of the first non-numeric character **>NUMBER** encountered or, if the string was entirely converted, of the first character past the end of the string. The double-precision integer will contain data from all digits converted thus far.

An example of the use of **>NUMBER** is:

```
: INPUT ( -- n )    PAD 5 BLANK   PAD 5 ACCEPT >R
     0. PAD R> >NUMBER  2DROP DROP ;
```

This initializes a region of **PAD** to blanks, and awaits up to five digits which will be stored there. **0.** provides an initial double-precision value, and **PAD R>** provides the address and actual count for **>NUMBER.** The phrase **2DROP DROP** discards the address and count returned by **>NUMBER** and the high-order part of the converted number.

INPUT will not convert input strings with a leading minus sign, because a minus is not a digit. If negative input is necessary, the above definition can be extended to check the first character before beginning the conversion; if it is a minus sign, start **>NUMBER** with the next character and negate the result.

>NUMBER returns the address of the string's next byte, so it may be called in a loop. The text interpreter's number conversion routine calls **>NUMBER** in just this way.

An application similar to this is parsing a packet of data received over a communications line or from a tape record, in which numeric fields are separated by an arbitrary delimiter such as **//**. To skip punctuation or fields that are not of interest, the appropriate number of bytes may simply be given as an argument to **/STRING** (Section 3.4) to space forward in the string.

Sometimes numbers may be in fields of known length but not separated by any delimiter. In such cases, the best solution may be to move groups of digits to **PAD**, where they may be converted easily by **>NUMBER.**

>NUMBER is a fairly low-level operator. Most implementations have added higher-level input number conversion words which are usually more convenient; they are not standardized, however. Common high-level input number conversions words are given in the glossary below.

Glossary

>NUMBER (ud_1 c-addr$_1$ u_1 – ud_2 c-addr$_2$ u_2) Core

Convert the characters in the string at *c-addr*$_1$, whose length is u_1, into digits, using the radix in **BASE**. The first digit is added to ud_1. Subsequent digits are added to ud_1 after multiplying ud_1 by the number in

BASE. Conversion continues until a non-convertible character (including an algebraic sign) is encountered or the entire string is converted; the result is ud_2. $c\text{-}addr_2$ is the location of the first unconverted character or, if the entire string was converted, of the first character beyond the string. u_2 is the number of unconverted characters in the string. "to-number"

NUMBER (c-addr u – n | d) Common usage

Attempt to convert a string at *c-addr* of length *u* into digits, using the radix (e.g., 10 for decimal, 16 for hex) in **BASE**. If valid punctuation (, . + - / :) is found, return *d*; if there is no punctuation, return *n*. If conversion fails due to a character that is neither a digit nor punctuation, an **ABORT** occurs.

NUMBER? (a n - 0 | n 1 | d 2) Common usage

Like **NUMBER**, but returns a flag above the result (if any) describing the result:

Table 7: Conversion results from NUMBER?

Flag value	Result
0	Failure (no **ABORT** occurs)
1	No punctuation, single number
2	Punctuation, double number.

References

Numeric input, Section 1.1.6
String moves, Section 3.4
ACCEPT, Section 5.4.1
PAD, Section 3.1.2

3.6.2 Numeric Output

Numeric output words allow the display of numeric quantities as ASCII characters. This output is generally directed to the terminal.

Numeric output words are divided into two categories: normal output words and conversion output words. The latter allow the *picturing* of ASCII text in a manner that somewhat resembles COBOL picturing.

All numeric output words produce ASCII text, which is the ASCII number expressed in the current **BASE**. **BASE** is a user variable, meaning that in a multitasked implementation each task may have its own copy. It contains the current conversion radix and is controlled with the appropriate radix word (e.g., **DECIMAL** or **HEX**) or by setting its value directly. For example, **BASE** may be set to binary by:

```
2 BASE !
```

References

Numbers, Section 1.1.6

3.6.2.1 Standard Numeric Output Words

Several standard words allow displaying single- or double-precision signed numbers in various formats. All of them remove their arguments from the stack. To preserve a number you are about to display, **DUP** it first. Each display word produces an output string that consists of the following characters:

1. If the number is negative, a leading minus sign (hyphen).
2. The absolute value of the number, with leading zeroes suppressed. (The number zero results in a single zero in the output.)
3. In some cases, a trailing blank.

The standard numeric output words are:

Glossary

. (n –) Core

Remove the top of stack item and display it as a signed single-precision integer followed by one space. "dot"

.R (n_1 $+n_2$ –) Core Ext

Display the signed single-precision integer n_1 with enough leading spaces to fill a field of width $+n_2$. This word expects a positive integer n_2 on top of the stack to specify the length of the output field. The width of the printed string that would be output by **.** is used to determine the number of leading blanks. No trailing blanks are printed. If the magnitude of the number to be printed prevents printing within the number of spaces specified, all digits are displayed with no leading spaces in a field as wide as necessary. "dot-R"

? (a-addr –) Tools

Display the contents of the address on the stack. "question"

? is equivalent to the phrase: **@ .**

D. (d –) Double

Display the top cell pair on the stack as a signed double-precision integer. "D-dot"

D.R (d +n –) Double

Display the top cell pair on the stack as a signed double-precision integer in a field of width *+n*, as for **.R**. "D-dot-R"

U. (u –) Core

Display the top stack item as an unsigned single-precision integer followed by one space. "U-dot"

U.R (u +n –) Core Ext

Similar to **.R** but unsigned. Display the unsigned single-precision integer *u* with enough leading spaces to fill a field of width *+n*. "U-dot-R"

3.6.2.2 Pictured Number Conversion

Forth converts numeric quantities to strings through a set of "pictured format" control words. These let the programmer specify field sizes, embedded punctuation, etc.

In Forth, the description of the desired output format starts with the rightmost (least-significant) character and continues to the left. Although this is the reverse of the method apparently used in other languages, it is the *actual* conversion process in all languages.

Binary numbers on the stack will be converted to ASCII character strings formatted according to the picture specifications. The string is built in a temporary area in memory large enough to accommodate at least 66 characters of output (on 32-bit CPUs) or 34 characters (on 16-bit CPUs).

After the picture conversion, the address of the beginning of the string and its length are returned on the stack. At this point, the converted string can be displayed, sent to a serial-type device with **TYPE**, moved to a buffer, saved to disk, or used in some other way.

The standard numeric output words (see previous section) use the same temporary region in the user's partition as the pictured format words. As a result, they may not be executed while a pictured output conversion is in process (e.g., during debugging). Furthermore, you must not make new definitions during the pictured conversion process; on many systems the buffer used for this purpose is defined by an offset from the current top of the dictionary and, therefore, modifying the dictionary will cause the buffer to move.

References

Standard numeric output, Section 3.6.2.1
TYPE, Section 5.4.3

3.6.2.3 Using Pictured Numeric Output Words

These words provide control over the conversion of binary numbers into digits. This section describes only pictured words with numeric output (digits); following sections describe the output of non-numeric punctuation such as periods and commas.

All the pictured numeric output words operate on an *unsigned double-precision integer* on the data stack. Throughout the process, this number remains on the stack, where it is repeatedly divided by **BASE** as digits are converted; it is finally discarded by **#>** at the end of the process. If you intend to append a possible sign to the number, you need to keep a signed value in the third stack position for that purpose.

Depending on the kind of number you begin with, the formula to get the required stack arrangement may be found in Table 8.

Table 8: Pre-processing for output number conversion

If you start with...	Use this phrase
Unsigned single precision	**0** (adds dummy high-order part)
Signed single precision	**DUP ABS 0**
Unsigned double precision	(no steps needed)
Signed double precision	**SWAP OVER DABS**

As an example of the use of these words, consider a definition of the standard Forth word **.** ("dot"):

```
: . ( n -- )   DUP ABS 0  <# #S ROT SIGN #>  TYPE SPACE ;
```

DUP ABS leaves two numbers on the stack: the absolute value of the number is on top of the original number, which is now useful only for its sign. **0** adds a cell on top of the stack, so the **0** cell and the **ABS** cell form the required double-precision integer to be used by the **<#** ... **#>** conversion routines. **<#** initializes the conversion process, then **#S** and **SIGN** assemble the string. **#>** completes the conversion and leaves the address and count of the ASCII string on the stack, suitable as input to **TYPE**.

To print a signed double-precision integer with the low-order three digits always appearing, regardless of the value, you could use the following definition:

```
: NNN ( d -- )   SWAP OVER DABS   <# # # #S
   ROT SIGN  #>  TYPE SPACE ;
```

The **SWAP OVER DABS** phrase establishes the signed value beneath the absolute value of the number to be printed, for the word **SIGN**. The sequence **# #** converts the low-order two digits, regardless of value. The word **#S** converts the remaining digits and always results in at least one character of output, even if the value is zero.

From the time the initialization word **<#** executes until the terminating word **#>** executes, the number being converted remains on the stack. It is possible to use the stack for intermediate results during pictured processing but any item placed on the stack must be removed before any subsequent picture editing or fill characters may be processed.

Glossary

<# (ud – ud) ***or*** (n ud – n ud) Core

Initialize pictured output of an unsigned double-precision integer. If the output is to be signed, a signed value *n* must be preserved somewhere, typically immediately beneath this integer, where it may later be passed to **SIGN** (below). "bracket-number"

(ud_1 – ud_2) Core

Divide ud_1 by **BASE**, giving the quotient ud_2 and the remainder *n*. Convert *n* to an ASCII character and append it to the beginning of the existing output string. Must be used after **<#** and before **#>**. The first digit added is the lowest-order digit (units), the next digit is the **BASE** digit, etc. A character is generated each time **#** is used, even if the number to be converted is zero. "number-sign"

#S (ud_1 – ud_2) Core

Convert digits from ud_1 repetitively until all significant digits in the source item have been converted, at which point conversion is complete, leaving ud_2 (which is zero). Must be used after **<#** and before **#>**. **#S** always results in at least one output character, even if the number to be converted is zero. "number-sign-S"

SIGN (n –) Core

Insert a minus sign at the current position in the string being converted if the signed value *n* is negative. This signed value *n* is a single-precision number; if the high-order bit is set, a minus sign will be introduced into the output as the leftmost non-blank character. The magnitude of the signed value is irrelevant. In order for the sign to appear at the left of the number (the usual place), **SIGN** must be called after all digits have been converted.

#> (ud – c-addr u) Core

Complete the conversion process after all digits have been converted. Discard the (presumably) exhausted double-precision number, and push onto the stack the address of the output string, with the count of bytes in this string above it. "number-bracket"

References

TYPE, Section 5.4.3

3.6.2.4 Using Pictured Fill Characters

In addition to pictured numeric output, it is possible to introduce arbitrary fill characters (or punctuation) into the output string at any point through the use of **HOLD**. **HOLD** requires as a parameter the numeric value of the ASCII character to be inserted. Thus,

> **2F HOLD**
> (value given in hex) or, more readably:
>
> **CHAR / HOLD**
> (value obtained by **CHAR** from the ASCII character following it)

...inserts the character / into the output string at the point where **HOLD** is executed. The phrase <value> **HOLD** may be executed as many times as desired in a given output conversion sequence.

Because this is normally done inside a colon definition, you would use **[CHAR]** (which compiles the character value as a literal) instead of **CHAR**.

.

If fill characters are likely to be used in several definitions, you may wish to add specific commands for them. The following format may be used for such a definition:

```
: '<name>'    <char-value> HOLD ;
```

...where *char-value* is the ASCII value of the character in the current radix and **'***name***'** is the name of the word to be defined. There are no restrictions on the format of the name, **'***name***'** is merely an often-used convention that includes the specified character appearing in the name itself. For example, a word that inserts a comma might be called **','**. **HOLD** is defined in such a way that executing **'***name***'** during pictured editing causes the indicated fill character to be inserted at the current point in the string being constructed.

In the following example, **'.'** produces a decimal point at the current position in the pictured numeric output. Then **.$** is defined to print double-precision integers as signed amounts with two decimal places:

```
: '.'    [CHAR] . HOLD ;
: .$ ( d -- )   SWAP OVER DABS  <# # # '.'
   #S ROT SIGN #> TYPE  SPACE ;
```

The word **[CHAR]** is only used in definitions. At run time, it places on the stack the ASCII value of the first character in the word following it. **CHAR** is similar, but is only used interpretively (i.e., not in definitions).

Glossary

HOLD (char –) Core
While constructing a pictured numeric output string, insert *char* at the current position. **HOLD** must occur only inside a **<#** ... **#>** number conversion sequence.

References

CHAR and **[CHAR]**, Section 3.1.1

3.6.3 Processing Special Characters

The normal pictured output capabilities described in the preceding two sections can handle most output requirements. But special cases, such as introducing commas in a number or "floating" a character (e.g., **$**) to the left of all significant digits, require special processing.

To perform certain of these operations, it is necessary to refer to the unconverted portion of a number being printed. This unconverted portion is equivalent to the original number divided by the current radix, for each numeric digit already generated. For example, if the initial number is 123 and the radix is 10, the intermediate number is 12 (following the conversion of the first digit) and 1 (following conversion of the second digit).

The value of this number may be tested and logical decisions may be based on its value. To illustrate, consider the following definitions. The word **D.ENG** prints a double-precision integer in U.S. engineering format (i.e., a comma after every three decimal places):

```
VARIABLE #PLACES                    \ Counts number of digits

: ',' ( -- )  [CHAR] , HOLD ;       \ Inserts a comma

: (D.ENG) ( d -- c-addr n)          \ Formats the string
   SWAP OVER DABS                   \ Set up stack
   0 #PLACES !                      \ Initialize place counter
   <#  BEGIN                        \ Start the conversion
```

```
      #  1 #PLACES +!          \ Increment counter
      2DUP D0= NOT WHILE       \ More significant digits?
      #PLACES 3 MOD 0= IF      \ Every 3 digits...
         ',' THEN   REPEAT     \  ... insert a comma
   ROT SIGN #> ;               \ Append sign, finish

: D.ENG ( d -- )   (D.ENG)  TYPE  SPACE ;
```

Using techniques similar to those above, you can do any kind of numeric output editing in Forth.

4. Structured Programming

The concept of *structured programming* was introduced by Edsger W. Dijkstra in a seminal series of papers beginning in 1968. Structured programming provides a uniform way to break a complicated structure into simple parts. The basic principles are:

1. Things must be defined before they are referenced.
2. A routine should have only one entry point and one exit.
3. Flow-of-control is restricted to sequential, conditional, and iterative (no arbitrary branching).

Forth's architecture strongly encourages adherence to these principles in both high-level code and in assembler. This section focuses on the flow-of-control issue.

4.1 Controlling Program Flow

Forth provides a set of words used to establish program loops and to alter the normal, sequential execution of words. Similar words for use in **CODE** definitions are available in some Forth assemblers.

The words that manage flow of control must be used within a colon definition. They will not operate properly when typed from a keyboard, because the text interpreter—processing the input stream sequentially—has no way to know where a forward branch should terminate. Loops must be opened and closed within the same definition. Loops may be nested to any depth, although deeply nested loops (above two or three levels) are difficult to test and not recommended.

Some words in this section are called *compiler directives*. When the compiler sees other words, it compiles references to those words' run-time behaviors. But when the compiler sees a compiler directive, it executes it immediately instead of compiling it. Forth is extensible, so you may define your own compiler directives; specific techniques appear in the section referenced below.

References

Compiler directives, Section 6.4

4.2 Comparison and Testing Operations

The words in this section perform logical operations that may be the basis for decisions involving flow of control.

These words test the contents of one or more items on the stack and leave a resulting truth value, or flag. In general, the test is destructive: it removes the item(s) tested and leaves only a numerical result flag. All numbers in Forth may be interpreted as *true* or *false* values: zero equals *false,* and *any* non-zero value equals *true.* Each word below performs a specific test and returns a "well-formed flag" (-1 for *true).*

Comparison and testing operations often precede an **IF**, **WHILE**, or **UNTIL** construct. Because they return well-formed flags, they may also be combined using the Boolean operators **AND**, **OR**, or **XOR**.

Glossary

0< (n – flag) Core
Return *flag*, which is *true* if and only if *n* is less than zero. "zero-less-than"

0<> (n – flag) Core Ext
Return *flag*, which is *true* if and only if *n* is not equal to zero. "zero-not-equal"

0= (n – flag) Core
Return *flag*, which is *true* if and only if *n* is equal to zero. "zero-equal"

0> (n – flag) Core Ext
Return *flag*, which is *true* if and only if *n* is greater than zero. "zero-greater-than"

< (n_1 n_2 – flag) Core
Return *flag*, which is *true* if and only if n_1 is less than n_2. "less-than"

<> (n_1 n_2 – flag) Core Ext
Return *flag*, which is *true* if and only if n_1 is not equal to n_2. "not-equal"

= (n_1 n_2 – flag) Core
Return *flag*, which is *true* if and only if n_1 is equal to n_2. "equal"

> (n_1 n_2 – flag) Core
Return *flag*, which is *true* if and only if n_1 is greater than n_2. "greater-than"

D0< `( d – flag )` Double

Return *flag*, which is *true* if and only if the double-precision value *d* is less than zero. "D-zero-less"

D0= `( d – flag )` Double

Return *flag*, which is *true* if and only if the double-precision value *d* is equal to zero. "D-zero-equal"

D< `( d1 d2 – flag )` Double

Return *flag*, which is *true* if and only if d_1 is less than d_2. "D-less-than"

D= `( d1 d2 – flag )` Double

Return *flag*, which is *true* if and only if d_1 is equal to d_2. "D-equals"

DU< `( ud1 ud2 – flag )` Double Ext

Return *flag*, which is *true* if and only if ud_1 is less than ud_2. "D-U-less"

FALSE `( – flag )` Core Ext

Return a *flag* that is *false* (binary zero).

NOT `( x – flag )` Common usage

Identical to **0=**, used for program clarity to reverse the results of a previous test.

TRUE `( – flag )` Core Ext

Return a *flag* that is *true* (single-cell value with all bits set).

U< `( u1 u2 – flag )` Core

Return *flag*, which is *true* if and only if u_1 is less than u_2. "U-less-than"

U> `( u1 u2 – flag )` Core Ext

Return *flag*, which is *true* if and only if u_1 is greater than u_2. "U-greater-than"

References

Conditionals, Section 4.3
MAX and **MIN**, Section 2.2.2
Post-testing loops, Section 4.5
Pre-testing loops, Section 4.3
String comparisons, Section 3.5

4.3 Conditionals

The words described in this section allow conditional execution of words within a single definition. They may only appear within a colon definition and may not be used in interpretive text or in text executed by direct entry from a terminal. Other, similar conditional words can be used interpretively (see Section 6.1.5).

The general usage of these words is:

`<test value>` **`IF`** `<true clause>` **`ELSE`** `<false clause>` **`THEN`**
or
`<test value>` **`IF`** `<true clause>` **`THEN`**

When **`IF`** is executed, the item on top of the stack is *removed* and examined. If *test value* is *true* (non-zero), execution continues with the words after **`IF`** (the *true clause*). If *test value* is *false* (zero), execution resumes with the words after **`ELSE`** (the *false clause*) or, if **`ELSE`** is not present, with the words after **`THEN`**. Execution of the *true clause* terminates with the word **`ELSE`**, if present, and resumes with the word after **`THEN`**. The logical flow is diagrammed in Figure 14.

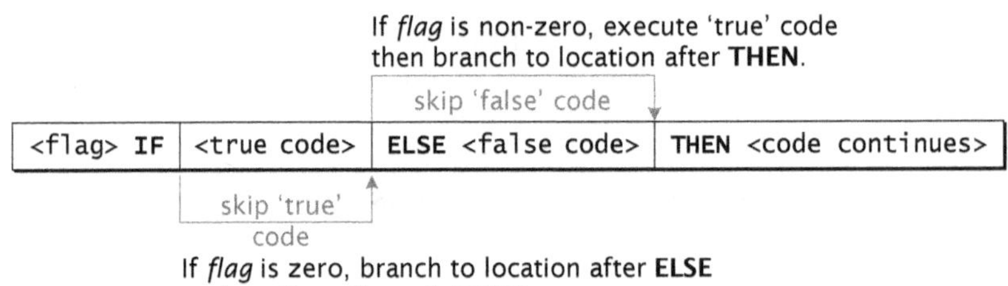

Figure 14. Logical flow of a conditional structure

Both the *true clause* and the *false clause* may be any group of previously defined Forth words. Either clause may contain **`DO`** ... **`LOOP`**s, **`BEGIN`** ... **`UNTIL`** loops, and/or other **`IF`** ... **`ELSE`** ... **`THEN`** structures—as long as the entire conditional is contained within the same parent clause. Similarly, one **`IF`** ... **`THEN`** structure may be nested inside another structure of any kind, so long as the **`THEN`** that terminates it appears within the same clause as its **`IF`**.

The **`ELSE`** clause (**`ELSE`** and the words that follow it) is optional, if the *true* clause is the only one of interest. However, every **IF** must have a **THEN** to terminate the structure. If only the *false* clause is of interest, it is good style to reverse your test, so that you don't have an empty or trivial *true* clause. For example, if you only want to process non-zero values, you might write:

```
: TEST ( n -- )    DUP 0= IF DROP ELSE PROCESS THEN ;
```

However, it would be both clearer and more efficient to use:

```
: TEST ( n -- )    ?DUP IF  PROCESS THEN ;
```

The comparison words in Section 4.2 are often used to produce a flag for **IF**, but you should also remember that **IF** will regard any non-zero value as *true*. In other words, it has a built-in **0<>**.

The glossary below describes the functional behavior of the words used in conditional structures. Their behavior as compiler directives is considered further in Section 6.4.1.

Glossary

ELSE (–) Core

Mark the end of the *true* part of a conditional structure, and commence the *false* part. May be omitted if there are no words to be executed in the *false* case.

IF (x –) Core

If *x* is zero, branch to the code immediately following an **ELSE** if one is present; if **ELSE** is omitted, branch to the point following **THEN**. If *x* is non-zero, continue execution with the code immediately following the **IF** and branch over any code following an **ELSE** to the point following **THEN**.

THEN (–) Core

Mark the point at which the *true* and *false* portions of an **IF** structure merge (the end of the structure).

References

Comparison operations, Section 4.2

Control-flow stack, Section 6.4.2

Text interpreter directives, Section 6.1.5

4.4 Indefinite Loops

The loop structures described in this section are generally referred to as "indefinite loops." It is not possible to know in advance how many times, or even the maximum number of times, the looping behavior needs to be repeated. Common situations include running a process until a switch is thrown or a key is pressed, waiting for a device to be turned on before accepting data from it, and converting digits to binary until a non-digit is detected.

The indefinite loop structures described in this section begin with the word **BEGIN**. **BEGIN** marks the location to which a subsequent branching word (e.g., **UNTIL**, **REPEAT**, **AGAIN**) will return to repeat the loop.

All the indefinite loop words are summarized in a single glossary at the end of this section.

4.4.1 Infinite loops

The simplest looping method available in Forth is the **BEGIN** ... **AGAIN** loop. This loop endlessly repeats any code between **BEGIN** and **AGAIN**. **BEGIN** ... **AGAIN** loops are used for control activities which are not expected to stop. Commonly, these are used to define the power-up behavior of an embedded system, or for a loop that will only terminate if an error condition causes a **THROW**. Examples of such applications include process-control loops and computer-sequenced machinery. **BEGIN** ... **AGAIN** is also used in **QUIT**, the highest-level word of an interactive Forth system. Loops with no exit can only be used at the highest level in a program.

An example of the outermost loop in a program to control an industrial process might be:

```
: REACTION ( -- )    CONTROLS CLEAR
   BEGIN  DATA  ERROR  CORRECT  AGAIN ;
```

This process-control loop clears the controls, then enters an infinite loop which continuously collects data, calculates an error quantity, and applies a correction function. Usually, such a program is run asynchronously by a background task, and the operator can stop it with an application command built from task-control words.

4.4.2 Post-testing loops

BEGIN and **UNTIL** allow the user to set up a loop to be executed repetitively—similar to **BEGIN** ... **AGAIN** loops, but a test is performed before the loop repeats. This structure is appropriate when you want to continue looping *until* an event occurs.

The form of a **BEGIN** ... **UNTIL** construct is:

```
BEGIN  <words to execute repeatedly>  <test value>  UNTIL
```

When execution reaches the word **UNTIL**, the test value on top of the stack is removed and examined. If this value is *false* (zero), execution returns to the word that follows **BEGIN**; if the value is *true* (non-zero), execution continues with the word that follows **UNTIL**.

UNTIL is similar to **IF** in that:

- its argument is removed from the stack, and
- any non-zero value will be considered *true.*

As is the case with **IF**, you may wish to use a comparison operator from the list in Section 4.2 before **UNTIL**.

The logical flow of a **BEGIN** ... **UNTIL** loop is diagrammed in Figure 15.

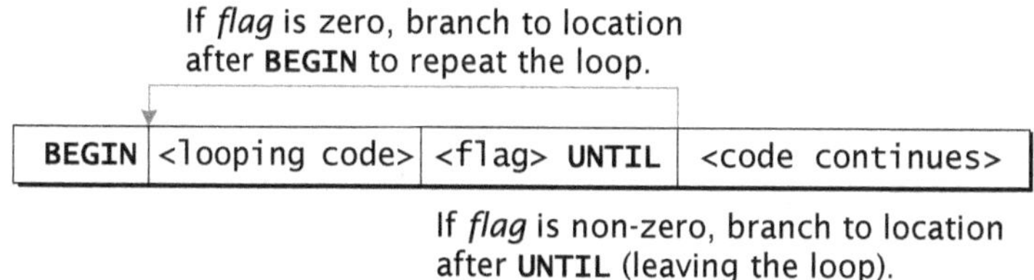

Figure 15. Logical flow of a post-test indefinite loop

Like other structures in Forth, **BEGIN** ... **UNTIL** may only be used within a definition. It may not be executed interpretively from a terminal.

References

Comparison operations, Section 4.2

4.4.3 Pre-testing loops

Pre-testing indefinite loops are similar to **BEGIN** ... **UNTIL** loops, except the test to leave the loop is performed *before* the end of the loop code. This structure is appropriate when you want to continue looping *while* some condition remains true. It also makes it possible to execute the conditional words zero times (if the condition fails on the first try).

The syntax of the Forth pre-testing loop is:

```
BEGIN  <executed every iteration>  <test> WHILE
   <not executed on the last iteration> REPEAT
```

WHILE removes the top number from the stack and tests it, then leaves the loop if the value is *false* (zero), skipping the words between **WHILE** and **REPEAT**. If the value on the stack is *true* (non-zero), **WHILE** continues to the next word in the loop. When program execution reaches **REPEAT**, it branches unconditionally back to the words immediately after **BEGIN** and repeats the loop. There may be no code before **WHILE** except the test; however you must take care that a new test value is left on the stack by code within the loop, because it is removed each time **WHILE** executes.

The logical flow of a **BEGIN** ... **WHILE** ... **REPEAT** structure is diagrammed in Figure 16.

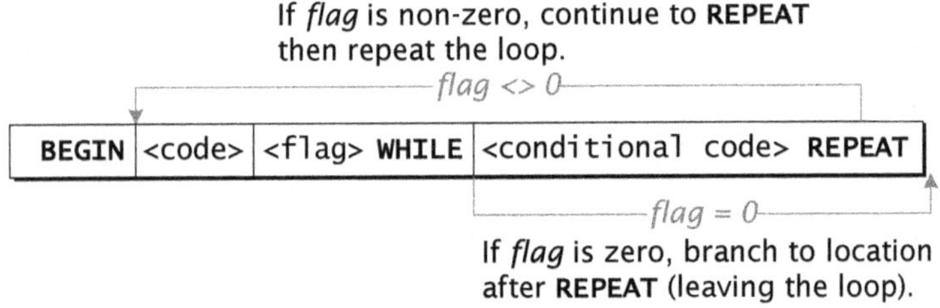

Figure 16. Logical flow of a pre-test indefinite loop

For an example, consider a word that counts fruit in a mechanical sorter:

```
: GOOD ( -- n )   0  BEGIN
   FETCH FRUIT ?GOOD WHILE
      KEEP 1+  REPEAT ;
```

As long as the machine sees good fruit in the test cell (as indicated by a flag returned by **?GOOD**), the loop continues and the machine considers the next fruit. When the test fails, the fruit remains in the test cell, to be evaluated by some process other than the word **?GOOD**.

In situations when both structures are equally convenient, the **BEGIN** … **UNTIL** loop is faster and requires slightly fewer bytes, and thus is preferable to the **BEGIN** … **WHILE** … **REPEAT** loop.

Glossary

AGAIN (–) Core Ext
Unconditionally branch back to the point immediately following the nearest previous **BEGIN**.

BEGIN (–) Core
Mark the destination of a backward branch for use by the other indefinite structure words **UNTIL** or **REPEAT**.

REPEAT (–) Core
In a **BEGIN** … **WHILE** … **REPEAT** structure, unconditionally branch back to the location following the nearest previous **BEGIN**.

UNTIL (x –) Core
If *x* is zero, branch back to the location immediately following the nearest previous **BEGIN**; otherwise, continue execution beyond the **UNTIL**.

WHILE (x –) Core
If *x* is zero, branch to the location immediately following the nearest **REPEAT**; otherwise, continue execution beyond the **WHILE**.

References

Comparison operations, Section 4.2
Control-flow stack, Section 6.4.2
Error handling with **THROW**, Section 5.3

4.5 Counting (Finite) Loops

The words described in this section are appropriate for constructing loops when it is clear how many times you wish the loop to execute (or, at least, the maximum number of times). The words associated with counting loops are given in the glossary at the end of this section.

The possible forms of a finite loop in Forth are as follows:

<limit> <initial> **DO** <words to repeat> **LOOP**
or <limit> <initial> **DO** <words to repeat> <value> **+LOOP**

A **DO** ... **LOOP** increments its index value by one and always runs in the positive direction. A **DO** ... **+LOOP** increments its index by the given integer *value*, which may be positive or negative.

To illustrate the use of loops, the word **SUM** is defined to add the values of the integers 1 to 100 and to leave the result on the stack:

```
: SUM   0  101 1 DO  I +  LOOP ;
```

The limit value is specified as 101, not 100, because the loop code **I +** executes first and then the loop index is incremented. The exit test is performed by **LOOP**, so the loop code will not be executed when the loop index equals 101.

The word **I** returns the current loop index on the stack. Loops may be nested to any depth, limited only by the capacity of the return stack. At each point in a nested loop, the word **I** returns the index of the innermost active loop, and the word **J** returns the index of the next outer loop.

+LOOP allows the programmer to specify the integer number by which the loop index will be incremented on each repetition of the loop. A negative value for this increment permits descending index values to be used. When an index value is descending, however, the loop is terminated when the limit is *passed* (not merely reached). When the index value is ascending (i.e., the increment value specified for **+LOOP** is positive), the loop terminates when the index value is reached, as for **LOOP**.

To illustrate the use of **+LOOP** with descending index values, the following definition is equivalent to the first definition of **SUM**:

```
: SUM   0  1 100 DO  I +  -1 +LOOP ;
```

Here the initial value of the index is 100 and the final value is 1.

Loop parameters usually are kept on the return stack (see glossary entry for **DO**, below), and are not affected by structures other than **DO** ... **LOOP**.

Loop parameters are checked at the end of the loop, so any loop will always execute at least once, regardless of the initial values of the parameters. Because a **DO** loop with equal input parameters will execute not once but a very large number of times—equal to the largest possible single-cell unsigned number—the word **?DO** should be used in preference to **DO** if the loop parameters are being calculated or if the upper limit is supplied as a parameter and might be equal (e.g., both zero).

DO ... **LOOP**s are frequently used to manage arrays and strings. Consider this example (using a hypothetical word **A/D** to read a value from an analog device and leave it on the stack):

```
1000 CONSTANT SIZE
CREATE DATA  SIZE CELLS ALLOT  DATA SIZE CELLS ERASE
: FILL ( -- )    SIZE 0 DO
      A/D  DATA I CELLS + ! \ Read value, put in Ith cell
   LOOP ;
: SHOW ( -- )    SIZE 0 DO
      I 10 MOD 0= IF  CR THEN          \ CR every 10th line
      DATA I CELLS + @ .               \ Display Ith value
   LOOP  CR ;
```

In this example, the constant **SIZE** is used both to define the array of cell-wide items and to manage the loops that fill and display the data. Should you need to change the size, you have only to change that constant and recompile.

The array is defined and initialized to zeroes. When **FILL** is executed, it will read **SIZE** values and store them in consecutive cells in the array. **SHOW** will display the data, 10 values per line.

Loops and conditionals in Forth may be nested, providing you nest an entire structure within an outer structure. That is, you must not attempt to branch into or out of a loop. Two forms of indefinite loops (**BEGIN** ... **UNTIL** and **BEGIN** ... **WHILE** ... **REPEAT**) incorporate mechanisms for deciding when to exit the loop. If you wish to exit from a finite loop, the appropriate mechanism is to use **LEAVE** inside an **IF** ... **THEN** structure. For example, suppose you're searching a table of **SIZE** items for a match on a string:

```
: FIND-IT ( addr len -- 0 | index )
   0 -ROT  SIZE 1+ 1 DO 2DUP FIND-ITEM IF
     ROT DROP I -ROT  LEAVE THEN
   LOOP  2DROP ;
```

Here we place a *false* flag on the stack below the address and length of the key we're searching for. If we find a match, we'll discard that and replace it with the index of the matching item. At the end of the loop, we discard the string parameters of the key, leaving only the index of the found item or *false*. Note that in this case the index starts with 1 rather than 0, so if we find a match on the first item it's still non-zero.

Glossary

DO (n_1 n_2 –) Core

Establish the loop parameters. This word expects the initial loop index n_2 on top of the stack, with the limit value n_1 beneath it. These values are removed from the stack and stored elsewhere, usually on the return stack, when **DO** is executed. If conditions could occur in which the limit will equal the initial loop index, consider **?DO** instead.

?DO (n_1 n_2 –) Core Ext

Like **DO**, but check whether the limit value and initial loop index are equal. If they are, continue execution immediately following the next **LOOP** or **+LOOP**; otherwise, set up the loop values and continue execution immediately following **?DO**. This word should be used in preference to **DO** whenever the parameters may be equal. "question-do"

LOOP (–) Core

Increment the index value by one and compare it with the limit value. If the index value is equal to the limit value, the loop is terminated, the parameters are discarded, and execution resumes with the next word. Otherwise, control returns to the word that follows the **DO** or **?DO** that opened the loop.

+LOOP (n –) Core

Like **LOOP**, but increment the index by the specified signed value *n*. After incrementing, if the index crossed the boundary between the loop limit minus one and the loop limit, the loop is terminated as with **LOOP**. "plus-loop"

I (– n) Core

Push a copy of the current value of the index onto the data stack. This word may only be used for this purpose within the definition that opened the loop, not in definitions the loop invokes. That is because nested colon definitions may cause a return address to be put on the stack—on top of the loop index. If the code in the body of the loop places any values explicitly on the return stack, they must be removed before **I** is executed; otherwise, an erroneous index value may result.

J (– n) Core
Push a copy of the next-outer loop index onto the data stack. When two **DO** ... **LOOP**s are nested, this obtains the value of the outer index from inside the inner loop.

LEAVE (–) Core
Discard loop parameters and continue execution immediately following the next **LOOP** or **+LOOP** containing this **LEAVE**.

UNLOOP (–) Core
Discard the loop parameters for the current nesting level. This word is not needed when a **DO** ... **LOOP** completes normally, but it is required before leaving a definition by calling **EXIT**. One **UNLOOP** call for each level of loop nesting is required before leaving a definition.

References

EXIT and un-nesting definitions, Section 4.8
Control-flow stack, Section 6.4.2

4.6 Finite vs. Indefinite Loops

We have seen three styles of indefinite loops and one class of finite loops (with several variations). Ignoring the infinite loop, which is a specialized structure, there are general guidelines for deciding which form to use:

- Use **DO** ... **LOOP** if:

  You know how many times you want to do it;
  You know the maximum number of times you want to do it;
  You need access to the loop index.

- Use an indefinite loop if:

  You want to do it until some event occurs;
  You want to do it while a condition exists;
  You have no idea how long either of these intervals may be;
  You don't need a loop counter;

- Use **BEGIN** ... **WHILE** ... **REPEAT** if:

  You have a requirement for indefinite loops and need to be

able to perform the "repeating" code zero times if the situation warrants.

- Use **?DO** ... **LOOP** if:

  You need to do something a specified number of times, and that number might be zero.

4.7 Case Statement

A high-level **CASE** statement structure is available for situations in which an input condition needs to be checked against more than one or two possible values. The usual syntax is:

```
CASE
   <x1> OF <x1 action> ENDOF
   <x2> OF <x2 action> ENDOF
   ...
   <default action> ENDCASE
```

The structure begins with the word **CASE**. When it executes, a case selector *x* must be on the stack. A series of **OF** ... **ENDOF** clauses follows, each **OF** preceded by a test value on the stack (x_1, x_2, etc.). The case selector is compared against the test values in order. If it matches one, the corresponding code between that **OF** and **ENDOF** is executed, and execution branches beyond the **ENDCASE**. If the case selector does not match any of the test values, it remains on the stack after the last **ENDOF**, and some default action may be taken. Any action should preserve the stack depth (use **DUP** if necessary), because **ENDCASE** performs a **DROP** (presumably on the case selector) and then continues execution beyond **ENDCASE**.

For example:

```
: TEST ( n - )   CASE  ." Value is "
                   1 OF ." One" ENDOF
                   2 OF ." Two" ENDOF
                   3 OF ." Three" ENDOF
                   DUP .
                ENDCASE ;
```

This structure is flexible, and is more readable than nested **IF** statements if there are more than two or so comparisons. However, it may use more memory than nested **IF**s. Note also that the comparison values (1, 2, and 3 in the above example) must be constants or literal values, and not expressions.

CASE statements may be nested; there may be any number of **OF** ... **ENDOF** pairs; and there may be any amount of logic inside an **OF** ... **ENDOF** clause, including computation of the next test value. However, if the content of an **OF** ... **ENDOF** clause is complex, it is highly recommended that you factor it into a separate definition to facilitate testing and to improve readability.

Glossary

CASE (–) Core Ext
Mark the start of a **CASE** ... **OF** ... **ENDOF** ... **ENDCASE** structure.

ENDCASE (x –) Core Ext
Discard the top stack value *x* (presumably the case selector) and continue execution.

ENDOF (–) Core Ext
Unconditionally branch to the instruction immediately following the next **ENDCASE**.

OF (x_1 x_2 – | x_1) Core Ext
If the test value x_2 is not equal to case selector x_1, discard x_2 and branch forward to the location immediately following the next **ENDOF** (presumably another **OF** or default code, if any, before an **ENDCASE**); otherwise, discard *both values* and continue execution beyond the **OF**.

References

Logic operations, Section 2.2.2
Control-flow stack, Section 6.4.2

4.8 Nesting Structures

In Forth, any structure may be nested inside any other structure, providing the entire structure is nested. That is, you may not "straddle" structures or, for example, attempt to use a conditional to branch into or out of a finite or indefinite loop.

Examples of legal and illegal nesting strategies are shown in Figure 17.

In general, strive to keep your definitions short and simple, and avoid nesting structures more than a couple of layers, as this makes testing and maintenance more difficult.

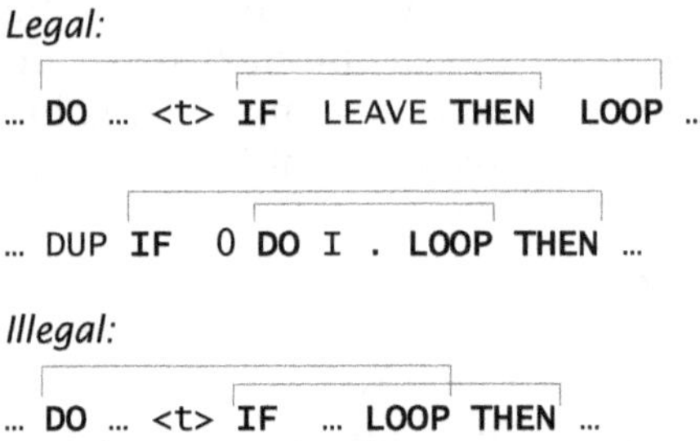

Legal:
... DO ... <t> IF LEAVE THEN LOOP ...
... DUP IF 0 DO I . LOOP THEN ...
Illegal:
... DO ... <t> IF ... LOOP THEN ...

Figure 17. Examples of legal and illegal nested structures.

For this reason, the **DO** … **LOOP** words don't include a mechanism for accessing loop indices beyond one level of nesting (**I** and **J**). Programs with many nested structures become very difficult to test thoroughly.

4.9 Nesting and Un-nesting Structures and Definitions

When a high-level definition calls another, it is said to *nest* the calls, because the return will normally be to the next location in the calling definition. The called definition *un-nests* when it is finished executing, to effect this return.

It is possible to force an exit from a definition at any point, even inside a structure, by using the word **EXIT**. **EXIT** will immediately leave the current definition and return to whatever called it. However, because return addresses are usually stored on the return stack, **EXIT** must be used with caution, following these rules:

- If **EXIT** is called with a **DO** … **LOOP** structure, you must first discard the loop's parameters using **UNLOOP**.
- If you have placed any temporary values on the return stack (using **>R**), you must remove them before calling **EXIT**.

Here is a trivial example of the use of **EXIT**:

```
: TEST ( n)   1 . IF EXIT THEN  2 . ;

0 TEST 1 2
1 TEST 1
```

Frequently, words containing **EXIT** will have different stack results depending on whether the word **EXIT**s or not. The standard stack notation for such a situation is:

```
( input-arguments -- EXIT-case | normal-case )
```

EXIT is the only Forth word which permits unstructured programs (modules with multiple exit points). Because unstructured techniques tend to impair code's readability and maintainability, they should be used sparingly—only when the overall effect is to simplify the code. It is considered bad form to use **EXIT** more than once in a word; if you believe you need to do so, try factoring that word into several words.

Glossary

EXIT (–); (R: nest-sys –) Core

Return control immediately to the calling definition specified by *nest-sys*. Before executing **EXIT**, a program must remove any items explicitly stored on the return stack. If **EXIT** is called within a **DO** … **LOOP**, **UNLOOP** must be executed first to discard the loop-control parameters.

References

Interpreter pointer, Section 1.1.7

Text interpreter, Section 1.1.5

UNLOOP, Section 4.5

5. SYSTEM FUNCTIONS

Forth is more than a programming language. The earliest versions of Forth ran standalone on primitive minicomputers and early microprocessors in the 1970s, providing an integrated system, language, and application functions in a single package. This heritage persists in the Forth *virtual machine*, even though today it is frequently implemented on top of a conventional operating system.

This section describes words used to load, organize, and manage Forth applications, as well as to interact with standard system devices (e.g., disk, terminal, and clock). But before considering details of various Forth system functions, the next section will present a fundamental concept commonly used to implement system functions.

5.1 VECTORED EXECUTION

Normal Forth usage (as well as good programming practice) emphasizes the *structured programming* modes of sequential, iterative, and conditional execution. But sometimes it is desirable to direct Forth to execute a specific function in response to some external stimulus. This technique may be used, for example, by a report that searches a database, selecting records according to a criterion that may need to vary; by a bank of push-buttons, each attached to a particular Forth word; or by a routine that computes the address of a function to be executed.

5.1.1 Execution Tokens

The word **EXECUTE** expects an *execution token* on the stack. An execution token is a value, typically an address, that points to the execution behavior of a definition. **EXECUTE** removes the token from the stack and uses it to cause the associated definition to execute.

You may find the execution token of a word by using:

```
' <name>
```

...interpretively, in which case the execution token for *name* is returned on the stack. Inside a definition, you may use **['] <name>** to compile the execution token for *name* as a literal.

Execution tokens may be used as single function pointers or in tables of execution vectors. In stack comments, an execution token is indicated as *xt*.

Glossary

' <name> (-- xt) Core

Search the dictionary for *name* and leave its execution token on the stack. Abort if *name* cannot be found. "tick"

['] <name> (-- xt) Core

Used in a definition, **[']** finds the word *name* in the dictionary and compiles its execution token as a literal to be pushed on the stack when the definition in which it appears is executed. If *name* is not in the dictionary, **[']** aborts. "bracket-tick"

EXECUTE (i*x xt -- j*x) Core

Remove execution token *xt* from the stack and perform the execution behavior it identifies. Other stack effects are due to the word that is **EXECUTE**d. The stack notation *i*x and j*x is a reminder that there may be a stack effect for the word being* **EXECUTE***d, but it is not affected by* **EXECUTE** *itself.*

@EXECUTE (i*x addr -- j*x) Common usage

Perform the execution behavior identified by an execution token stored in *addr*. Equivalent to **@ EXECUTE**, except it's a no-op if *addr* contains zero, instead of an error. "fetch-execute"

In some Forth implementations, this function is known by the synonym **PERFORM**.

5.1.2 Single Function Pointers

A single function pointer in Forth is equivalent to a variable whose contents is an execution token.

Consider the following example:

```
VARIABLE NUMERAL
: T1   1 . ;
: T2   2 . ;
: ONE    ['] T1  NUMERAL ! ;    \ Stores the xt of T1.
: TWO    ['] T2  NUMERAL ! ;    \ Stores the xt of T2.
: N   NUMERAL @ EXECUTE ;
```

If the user types:

```
ONE N
```

...the system will display **1**. Typing:

```
TWO N
```

...will produce **2**.

The stack effect must be the same for each member of a set of words to be **EXECUTE**d in a particular context. That is, each must require and leave the same number of items on the stack as all the other words.

The word **DEFER** provides a convenient means of managing a single execution vector. The syntax is:

```
DEFER <name>
```

This creates a dictionary entry for *name* and makes it an *execution variable. name* is similar to a variable but specifically contains the execution token of another word; the other word is executed when *name* is executed. The execution token of the other word to be executed is stored into the data area of *name* by the word **IS**[1].

In the example above, you will get unpredictable results if the **VARIABLE** is not initialized to a valid execution token. However, **DEFER** will initialize its instances to the execution token of a word that will abort with a message.

DEFER lets you change the execution of previously defined commands by creating a slot which can be loaded with different behaviors at different times. The preceding example would be defined this way using **DEFER**:

1. Some systems use **TO** for changing a **DEFER**. We believe **IS** is the preferred usage.

```
DEFER NUMERAL
: T1   1 . ;
: T2   2 . ;
: ONE    ['] T1  IS NUMERAL ;
: TWO    ['] T2  IS NUMERAL ;
```

Then, typing:

```
ONE NUMERAL
```

...displays **1**, and

```
TWO NUMERAL
```

...displays **2**.

Like **VARIABLE**s, **DEFER**s are global in scope. A similar strategy is used in multitasking versions of Forth to make function pointers that may have a different value for each task. See Section 5.1.4 for details.

Glossary

DEFER <name> (–) Common usage

Define a function pointer with an initial behavior that will abort safely if it is executed before being initialized. The content of a **DEFER** can be changed using **IS**.

> name (i*x – j*x)
> Execute the word whose execution token is stored in *name*'s data space. Stack effects depend on the word being executed.

IS <defer-name> (xt –) Common usage

Store the *xt* in the data space for *defer-name*, which must be the name of an instance of **DEFER**.

5.1.3 Execution Vector Tables

Most uses of **EXECUTE** are for implementing a variable function, as described in the previous sections. The ability to generate and manage a table of execution addresses is also extremely useful for such purposes as managing a function-button pad, a menu on a graphics tablet, etc. The following example outlines a simple button-response application which may serve as a model for similar situations.

Let us assume we are programming a device which is controlled by a panel containing five buttons. Each button is wired to return a value 0-4. The hypothetical word **BUTTON?** waits for a button to be pressed and returns its value. Now imagine that you've defined five functions, each to be associated with one of these buttons: Button 0 is **START**, 1 is **SLOW**, 2 is **MED**, 3 is **FAST**, and 4 is **FINISH**.

Now we can construct a table of behaviors, using the words described in Section 2.3.3:

```
CREATE BUTTONS   ' START ,   ' SLOW ,   ' MED ,
   ' FAST , ' FINISH ,
```

BUTTONS returns the address of the start of a table five cells long, containing the execution tokens of each of the button response words. Here's how we might handle these buttons:

```
: BUTTON ( -- )   BUTTON?  CELLS BUTTONS + @EXECUTE ;
```

BUTTON gets a button number and converts it to a cell offset that can be added to the table address (returned by **BUTTONS**) to get the location of an *xt* that can be passed to **@EXECUTE**.

This could also be achieved using **CASE** (Section 4.7), but this version is significantly smaller and faster. It also has a unique advantage that allows you to store an *xt* in the table after **BUTTONS**, and even after **BUTTON**, have been defined. In other words, if you have a later definition for one of those words—even a temporary one entered from the keyboard during debugging—you can patch it in.

A disadvantage of this approach, however, is that it assumes that the selector values (button numbers, in this example) are either sequential or at least dense. If they're completely arbitrary values, **CASE** may be more convenient.

References

['], Section 5.1.2
CASE, Section 4.7

5.1.4 Vectored System Routines

It is often desirable to modify or re-direct system functions—perhaps because of changing hardware or application requirements—without recompiling the system kernel. Forth facilitates this by providing *execution vectors* containing the addresses of the current versions of these system-level functions. There are two groups of vectored routines: system-wide functions and terminal-dependent functions (i.e., those whose behavior differs between different kinds of CRT or between keyboard/display and printer). For each vectored function, there are at least three Forth words: the function itself (which executes the vector), the vector itself, and at least one routine to be executed.

Examples of functions that are typically vectored on a system-wide basis include basic disk access, compiler functions (e.g., to facilitate adding an optimizing compiler), input number conversions (e.g., to facilitate adding floating point), and other generically global issues.

In addition, some routines in multitasking systems are vectored through user variables for differing task-specific functions. Typically, these control different kinds of "display" devices, such as printers and other serial peripherals.

Refer to your product documentation for specific details of vectored system functions on your implementation.

References

@EXECUTE, Section 5.1.1
Support of special terminal functions, Section 5.4.3
TYPE, Section 5.4.2

5.2 System Environment

Standard Forth systems provide a mechanism for inquiring about the configuration and parameters of a particular system, either interactively or within program code. The word **ENVIRONMENT?** expects to find on the stack the address and length of a text string referring to an option or parameter, and returns either a single *false* flag (parameter/option is unknown), or a *true* flag (known) on top of the stack, with a second flag or data value beneath. The word **S"** (see Section 6.1.5), which returns the address and length of a string, is often used with **ENVIRONMENT?**. For example, the string **STACK-CELLS** is defined as indicating the maximum number of cells in the data stack. You might type at the keyboard, or include in a definition, the phrase:

```
S" STACK-CELLS" ENVIRONMENT?
```

...which might return:

```
256 -1
```

...where the **-1** (true) indicates that the system recognized the **STACK-CELLS** string, and the **256** shows that the maximum size of the stack is 256 cells. Table 9 lists the standard strings available for environmental queries and the data values they may return. The data type is the type of the associated data or second flag.

Most ANS Forth word sets contain a basic part and extensions whose presence may be tested for individually. For example, in this table, **BLOCK** and **BLOCK-EXT** separately test for the presence of the basic block word set and the block extensions word set.

Table 9: Environmental query strings and associated data

String	Type	Meaning
/COUNTED-STRING	n	Maximum size of a counted string, in characters.
/HOLD	n	Maximum size of pictured numeric output string, in characters.
/PAD	n	Size of the scratch area **PAD** in characters.
BLOCK	flag	*true* if block word set is present.
BLOCK-EXT	flag	*true* if block extensions word set is present.
CORE	flag	*true* if complete Standard Forth core word set is present.
CORE-EXT	flag	*true* if complete Standard Forth core extensions word set is present.
DOUBLE	flag	*true* if double number integer word set is present.
DOUBLE-EXT	flag	*true* if double-number extensions integer word set is present.
EXCEPTION	flag	*true* if exception word set is present.
EXCEPTION-EXT	flag	*true* if exception extensions word set is present.
FACILITY	flag	*true* if facility word set is present.

Table 9: Environmental query strings and associated data *(continued)*

String	Type	Meaning
FACILITY-EXT	flag	*true* if facility extensions word set is present.
FILE	flag	*true* if file word set is present.
FILE-EXT	flag	*true* if file extensions word set is present.
FLOATING	flag	*true* if floating-point word set is present.
FLOATING-EXT	flag	*true* if floating-point extensions word set is present.
FLOATING-STACK	n	If *n*=0, floating-point numbers are kept on the data stack; otherwise, *n* is the maximum depth of the separate floating-point stack.
FLOORED	flag	*true* if floored division is the default, *false* if symmetric division is the default.
MAX-CHAR	u	Maximum value of a character in the implementation-defined character set.
MAX-D	d	Largest usable signed double number.
MAX-FLOAT	r	Largest usable floating-point number.
MAX-N	n	Largest usable signed integer.
MAX-U	u	Largest usable unsigned integer.
MAX-UD	ud	Largest usable unsigned double number.
MEMORY-ALLOC	flag	*true* if memory-allocation word set is present.
RETURN-STACK-CELLS	n	Maximum size of the return stack, in cells.
STACK-CELLS	n	Maximum size of the data stack, in cells.
SEARCH-ORDER	flag	*true* if search-order word set is present.
SEARCH-ORDER-EXT	flag	*true* if search-order extensions word set is present.
STRING	flag	*true* if string word set is present.
TOOLS	flag	*true* if programming tools word set is present.
TOOLS-EXT	flag	*true* if programming tools extensions word set is present.
WORDLISTS	n	Maximum number of word lists usable in the search order.

Because a system may load options in any order, some environmental queries could return either *false* or *true*, depending on when they were executed. The Standard Forth requirements are:

- If a query returns *false* (unknown) in response to a string, subsequent queries with that string *may return true*, because additional capabilities may have been acquired.
- If a query returns *true* (known) and a numerical value, subsequent queries with the same string *must also return true* and the same numerical value. In other words, added capabilities may not take away or fundamentally alter entitlements already presented to the program.
- Flags indicating the presence or absence of optional word sets *may* change; the flag indicating floored or symmetric division *may not* change.

Glossary

ENVIRONMENT? (c-addr u – false | i*x true) Core
Return information about the system software configuration. The character string specified by *c-addr u* should contain one of the strings from Table 9. If it does not, return *false*; otherwise, return *true* and data specified in Table 9 for that string. "environment-query"

5.3 Exception Handling

Forth provides several methods for error handling. **ABORT** and **ABORT"** may be used to detect errors. However, they are relatively inflexible, in that they unconditionally terminate program execution and return to the idle state. Frequently, when a terminal task aborts, it is desirable to display a message, clear the stacks, and re-enter a default state awaiting user commands. This is the primary use of **ABORT"**.

CATCH and **THROW**, discussed in this section, provide a method for propagating error handling to any desired level in an application program. **THROW** may be thought of as a multi-level **EXIT** from a definition, with **CATCH** marking the location to which the **THROW** returns.

Suppose that, at some point, word A calls word B, whose execution may cause an error to occur. Instead of just executing word B's name, word A calls word B using the word **CATCH**. Somewhere in word B's definition (or in words that B's definition may call), there is at least one instance of the word **THROW** to be executed if an error occurs, leaving a numerical *throw code* identifier on the stack. After word B has executed and program execution returns to word A just beyond the **CATCH**, the throw code is on the stack to assist word A in resolving the error. If the **THROW** was not executed, the top stack item after the **CATCH** is zero.

When **CATCH** executes, it requires the execution token of the lower-level routine it calls to be on top of the stack:

```
... ['] <name> CATCH ...
```

...is appropriate usage (inside a definition). At the time **CATCH** executes, there may be other items on the data stack, such as parameters that *name* is expecting.

After the lower-level routine executes and control returns to the routine that will handle any errors, the data stack will have one of two behaviors. If the lower-level routine (and any words it called) did not cause a **THROW** to execute, the top stack item after the **CATCH** will be zero and the remainder of the data stack may be different than it was before, changed by the behavior of the lower-level routine. If a **THROW** did occur, the top stack item after the **CATCH** will contain the throw code, and the remainder of the data stack will be restored to the same *depth*—although *not necessarily to the same data*—it had just before the **CATCH**. The return stack will also be restored to the depth it had before the **CATCH**.

When **THROW** executes, it requires a throw code on top of the stack. If this code is zero, **THROW** does nothing except remove the zero from the stack; the remainder of the stack is unchanged. If the throw code is non-zero, **THROW** returns the code on top of the stack, restores the data stack *depth* (but not necessarily the data) to its value when **CATCH** was executed, restores the return stack depth, and passes control to the error-handling routine. If a non-zero **THROW** occurs without a corresponding **CATCH** to return to in the application, it is treated as an **ABORT**.

The set of information (e.g., stack depths) that may be needed for restoration is called an *exception frame*. Exception frames are placed on an *exception stack* in order to allow nesting of **CATCH**es and **THROW**s. Each use of **CATCH** pushes an exception frame onto the exception stack. If execution proceeds normally, **CATCH** pops the frame; if an error occurs, **THROW** pops the frame and uses its information for restoration.

An example of **CATCH** and **THROW** taken from Standard Forth is:

```
: COULD-FAIL ( -- c)   KEY DUP  [CHAR] Q = IF
   1 THROW  THEN ;

: DO-IT ( n n -- c)   2DROP  COULD-FAIL ;

: TRY-IT ( -- )   1 2  ['] DO-IT CATCH  IF
   2DROP ." There was an exception"  CR
   ELSE ." The character was " EMIT CR  THEN ;
```

The higher-level word **TRY-IT** calls the high-risk operation **DO-IT** (which in turn calls **COULD-FAIL**) using **CATCH**. Following the **CATCH**, the data stack contains either the character returned by **KEY** and a zero on top, or two otherwise-undefined items (to restore it to the depth before the **CATCH**) and a one on top. Because any non-zero value is interpreted as *true*, the returned throw code is suitable for direct input to the **IF** clause in **TRY-IT**.

Standard Forth reserves negative throw codes for system implementors. Throw codes -1 through -255 are reserved for assignment by the Standard itself in order to specify common types of errors, so different Forth implementations will have compatible associated behaviors. See Table 10 for a list of existing assignments. The remaining negative throw codes may be used for implementation-specific system exceptions. All positive throw codes are available for application use.

Table 10: ANS Forth reserved throw codes

Code	Meaning	Code	Meaning
-1	**ABORT**	-30	obsolescent feature
-2	**ABORT"**	-31	**>BODY** used on non-**CREATE**d definition
-3	stack overflow	-32	invalid name argument (e.g., **TO** <xxx>)
-4	stack underflow	-33	block read exception
-5	return stack overflow	-34	block write exception
-6	return stack underflow	-35	invalid block number
-7	do-loops nested too deeply	-36	invalid file position
-8	dictionary overflow	-37	file I/O exception

Table 10: ANS Forth reserved throw codes *(continued)*

Code	Meaning	Code	Meaning
-9	invalid memory address	-38	non-existent file
-10	division by zero	-39	unexpected end of file
-11	result out of range	-40	invalid **BASE** for floating point
-12	argument type mismatch	-41	loss of precision
-13	undefined word	-42	floating-point divide by zero
-14	interpreting a compile-only word	-43	floating-point result out of range
-15	invalid **FORGET**	-44	floating-point stack overflow
-16	attempt to use zero-length string as a name	-45	floating-point stack underflow
-17	pictured numeric output string overflow	-46	floating-point invalid argument
-18	parsed string overflow	-47	compilation word list deleted
-19	definition name too long	-48	invalid **POSTPONE**
-20	write to a read-only location	-49	search-order overflow
-21	unsupported operation	-50	search-order underflow
-22	control structure mismatch	-51	compilation word list changed
-23	address alignment exception	-52	control-flow stack overflow
-24	invalid numeric argument	-53	exception stack overflow
-25	return stack imbalance	-54	floating-point underflow
-26	loop parameters unavailable	-55	floating-point unidentified fault
-27	invalid recursion	-56	**QUIT**
-28	user interrupt	-57	exception sending or receiving a character
-29	compiler nesting		

Glossary

ABORT (i*x –); (R: j*x –) Core, Exception Ext

Unconditionally terminate execution, empty both stacks, and return to the task's idle behavior (usually **QUIT**—see Section 6.1.2). No message is issued. May be executed by any task in a multitasking implementation.

ABORT" <text>" (i*x flag –); (R: j*x –) Core, Exception Ext

If *flag* is *true* (non-zero), type the specified *text* at the user's terminal, clear both stacks, and return to the task's idle behavior. Must be used inside a definition.For example:

```
: CHECK ( n -- n)   1000 OVER <
   ABORT" TOO BIG" ;
```

The definition of **ABORT"** concludes with the word **ABORT** (or otherwise includes its functionality). On many systems it echoes the word being interpreted when the error occurred. "abort-quote"

CATCH (i*x xt – j*x 0 | i*x n) Exception

Save information about the depth of the data and return stacks in an exception frame and push the frame on the exception stack. Execute the execution token *xt* (as with **EXECUTE**). If the execution of *xt* completes normally (i.e., a non-zero **THROW** is not executed), pop the exception frame and return zero on top of the data stack—above whatever stack items were returned by *xt* **EXECUTE**—and delete the stack-depth information. Otherwise, see the definition of **THROW** for completion of the exception-processing behavior.

THROW (k*x n – k*x | i*x n) Exception

If *n* is zero, simply remove *n* from the data stack. If *n* is non-zero, pop the topmost frame from the exception stack, restore the input source specification that was in use before the corresponding **CATCH**, and adjust the depths of all stacks so they are the same as the depths saved in the exception frame (the value of *i* in **THROW**'s stack comments is the same as the value of *i* in **CATCH**'s comments). Place *n* on top of the data stack and transfer control to a point just beyond the **CATCH** that pushed the exception frame.

References

Execution tokens, Section 5.1.1

5.4 Serial I/O

Forth supports a variety of means to perform I/O with a terminal, printer, or other serial-type I/O device. In addition, a simplified method is provided to make use of cursor positioning and other hardware-dependent features without forcing the use of particular terminal models.

5.4.1 Terminal Input

The words described in this section handle character input from devices. The input is received from the *current input device* (e.g., keyboard, serial port). Selection of the current input device is system dependent.

The command **KEY** awaits one character and leaves it on the stack. **KEY** does not edit or echo. As this is a "blocking" word (i.e., it waits for input), you may wish to use **KEY?**, which will return *true* if a key is available for input. If **KEY?** returns true, a subsequent call to **KEY** will return the character without waiting.

Technically, **KEY** and **KEY?** only respond to 7-bit ASCII keys, although many implementations will return 8-bit ASCII values. A similar pair of words is available to receive "keyboard events" of a more generic nature (e.g., mouse clicks, function keys, etc.). These are **EKEY** and **EKEY?**. Whereas **KEY** returns a character in the low-order bits of the top stack item, **EKEY** returns a full cell, which may have information in the high-order bits for extended character sets, formatting information, etc. The exact nature of the characters returned by **EKEY** is platform-dependent (naturally, as its primary purpose is to let a program receive unfiltered data).

ACCEPT awaits a character *string* from the terminal or other serial device, given the maximum number of characters and the address where they are to be stored. Input is terminated by a return ($0D_H$). If the terminator is not received before the maximum character count is reached, the excess characters are discarded. **ACCEPT** returns the length of the character string that was stored at the given address. For example,

```
PAD 10 ACCEPT
```

...will await up to ten characters, place them at **PAD**, and return the actual character count on the stack.

On most systems, incoming characters are checked for the return, which terminates input; and for backspace (08) or DEL ($7F_H$), which cause the character pointer to be "backed up" one and a backspace (or equivalent) to be sent to the terminal. All other characters are echoed to the terminal. Because **ACCEPT** edits for special keys, it is not appropriate for receiving binary data on a serial port. The recommended procedure is to use **KEY** in a loop for this purpose.

ACCEPT should not be executed if there is no terminal or serial device capable of providing input for the task.

No indication is provided at the terminal that the system is awaiting input as a result of an **ACCEPT** request. The programmer should indicate this fact through some output message issued prior to the **ACCEPT** request.

The conventional place to put incoming strings is the input message buffer. At least 80 bytes are available. The system text interpreter **ACCEPT**s 80 bytes into the input message buffer and performs the necessary housekeeping to process the text. The text interpreter is called by **QUIT**, which performs a terminal's basic idle loop behavior.

However, you can use any memory region as a buffer for **ACCEPT**. Another handy temporary storage place is **PAD**. Here's an example of the use of **PAD** for input:

```
: GET-STRING ( -- n )   PAD 40 ACCEPT ;
: SHOW-STRING ( -- )   GET-STRING  PAD SWAP TYPE ;
```

The word **SHOW-STRING** obtains the string, whose actual length is returned by **GET-STRING**, and displays it. More commonly, you might use this string to search or store in a database.

Glossary

ACCEPT (c-addr +n1 – +n2) Core

Get, at most, $+n_1$ characters from the current input device, echo each, and place them in memory beginning at *c-addr*. The process continues until **ACCEPT** encounters a carriage return (line terminator). If the line terminator is not received before a count of $+n_1$ is reached, any excess characters are discarded. Return the actual count $+n_2$ of characters received. An example of use is:

```
PAD 10 ACCEPT <cr> 12345 ok
. 5 ok
```

ACCEPT is used for most terminal input. On most systems, **ACCEPT** will back up over previously input characters in response to the backspace (08) or DEL ($7F) key. When the character pointer points to *c-addr*, the original address, **ACCEPT** stops backing up and may thereafter emit a tone for each backspace or DEL it receives.

EKEY (– u) Facility Ext

Receive one keyboard event and place the result on the stack. The encoding of keyboard events is system dependent. "E-key"

EKEY>CHAR (u – u 0 | char -1) Facility Ext

Attempt to convert a keyboard event into a character. If successful, return the character and *true*, otherwise return the event and *false*. "E-key-to-care"

EKEY? (– flag) Facility Ext

Check whether a valid keyboard event has been received on the task's serial device since the last call to **ACCEPT**, **KEY**, or **EKEY**. If so, return *true*, otherwise return *false*. The value of the event may be obtained by the next execution of **EKEY**. After **EKEY?** returns with a value of *true*, subsequent executions of **EKEY?** before executing **KEY**, **KEY?**, or **EKEY** will also return *true*, because they refer to the same event. "E-key-question"

KEY (– b) Core

Await exactly one character from the input device and place its value on the stack. **KEY** does not echo. **KEY** is sometimes used for input prompting and in serial protocols. **KEY** is also often useful to interactively determine the ASCII numeric value of a character. For example, if you type:

```
KEY .
```

...the system will wait for you to press one key and will display its ASCII value.

KEY? (– flag) Facility

Check whether a character has been received on the current input device since the last call to **ACCEPT**, **KEY**, or **EKEY**. If so, return *true*, otherwise return *false*. Invalid (non-character) keyboard events occurring before a valid character are discarded and made unavailable. The value of the character received may be obtained by the next execution of **KEY**. After **KEY?** returns with a value of *true*, subsequent executions of **KEY?** before executing **KEY** or **EKEY** will also return *true*, without discarding keyboard events. "key-question"

References

String operations, Section 3

Input number conversion, Section 3.6.1

QUIT, Section 6.1.2

PAD, Section 3.1.2

TYPE, Section 5.4.2

5.4.2 Terminal Output

Forth provides words to output character strings, as well as single characters. The output is sent to the *current output device* (e.g., the display or printer). Selection of the current output device is system dependent.

The command **EMIT** will transmit a single ASCII character, given its value on the stack. Thus,

```
65 EMIT
```

...will output an "A".

TYPE outputs a character string to the current output device. The character string is emitted exactly as it appears in storage.

The length of the string, in bytes, must be on top of the stack, with the address of the first byte of the string beneath it.

For example, you could use the following phrase to display thirty-two characters from **PAD** on the terminal:

```
PAD 32 TYPE
```

Glossary

EMIT (b –) Core

Output one character from the least-significant byte of the top item on the stack, then pop the stack. **EMIT** is often useful for initial "cut-and-try" definitions.

EMIT? (– flag) Facility Ext

Check that it is okay to output a character (e.g., the device is ready). Return *flag*, which is *false* if it is known that the execution of **EMIT** instead of **EMIT?** would suffer an indefinite delay; otherwise, return *true*, including the case where the device status is indeterminate. Used, for example, in modem protocols with the RTS line. "emit-question"

TYPE (c-addr u –) Core

Output the character string at *c-addr*, length *u*.

References

PAD, Section 3.1.2

Scanning strings, Section 6.1.5

Vectored I/O words, Section 5.1.4

5.4.3 Support of Special Terminal Features

Each terminal task in a Forth system may have unique user variables, including a port address or other device- and system-specific parameters. Each task may require different control character sequences for functions such as **CR** (go to beginning of next line) and **PAGE** (go to top of next page).

The standard Forth words that perform terminal functions are listed in this section. The method of vectoring these functions to the particular output sequences required for given devices is system dependent.

Glossary

AT-XY (u_1 u_2 –) Facility

Configure the current output device so the next character displayed will appear in column u_1, row u_2 of the device's output area. The upper-left corner of this area is at $u_1 = 0$, $u_2 = 0$. "at-X-Y"

CR (–) Core

Cause subsequent output to appear at the beginning of the next line on the current output device. "C-R"

GET-XY (– u_1 u_2) Common usage

Return the current cursor position (column u_1, row u_2) from the current input device. "get-X-Y"

PAGE (–) Facility

Move to another page for output on the current device. On a CRT, clear the screen and reset the cursor position to the upper-left corner. On a printer, perform a form feed.

SPACE (–) Core

Display one space on the current output device.

SPACES (u –) Core

Display *u* spaces on the current output device.

5.5 File-Based Disk Access

Forth systems provide access to mass storage using a block-based or file-based method. This section discusses words that access mass storage using files. Appendix C discusses words used to access and manage disk blocks and block buffers in Forth.

Many items discussed in this section—the specific value and meaning of non-zero I/O result codes, allowable forms of filenames, values of line terminators, etc.—are system dependent. Consult your product documentation for details.

5.5.1 Overview

Forth words described in this section provide access to mass storage in the form of *files*, under the following conditions and assumptions:

- Files are provided by a host operating system.
- File state information (e.g., current position in file, size) is managed by the host operating system. File sizes are dynamically variable, so write operations will change the size of a file as necessary.

- Filenames are represented as character strings whose format is determined by the host operating system. Filenames may include system-specific pathnames.
- A *file identifier* (*fileid*) is a single-cell value passed to file operators to refer to specific files. Opening a file assigns it a file identifier, which remains valid until the file is closed. When the text interpreter is using a file as input, its *fileid* will be returned by **SOURCE-ID**. The other possible values that **SOURCE-ID** can return are zero (if the user input device is the source) and -1 (if the source is a character string passed by **EVALUATE**).
- File contents are accessed as a sequence of characters. The *file position* is the character offset from the start of the file. The file position is updated by all read, write, and re-position commands.
- File read operations return an *actual* transfer count, which can differ from the *requested* transfer count.
- A *file access method* (*fam*) is a single-cell value indicating the permissible means of accessing a specific file, such as read/write or read-only.
- An *I/O result* (*ior*) is a single-cell value indicating the result of an I/O operation. A value of zero always indicates success; non-zero values are definition- and system-specific. An operation reaching the end of a file shall not consider it an error and shall return a zero *ior*.

5.5.2 Global File Operations

The words in this section manipulate files as entire entities.

Glossary

CLOSE-FILE (fileid — ior) File
Close the file identified by the *fileid*. Return an I/O result code.

CREATE-FILE (c-addr u fam — fileid ior) Core
Create a file, whose name is given by the character string at *c-addr* of length *u*, and open it using file access method *fam*. If the file already exists, re-create it as an empty file that replaces the pre-existing file of that name. If creation and opening are successful, return an *ior* of zero and the *fileid*. Otherwise, return a non-zero *ior* and an undefined value for *fileid*.

DELETE-FILE (c-addr u – ior) File

Delete the file whose name is given by the character string at *c-addr* and whose length is *u*. Return an I/O result code.

FLUSH-FILE (fileid – ior) File Ext

Force any buffered contents of the file referred to by *fileid* to be written to mass storage, and the size information for the file to be recorded by the system, if it changed. Return an *ior* of zero if successful; otherwise, return a system-dependent value.

OPEN-FILE (c-addr u fam – fileid ior) File

Open the file, whose name is given by the character string at *c-addr* of length *u*, using file access method *fam*. If successful, set the file position to zero, and return an *ior* of zero and the *fileid*; otherwise, return a non-zero *ior* and an undefined value for *fileid*.

RENAME-FILE ($c\text{-}addr_1$ u_1 $c\text{-}addr_2$ u_2 – ior) File Ext

Rename the file, whose current name is given by the character string at $c\text{-}addr_1$ of length u_1, to the name given by the character string at $c\text{-}addr_2$ of length u_2. Return an I/O result.

RESIZE-FILE (ud fileid – ior) File

Set the size of the file identified by *fileid* to *ud* and return an I/O result code. If the file size increases, the contents of the newly allocated space is indeterminate. After this operation (if successful), **FILE-SIZE** will return the same value for *ud*, and **FILE-POSITION** returns an undefined value.

5.5.3 File Reading and Writing

The words in this section are used to read or write to a specific file. Commands whose names include **INCLUDE** share the property of directing Forth's text interpreter to process the file as an alternate input stream. The **READ** and **WRITE** words are lower-level generic functions that access the file without assumptions about its contents.

Glossary

INCLUDE-FILE (fileid –) File

Read and interpret the given file, performing the following steps: Save the current input source specification. Store the given *fileid* in **SOURCE-ID**, set **BLK** to zero, and make this file the input source. Read a line from the file at the current file position, fill the input buffer with the contents of the line, set **>IN** to zero, and interpret the buffer contents. Continue reading lines until the end of the file is reached. When the end of file is reached, close the file and restore the previous input source specification.

INCLUDED (c-addr u –) File
Same as **INCLUDE-FILE**, except the file is specified by its name, which is stored at *c-addr* and is of length *u*. The file is opened and its *fileid* is stored in **SOURCE-ID**.

INCLUDE <filename> (–) Common usage
Same as **INCLUDE-FILE**, except the file is specified by the *filename* which follows in the input stream.

READ-FILE (c-addr u_1 fileid – u_2 ior) File
Read and store text from the given file—without interpretation—and update **FILE-POSITION**. Read u_1 consecutive characters from the current position in the file identified by *fileid*, storing them at *c-addr*. Return an *ior* and the number u_2 of characters successfully read. If no exception occurs, return an *ior* of zero and $u_2 = u_1$ or the number of characters actually read before encountering the end of the file, whichever is smaller. If **FILE-POSITION** was equal to **FILE-SIZE** before executing **READ-FILE**, u_2 is zero. If a non-zero *ior* is returned, u_2 is the number of characters successfully transferred before the exception occurred.

READ-LINE (c-addr u_1 fileid – u_2 flag ior) File
Read and store one line of text from the given file—without interpretation—and update **FILE-POSITION**: Read up to u_1 consecutive characters from the current position in the file identified by *fileid*, storing them at *c-addr*. Terminate the read if end-of-line delimiter(s) are encountered. Return an *ior* and the number u_2 of characters successfully read, not including any line delimiter(s). One or two line delimiter(s may be read into memory at the end of the line in addition to u_2; therefore, the buffer at *c-addr* should be at least u_1+2 characters long. If $u_2 = u_1$, the line delimiter was not reached. If no exception occurs, the returned *ior* is zero and *flag* is true. If **FILE-POSITION** was equal to **FILE-SIZE** before executing **READ-LINE**, *flag* is false, *ior* is zero, and u_2 is zero. If an non-zero *ior* is returned, other returned parameters are undefined.

REFILL (– flag) Block Ext, Core Ext, File Ext
When the input source is a text file, attempt to read the next line from

the current file. If successful, make the result the current input buffer, set **>IN** to zero, and return *true*; otherwise, return *false*.

WRITE-FILE (c-addr u fileid – ior) File
Write *u* characters from *c-addr* to the file identified by *fileid*, starting at its current file position. Increase **FILE-SIZE** if necessary. Return an I/O result code. After this operation, **FILE-POSITION** returns the next file position after the last character written to the file, and **FILE-SIZE** returns a value equal to or greater than **FILE-POSITION**.

WRITE-LINE (c-addr u fileid – ior) File
The same as **WRITE-FILE** except a line terminator is written to the file after the *u* characters.

5.5.4 File Support Words

The words in this section provide support for other file access functions.

Glossary

BIN (fam_1 – fam_2) File
Modify the given file access method fam_1 to additionally select a binary (not line-oriented) file access method, returning the modified access method fam_2.

FILE-POSITION (fileid – ud ior) File
Return the double-cell current file position *ud* for the file identified by *fileid*, and an I/O result code. If the *ior* is non-zero, the position *ud* is undefined.

FILE-SIZE (fileid – ud ior) File
Return the double-length file size *ud* for the file identified by *fileid*, and an I/O result code. This operation does not affect the value returned by **FILE-POSITION**. If the *ior* is non-zero, the size *ud* is undefined.

FILE-STATUS (c-addr u – x ior) File Ext
Return the status of the file whose name is given by the character string at *c-addr* of length *u*. The *ior* is zero if the file exists, otherwise it is a system-dependent value. Cell *x* contains system-dependent information about the file.

R/O (– fam) File
Return the read-only file access method. "R-O"

R/W (– fam) File
Return the read/write file access method. "R-W"

REPOSITION-FILE (ud fileid – ior) File
For the file identified by *fileid*, reset the file position to *ud* and return an I/O result code. After this operation (if successful), **FILE-POSITION** will return this same value for *ud*.

S" <string>" (– c-addr u) Core, File
Store *string* in a temporary buffer, which is at least 80 characters long, and return the address and length of the string. "S-quote"

This word normally compiles a string in a definition, returning its address and count when executed. In a file-based disk access system, this word is extended to operate interpretively with filenames. When interpreting, it looks ahead in the input stream to obtain a character string terminated by ".

W/O (– fam) File
Return the write-only file access method. "W-O"

5.6 Time and Timing Functions

Many Forth systems support an asynchronous, free-running milliseconds timer, and retrieval of date and time from a host operating system (if the host provides this function). The precision of the milliseconds timer depends both on the resolution of the system clock and on relevant hardware characteristics. A task executing **MS** is suspended until its time-out period has elapsed.

Glossary

MS (u –) Facility Ext
Wait for at least *u* milliseconds, but not more than *u* plus twice the resolution of the system clock. "M-S"

TIME&DATE (– u_1 u_2 u_3 u_4 u_5 u_6) Facility Ext
Return the current time and date: u_1=seconds (0–59), u_2=minutes (0–59), u_3=hours (0–23), u_4=days (0–31), u_5=months (1–12), and u_6=years (0–9999).

5.7 Dynamic Memory Management

Some applications require dynamic data storage. For example, a large number of asynchronous tasks may be taking data intermittently. When one of them receives a burst of data, it needs a temporary buffer to hold and process the data, but can relinquish the buffer when processing is complete.

The words in this section allocate, resize, and free regions of data space. Memory regions allocated this way are at arbitrary addresses, so they are useful only for data. They cannot be used, for example, for the Forth dictionary, because there is no way for an application to manage the dictionary pointer. Although a given region will be internally contiguous, it is not guaranteed to be contiguous with any other region, so no operation should attempt to cross a region's boundary.

Glossary

ALLOCATE `( u – a-addr ior )` Memory

Attempt to allocate *u* bytes of contiguous data space. The data space pointer is unaffected by this operation. The initial content of the allocated space is not defined. If the allocation is successful, the aligned starting address *a-addr* of the allocated space and an *ior* of zero is returned. If the allocation is not successful, *a-addr* is an undefined value and a system-dependent non-zero *ior* is returned.

FREE `( a-addr – ior )` Memory

Release the contiguous data space identified by *a-addr* to the system for later re-allocation. The address *a-addr* is a value previously returned by **ALLOCATE** or **RESIZE**. The data space pointer is unaffected by this operation. If the release operation succeeds, *ior* is zero; otherwise, it is a system-dependent non-zero value describing the failure.

RESIZE ($a\text{-}addr_1$ u – $a\text{-}addr_2$ ior) Memory

Change the size of a contiguous data space previously allocated by **ALLOCATE** or **RESIZE** at $a\text{-}addr_1$ to *u* bytes, where *u* may be either larger or smaller than the current size of the space. The data space pointer is unaffected by this operation. If the operation succeeds, $a\text{-}addr_2$ is the aligned starting address of the *u* bytes of allocated memory and *ior* is zero. $a\text{-}addr_2$ may be, but need not be, the same as $a\text{-}addr_1$. In any case, the contents of the area before and after the **RESIZE** are preserved up to *u* bytes or to the original size, whichever is smaller. If *a-addr*$_2$ is not the same as *a-addr*$_1$, the region of memory at *a-addr*$_1$ is released to the system as if by **FREE**. If the resize operation fails, *a-addr*$_2$ equals *a-addr*$_1$, the content of the region of memory at *a-addr*$_1$ is unaffected and a system-dependent non-zero *ior* code is returned.

5.8 Floating Point

Many Forth applications do not require floating-point math. Arithmetic that might seem to need floating-point calculations can often be done more simply, using less memory and executing faster, when coded with integer operators and with intelligent use of scaling words such as ***/**. This is especially true when hardware floating point is not available, often the case in embedded applications. The key issue is dynamic range in the variables of interest; if that is limited to fewer than 15 bits, say (as it usually will be if driven by I/O devices), integer math is usually the better choice unless hardware floating point is available.

For applications in which floating-point mathematics is essential and to take advantage of floating-point hardware, Forth defines a full set of optional floating-point operators. This section describes the general operators available on systems that comply with Standard Forth and support floating point. Their implementation is very system specific and may use floating-point hardware. Your implementation-specific documentation should be consulted for additional features that may be present (such as hardware-stack implementation and additional hardware error trapping).

References

Multi-stack notation, Section 2.1.1

5.8.1 Floating-Point System Guidelines

Floating-point packages may exist on systems with widely varying hardware capabilities, and thus may require different implementation strategies. Therefore, the basic Standard Forth floating-point word set is flexible in many areas. For details of a particular implementation, you will need to consult CPU-specific documentation. The following guidelines apply:

- The internal representation of a floating-point number, including the format and precision of both significand and exponent, is implementation specific, as is the largest usable floating-point number. For portability, supplementary words are defined that fetch and store to standard 32- or 64-bit IEEE floating-point number format (see ANSI/IEEE Standard 754 -1985).
- Because the length in memory of a floating-point number is implementation specific, the question of alignment arises. A *float-aligned address* (stack comment *f-addr*) is an address where a floating-point number can be accessed. Similarly, a *single-float aligned address* (*sf-addr*) or *double-float-aligned address* (*df-addr*) is an address where a single-precision (32-bit) or double-precision (64-bit) IEEE standard floating-point number can be accessed.
- There is a logically separate *floating-point stack*. Both the width and the depth are implementation specific, but the stack must be able to contain at least six items.
- The floating-point stack may be physically separate or it may be implemented using the data stack. If it uses the data stack, integer data and floating-point numbers can become mixed on the same stack. An application program intended to be portable across different implementations (with and without separate stacks) must order its operations carefully. For example, it must clear the floating-point stack of all items before trying to access any data stack items that may be underneath (and vice versa). It must also ensure that arguments to operations using both stacks (e.g., **F!**) are produced in the correct order. A program can determine whether floating-point numbers are kept on the data stack by passing the string FLOATING-STACK to **ENVIRONMENT?** (see Section 5.2). If the value returned is zero, the data stack is used; otherwise, the non-zero value indicates the maximum depth of the separate floating-point stack.
- For floating-point input and output, the current base must be **DECIMAL**; if the base is other than decimal, number conversion or display will not take place. Floating-point numbers to be interpreted by a system that complies with Standard Forth must contain an exponent indicator **E** or **e**. For example, one legitimate floating-point representation of the number 12300 is 1.23E4, where 1.23 is the *significand* and 4 is the *exponent*.
- Floating-point operators may address memory in data space

regions declared with **FVARIABLE**. These regions are *not necessarily contiguous* with subsequent regions allocated with **,** (comma) or **ALLOT**.

5.8.2 Input Number Conversion

A floating-point number in Forth must contain an E or an e (signifying an exponent), and must begin with a digit (optionally preceded by an algebraic sign). For example, -0.5e0 is valid, but .2e0 is not. A number does not need to contain a decimal point or a value for the exponent; if there is no exponent value, it is assumed to be zero (a multiplier of one). *Punctuation other than a decimal point is not allowed in a floating-point number.*

During number conversion, **BASE** must be **DECIMAL** so numbers such as **1E** are not interpreted as hexadecimal digits. If **BASE** is not **DECIMAL**, floating-point number conversion will not take place.

All the following are valid floating-point numbers:

```
3.14159E+00  -3E-07  1e  1.E  0.005e02
```

...but the following are double-precision integers (under the enhanced rules described in Section 1.1.6), not floating-point numbers:

```
3.14159  -1,000,000.12  -0.003
```

Input conversion of floating numbers is accomplished by adding an additional level to Standard Forth number conversion routines. First, an attempt is made to convert an input string to a floating-point number. If this succeeds, the number is returned on the floating-point stack; otherwise, control passes to the integer number conversion routines. Thus, **20.E** would be converted as a floating number and **20.** as a double-precision integer.

References

Input number conversion, Sections 1.1.6, 3.6.1

5.8.3 Output Formats

Three standard output formats are provided to display floating-point numbers. All of them remove the top item on the floating-point stack. The number of significant digits to display is set globally for all three formats and will remain in use until changed. There is also low-level support for custom output (and input) formatting; see Section 5.8.11.

Glossary

F. (F: r –) Floating Ext
Display the top number on the floating-point stack, followed by a space. Uses fixed-point notation (decimal point only, no exponent). The number of significant digits displayed is set by **SET-PRECISION**. "F-dot"

FE. (F: r –) Floating Ext
Display the top number on the floating-point stack, followed by a space. Uses engineering notation (the significand is greater than or equal to 1.0 and less than 1000.0, and the decimal exponent is a multiple of three). The number of significant digits displayed is set by **SET-PRECISION**. "F-E-dot"

FS. (F: r –) Floating Ext
Display the top number on the floating-point stack, followed by a space. Uses scientific notation (significand plus exponent), where the significand is greater than or equal to 1.0 and less than 10.0. The number of significant digits to display is set by **SET-PRECISION**. "F-S-dot"

PRECISION (– u) Floating Ext
Return the number of significant digits currently displayed by **F.**, **FE.**, or **FS.**.

SET-PRECISION (u –) Floating Ext
Set the number of significant digits to be used by **F.**, **FE.**, or **FS.** to *u*.

5.8.4 Floating-Point Constants, Variables, and Literals

There are floating-point counterparts to the integer Forth words **CONSTANT**, **VARIABLE**, and **LITERAL**. The memory storage requirements, maximum value, and precision of the floating-point versions are implementation specific.

Glossary

FCONSTANT <name> (F: r –) Floating

Define a floating-point constant with the given *name* whose value is *r*. For example:

```
3.14159E FCONSTANT PI.
```

name (– F: r)
When *name* is executed, the value *r* is returned on the floating-point stack. "F-constant"

FLITERAL (F: r –) Floating

Used only within a definition. When the definition is compiled and the word **FLITERAL** is reached, there must be a value *r* on the floating-point stack; it will be removed and added to the definition. When the definition is executed, **FLITERAL** returns the value *r* on the floating-point stack. "F-literal"

FVARIABLE <name> (–) Floating

Create a dictionary entry for *name*, associated with an amount of data space sufficient to store one floating-point number of the implementation-specified size.

ANS Forth cautions that subsequent allocations of memory with **,** or **ALLOT** may not be contiguous with the data space of an **FVARIABLE**. An **FVARIABLE** may be initialized with, e.g., **F!** (see below). "F-variable"

name (– f-addr)
Return the address of the data space associated with *name*.

5.8.5 Memory Access

Memory access words similar to those in other parts of a Forth system are provided for floating-point data types. These words obtain addresses from the data stack, and transfer data to and from the floating-point stack.

The requirement for float-alignment creates some issues in defining floating-point arrays. An object defined by **CREATE** returns a cell-aligned address, but it is not necessarily float-aligned. Therefore, you would create an array of ten floats this way:

```
CREATE MY-FLOATS  FALIGN 10 FLOATS ALLOT
```

Subsequently, you must use **FALIGNED** following any reference to **MY-FLOATS**. For example, to print them, you could write:

```
: SHOW-FLOATS ( -- )   MY-FLOATS FALIGNED
   10 0 DO DUP I FLOATS + F@ F.  LOOP DROP ;
```

A potential simplification would be to start with **FVARIABLE**:

```
FVARIABLE MY-FLOATS  9 FLOATS ALLOT
```

This version of **MY-FLOATS** is guaranteed to return a float-aligned address. ANS Forth cautions that the use of **ALLOT** or **,** following a **VARIABLE** or **FVARIABLE** does not necessarily allocate space contiguous to the variable's data space. But situations in which this is problematic are very rare. We advise checking your system's documentation in this regard. If the spaces will be contiguous, you can use this simpler approach (which avoids invoking **FALIGNED** every time you reference your array) and simply document your dependence on contiguity.

Glossary

F! (f-addr –); (F: r –) Floating
Store the floating-point value *r* at *f-addr*. In single-stack implementations, *f-addr* must be on top of the stack. "F-store"

F@ (f-addr –); (F: – r) Floating
Fetch the value stored at *f-addr* to the floating-point stack. "F-fetch"

DF! (df-addr –); (F: r –) Floating Ext
Store the floating-point value *r* as a 64-bit IEEE double-precision number at *df-addr*, rounding if the internal representation has more precision. In single-stack implementations, *df-addr* must be on top of the stack. "D-F-store"

DF@ (df-addr –); (F: – r) Floating Ext
Fetch the 64-bit IEEE double-precision number at *df-addr*, convert to internal representation and place on the floating-point stack, rounding if the internal representation has less than 64-bit precision. "D-F-fetch"

SF! (sf-addr –); (F: r –) Floating Ext
Store the floating-point value *r* as a 32-bit IEEE single-precision number at *sf-addr*, rounding if the internal representation has more precision. In single-stack implementations, *sf-addr* must be on top of the stack. "S-F-store"

SF@ (sf-addr –); (F: – r) Floating Ext

Fetch the 32-bit IEEE single-precision number at *sf-addr*, convert to internal representation and place on the floating-point stack, rounding if the internal representation has less than 32-bit precision. "S-F-fetch"

5.8.6 Floating-Point Stack Operators

The floating-point stack operators generally correspond to equivalent operators for the integer data stack. Operators are also provided for exchanging values between the data and floating-point stacks. Before coding complicated floating-point stack maneuvers, check your particular system's maximum floating-point stack depth—it may be small. On systems that keep floating-point numbers on the data stack, take care with the order of floating-point and integer operations.[1]

Glossary

D>F (d –); (F: – r) Floating

Convert a double-precision integer *d* to internal floating-point representation *r* and place it on the floating-point stack. "D-to-F"

F>D (– d); (F: r –) Floating

Convert a floating-point number *r* to a double-precision integer *d*, discarding the fractional part, and place it on the data stack. "F-to-D"

FDEPTH (– +n) Floating

Return the number *+n* of values on the floating-point stack. If floating-point numbers are kept on the data stack, *+n* is the maximum possible number of floating-point values given the current data stack depth in cells. "F-depth"

FDROP (F: r –) Floating

Drop the top item on the floating-point stack. "F-drop"

FDUP (F: r – r r) Floating

Duplicate the top item on the floating-point stack. "F-dupe"

FOVER (F: r_1 r_2 – r_1 r_2 r_1) Floating

Copy r_1 to the top of the floating-point stack. "F-over"

1. These operators function as described even if the system implements the floating-point stack on the data stack.

FROT (F: r_1 r_2 r_3 – r_2 r_3 r_1) Floating
Rotate the third item to the top of the floating-point stack. "F-rote"

FSWAP (F: r_1 r_2 – r_2 r_1) Floating
Exchange the top two items on the floating-point stack. "F-swap"

5.8.7 Floating-Point Arithmetic

The words in this section perform arithmetic on the floating-point stack. All operations are carried out to the full precision of the implementation-specific representation of a floating-point number.

Glossary

F* (F: r_1 r_2 – r_3) Floating
Multiply r_1 by r_2, giving r_3. "F-star"

F** (F: r_1 r_2 – r_3) Floating Ext
Raise r_1 to the power r_2, giving the result r_3. "F-star-star"

F+ (F: r_1 r_2 – r_3) Floating
Add r_1 to r_2, giving the sum r_3. "f-plus"

F- (F: r_1 r_2 – r_3) Floating
Subtract r_2 from r_1, giving the difference r_3. "F-minus"

F/ (F: r_1 r_2 – r_3) Floating
Divide r_1 by r_2, giving the quotient r_3. "F-slash"

FABS (F: r_1 – r_2) Floating Ext
Return r_2, the absolute value of r_1. "F-abs"

FLOOR (F: r_1 – r_2) Floating Ext
Round r_1 *toward negative infinity* to the next integral value, giving r_2. "floor"

FMAX (F: r_1 r_2 – r_3) Floating
Return r_3, the greater of r_1 and r_2. "F-max"

FMIN (F: r_1 r_2 – r_3) Floating
Return r_3, the lesser of r_1 and r_2. "F-min"

FNEGATE (F: r_1 – r_2) Floating

Return r_2, the negation of r_1. "F-negate"

FROUND (F: r_1 – r_2) Floating

Round r_1 *to the nearest integral value,* giving r_2. "F-round"

FSQRT (F: r_1 – r_2) Floating Ext

Return r_2, the square root of r_1. An error may occur if r_1 is less than zero. "F-square-root"

5.8.8 Floating-Point Conditionals

Conditional tests of floating-point numbers consume their argument(s) on the floating-point stack and return a truth flag to the data stack. The word **F~** provides both exact and near-equality testing. **F~** is usually preferable to **F0=** because a floating-point number may fail to be zero by an infinitesimal amount.

Glossary

F0< (– flag); (F: r –) Floating

Return *true* if and only if *r* is less than zero. "F-zero-less-than"

F0= (– flag); (F: r –) Floating

Return *true* if and only if *r* is exactly equal to zero. (See the definition of **F~** below.) "F-zero-equals"

F< (– flag); (F: r_1 r_2 –) Floating

Return *true* if and only if r_1 is less than r_2. "F-less-than"

F~ (– flag); (F: r_1 r_2 r_3 –) Floating Ext

Test for equality or near equality, on an absolute or relative basis. If the increment r_3 is positive, return *true* if and only if the absolute value of $[r_1 - r_2]$ is less than r_3. If the increment r_3 is zero, return *true* if and only if r_1 and r_2 are exactly identical (be aware that some implementations may encode positive zero and negative zero differently). If the increment r_3 is negative, return *true* if and only if the absolute value of $[r_1 - r_2]$ is less than the absolute value of r_3 times the sum of the absolute values of r_1 and r_2. "F-proximate"

5.8.9 Logarithmic and Trigonometric Functions

The words in this section provide a full set of logarithmic, exponential, and trigonometric functions. All angles are in radians. The function **FSINCOS** is a little unusual: it returns the sine *and* the cosine of the given angle (cosine on top). **FSINCOS** and **FATAN2** are complementary operators that convert angles to 2-vectors and vice versa. They correctly handle the conversion even when the tangent of the angle would be infinite. The pair of values returned by **FSINCOS** is a Cartesian unit 2-vector in the direction of the given angle, measured counter-clockwise from the positive X-axis. **FATAN2** takes arguments in the same order, converting a 2-vector back to a scalar angle. For all principal angles (-pi to +pi radians), the phrase **FSINCOS FATAN2** is an identity operation within the accuracy and range of the operators. The phrase **FSINCOS F/** is functionally equivalent to **FTAN**, but is useful only over a limited range of angles, whereas **FSINCOS** and **FATAN2** are useful for all angles.

Glossary

FACOS (F: r_1 – r_2) Floating Ext

Return r_2, the principal radian angle (zero to +pi) whose cosine is r_1. "F-A-cos"

FACOSH (F: r_1 – r_2) Floating Ext

Return r_2, the floating-point value whose hyperbolic cosine is r_1. "F-A-cosh"

FALOG (F: r_1 – r_2) Floating Ext

Raise 10 to the power r_1, giving r_2. "F-A-log"

FASIN (F: r_1 – r_2) Floating Ext

Return r_2, the principal radian angle (-pi/2 to +pi/2) whose sine is r_1. "F-A-sine"

FASINH (F: r_1 – r_2) Floating Ext

Return r_2, the floating-point value whose hyperbolic sine is r_1. "F-A-sine-H"

FATAN (F: r_1 – r_2) Floating Ext

Return r_2, the principal radian angle (-pi/2 to +pi/2) whose tangent is r_1. "F-A-tan"

FATAN2 (F: r1 r2 – r3) Floating Ext

Return r_3, the principal radian angle (-pi to +pi) whose tangent is r_1/r_2. The values r_1 and r_2 may be, but need not be, components of a unit vector. An error will occur if both r_1 and r_2 are zero (vector of zero magnitude). "F-A-tan-two"

FATANH (F: r_1 – r_2) Floating Ext

Return r_2, the floating-point value whose hyperbolic tangent is r_1. "F-A-tan-H"

FCOS (F: r_1 – r_2) Floating Ext

Return r_2, the cosine of the radian angle r_1. "F-cos"

FCOSH (F: r_1 – r_2) Floating Ext

Return r_2, the hyperbolic cosine of r_1. "F-cosh"

FEXP (F: r_1 – r_2) Floating Ext

Raise *e* (2.71828...) to the power r_1, giving r_2. "F-E-X-P"

FEXPM1 (F: r_1 – r_2) Floating Ext

Raise *e* (2.71828...) to the power r_1 and subtract one, giving r_2. This function provides increased accuracy over **FEXP** when the argument r_1 is close to zero. "F-E-X-P-M-one"

FLN (F: r_1 – r_2) Floating Ext

Return r_2, the natural logarithm of r_1. "F-L-N"

FLNP1 (F: r_1 – r_2) Floating Ext

Return r_2, the natural logarithm of $(1 + r_1)$. This function provides increased accuracy over **FLN** when the argument r_1 is close to zero. "F-L-N-P-one"

FLOG (F: r_1 – r_2) Floating Ext

Return r_2, the base-ten logarithm of r_1. "F-log"

FSIN (F: r_1 – r_2) Floating Ext

Return r_2, the sine of the radian angle r_1. "F-sine"

FSINCOS (F: r_1 – r_2 r_3) Floating Ext

Return r_2 (sine) and r_3 (cosine) of the radian angle r_1. "F-sine-cos"

FSINH (F: r_1 – r_2) Floating Ext

Return r_2, the hyperbolic sine of r_1. "F-sine-H"

FTAN (F: r_1 – r_2) Floating Ext

Return r_2, the tangent of the radian angle r_1. "F-tan"

FTANH (F: r_1 – r_2) Floating Ext

Return r_2, the hyperbolic tangent of r_1. "F-tan-H"

5.8.10 Address Management

The floating-point command set introduces three new data types: internal floating point, 32-bit IEEE single-precision floating point, and 64-bit IEEE double-precision floating point. An application creating data structures using any of these types should use the support words described in this section to manage the address space. For example, the length of an internal floating-point number should always be referred to indirectly with words such as **FLOAT+** or **FLOATS**, as the size may vary in different implementations.

When defining custom data structures, be aware that **CREATE** does not necessarily leave the data-space pointer aligned for the various floating-point data types. You can ensure alignment by explicitly specifying it both at compile time and at execution time. An example from Standard Forth is:

```
: FCONSTANT ( F: r -- )   CREATE  FALIGN  HERE
  1 FLOATS ALLOT  F!  DOES> ( F: - r)  FALIGNED  F@ ;
```

In this example, the **FALIGN** after **CREATE** ensures that the address returned by **HERE** is float-aligned for the **F!** operation. **FALIGN** may have needed to reserve extra data space to do this, so, when an example of **FCONSTANT** is executed (using the code following **DOES>**) and the example's address is returned, the word **FALIGNED** is used to skip any such extra space and access the floating-point value properly with **F@**.

In many implementations, alignment of floating-point data types requires nothing more than ordinary cell alignment. In such systems, words such as **FALIGN** and **FALIGNED** may simply be aliases for **ALIGN** and **ALIGNED**. An application should not rely on this equivalence, however, and should use the floating-point words in this section.

Glossary

FALIGN (—) Floating
If the data-space pointer is not float aligned, reserve enough data space to make it so. "F-align"

FALIGNED (addr — f-addr) Floating
Return *f-addr*, the first float-aligned address equal to or greater than *addr*. "F-aligned"

FLOAT+ ($f\text{-}addr_1$ — $f\text{-}addr_2$) Floating
Add the size in bytes of a floating-point number to $f\text{-}addr_1$, giving $f\text{-}addr_2$. "float-plus"

FLOATS (n_1 — n_2) Floating
Return n_2, the size in bytes of n_1 internal floating-point numbers.

DFALIGN (—) Floating Ext
If the data-space pointer is not double-float aligned, reserve enough data space to make it so. "D-F-align"

DFALIGNED (addr — df-addr) Floating Ext
Return *df-addr*, the first double-float-aligned address equal to or greater than *addr*. "D-F-aligned"

DFLOAT+ ($df\text{-}addr_1$ — $df\text{-}addr_2$) Floating Ext
Add the size in bytes of a 64-bit IEEE double-precision floating-point number to $df\text{-}addr_1$, giving $df\text{-}addr_2$. "D-float-plus"

DFLOATS (n_1 — n_2) Floating Ext
Return n_2, the size in bytes of n_1 64-bit IEEE double-precision floating-point numbers. "D-floats"

SFALIGN (—) Floating Ext
If the data-space pointer is not single-float aligned, reserve enough data space to make it so. "S-F-align"

SFALIGNED (addr — sf-addr) Floating Ext
Return *sf-addr*, the first single-float-aligned address equal to or greater than *addr*. "S-F-aligned"

SFLOAT+ ($sf\text{-}addr_1$ — $sf\text{-}addr_2$) Floating Ext
Add the size in bytes of a 32-bit IEEE single-precision floating-point number to $sf\text{-}addr_1$, giving $sf\text{-}addr_2$. "S-float-plus"

SFLOATS `( n1 - n2 )` Floating Ext

Return n_2, the size in bytes of n_1 32-bit IEEE single-precision floating-point numbers. "S-floats"

5.8.11 Custom I/O

The input number conversion routines in the text interpreter and the standard output words **F.**, **FE.**, and **FS.** can be used for most floating-point I/O, but in some cases more control over the process is desirable. The words **>FLOAT** (for input) and **REPRESENT** (for output) can be used as the basis for custom I/O routines. The input word **>FLOAT** is more flexible than the text interpreter routines (for example, an exponent marker **E** or **e** is not required), but it cannot distinguish between integers and floating-point numbers; it assumes the input string is to be converted as a floating-point number, if possible. **>FLOAT** is defined broadly to permit valid floating-point input from many standard programming environments.

Glossary

>FLOAT `( c-addr u - true | false ); ( F: - r | )` Floating

Attempt to convert the string specified by starting address *c-addr* and length *u* to internal floating-point representation. If the conversion is successful, its floating-point value *r* and *true* are returned. If it was not successful, only *false* is returned. A string of blanks should be converted as floating-point zero. "to float"

Nearly any reasonably constructed string will convert. Decimal base is assumed. A valid number has a significand and an optional exponent. The significand has an optional sign and at least one digit, with or without a decimal point. The exponent, if present, is signified by **E**, **e**, **D**, or **d** followed by an optional integer (signed or unsigned), or by a plain **+** or **-** followed by an optional integer. **>FLOAT** will convert all the following to valid floating-point numbers:

```
-1.23e-01  -1  .3  5D  -6.12+34  7+3  .456-  .006  9+00
```

REPRESENT `( c-addr u - n flag1 flag2 ); ( F: r - )`[1] Floating

Attempt to convert the significand of the floating-point number *r*. At

1. For single-stack systems, the order of the input arguments to **REPRESENT** is *r* on the bottom followed by *c-addr* and *u* (top).

c-addr, place an ASCII representation of the *u* most-significant digits of the significand. The string is to be interpreted as a decimal fraction, with an implied decimal point to the left of the first digit; the first digit is zero only if all digits are zero. Return on the stack the resulting decimal base exponent *n*, the sign of the floating-point number as $flag_1$ (*true* if *r* was negative), and a valid-result $flag_2$ (*true* if *r* was in the implementation-defined range of valid floating-point numbers). The significand is rounded to *u* digits using the round-to-nearest-integer rule, and *n* is adjusted as necessary after the rounding.

If $flag_2$ is false, *n*, $flag_1$, and the contents of *c-addr* are implementation specific. However, the string at *c-addr* shall consist of displayable characters. For example, a system might return the informative messages `+infinity` or `nan` ("not a number") to *c-addr*.

6. The Forth Interpreter and Compiler

Forth is primarily a development environment, usually presented as a fairly complete "integrated development environment" including programming tools, libraries, compiler, assembler, and in some cases an editor. This section describes features specific to the Forth compiler as well as Forth's uniquely powerful ability to construct data objects of various types. Unlike more conventional compilers, the Forth compiler uses a text interpreter that is also available to the programmer for application use. Moreover, the tools used inside the Forth compiler and interpreter are available, so you can modify and extend both.

6.1 The Text Interpreter

The text interpreter in Forth is used for terminal interaction and for processing text on disk (either in direct execution or in compilation). A brief description of its operation is given in Section 1.1.5. This section covers the text interpreter in more detail and discusses ways the programmer may use the text interpreter in application routines.

References

Text interpreter, Section 1.1.5

6.1.1 Input Sources

The text interpreter always interprets from an *input buffer (*also called an *input stream),* which may or may not be a physically separate location. There are up to four sources for input: the *user input device* (almost always a keyboard), a character string in memory, a text file, and a block file. The default source is the keyboard. All systems have a keyboard input buffer, typically 80 characters long. All systems can also treat a character string in memory as an input buffer, if given the string's address and length. When systems with source code in text files interpret from files, the current line in the current file is the input buffer. When systems with source code in blocks interpret from blocks, the current block (1024 bytes) is the input buffer.

Early Forth systems that ran without a host OS always kept source in blocks, and as more Forths were developed to run under operating systems many implementors and users found blocks to be convenient. In the 21st century most Forths use text files, but some block-based Forths still exist. The words **BLK** and **SOURCE-ID** constitute a bridge between block-oriented and text file-oriented Forths.

The word **SOURCE-ID** returns a value that identifies the input source, unless it is a block. On systems that implement blocks, the variable **BLK** contains the block number that is the current input source, or zero if the input is not a block. On systems with all four inputs, checking **BLK** first and then **SOURCE-ID** will uniquely identify the input. See Table 11 below:

Table 11: Identifying the input source

Input Source	SOURCE-ID	BLK @
User Input Device (keyboard)	0	0
Character String	-1	0
File	Text file *fileid*	0
Block	(undefined)	block number

Glossary

BLK (– a-addr) Block

Return the address of a cell containing zero or the number of the mass-storage block being interpreted. If **BLK** contains zero, the input source can be identified by **SOURCE-ID**. "B-L-K"

SOURCE-ID (– n) Core Ext, File

Return a value indicating the current input source. The value is 0 if the source is the user input device, -1 if the source is a character string, a *fileid* if the source is a file, and undefined if the source is a block.

References

File-based disk access, Section 5.5
Block-based disk access, Appendix C

6.1.2 Input Source Management

The word **QUIT** is the basic idle behavior of the terminal task that controls the user input device. Executing **QUIT** makes the user input device the current input source and awaits a line of input into the keyboard buffer. When the input is received, the character pointer **>IN** is set to zero and interpretation begins. If interpretation completes normally, the system-defined prompt is displayed (typically **OK**) and **QUIT** awaits the next line of input.

EVALUATE directs interpretation to take place from a specified character string. When **EVALUATE** is executed, the address and count of a character string must be on the stack. **EVALUATE** saves the current input source specification, makes the character string the input buffer, sets **>IN** to zero, and begins interpretation. When the parse area is empty (there are no more words to be interpreted in the string), the prior input source is restored.

Interpretation from a file usually is done with **INCLUDE-FILE**, **INCLUDE**, or **INCLUDED**. These and other file-handling words are described in detail in Section 5.5 of this manual.

Interpretation from blocks is done with **LOAD** or **THRU**. See Appendix C.2 for details of block reading and writing.

The support words in the following list are connected with text interpretation. In general, they are used at the system level to create custom text interpretation words and will not be needed by an application; for example, all standard source-selection words—such as **EVALUATE**, **INCLUDE**, and **LOAD**—automatically save and restore the current input source specification. Some lower-level words—such as **READ-FILE** and **READ-LINE**—do not, and might need explicit uses of **SAVE-INPUT** and **RESTORE-INPUT**.

Glossary

>IN (– a-addr) Core
Return the address of a cell containing the offset, in characters, from the start of the input buffer to the start of the current parse area. "to-in"

EVALUATE (i*x c-addr u – j*x) Core, Block
Save the current input source specification. Set **SOURCE-ID** to -1. Make the string at *c-addr*, whose length is *u*, the input source and input buf-

fer, set **>IN** to zero, and interpret. When the parse area is empty, restore the prior input source specification. Other stack effects are due to the word(s) that were **EVALUATE**d.

QUIT (i*x –); (R: j*x –) Core

Terminate execution of the current word (and all words that called it). Clear the return and data stacks. No indication is given to the terminal that a **QUIT** has occurred. Enter interpretation state and begin an infinite loop of awaiting a line of text from the input source and interpreting it. **QUIT** is the default idle behavior for terminals.

REFILL (– flag) Block Ext, Core Ext, File Ext

Attempt to fill the input buffer from the input source, returning a *flag* that is *true* if successful. If no input is available from the current source, return *false*.

If the input source is the keyboard, await a line of input. If successful (a line of zero characters—i.e., only CR was pressed—is successful), set **>IN** to zero and return *true*.

If the input source is a string from **EVALUATE**, return *false* and take no other action.

If the input source is a block, make the next block the input source and buffer by adding one to **BLK** and setting **>IN** to zero. Return *true* if the new value of **BLK** is a valid block number, otherwise *false*.

If the input source is a text file, attempt to read the next line from the file. If successful, make the result the current input buffer, set **>IN** to zero, and return *true*; otherwise, return *false*.

RESTORE-INPUT (x_n ... x_1 n – flag) Core Ext

Attempt to restore the input source specification to the state described by the parameters on the stack. The number and content of the parameters are system dependent. Return *true* if the input source *cannot* be so restored. It is an error if the input source represented by the arguments is not the same as the current input source (i.e., **SAVE-INPUT** and **RESTORE-INPUT** are intended for re-positioning within a given source, not for switching between sources).

SAVE-INPUT (– x_n ... x_1 n) Core Ext

Save *n* parameters (and *n* itself) describing the state of the current input source specification for later use by **RESTORE-INPUT**. The number and content of the parameters are system dependent. The parameters will include the value of **>IN** and others that are input-source dependent.

SOURCE (– c-addr u) Core

Return the address and length of the input buffer.

References

Text interpretation and **>IN**, Section 1.1.5

6.1.3 Parsing Text in the Input Stream

The normal behavior of a Forth system is to await text from some source (e.g., the keyboard or a text file) and process it. Text in the input stream may be parsed—that is, processed—by searching for a delimiter used to segregate portions of the input stream.

WORD and **PARSE** are the main workhorses of Forth's text interpreter. They are very similar but have two critical differences.

Both of these parsing words fetch characters from the input stream, starting at the offset given by the user variable **>IN**, until reaching a specified delimiter. This input stream, or current input source, is normally the terminal input buffer although it can be in other places, as described in Section 6.1.1. Both words also expect the delimiter character in the low-order byte of the top item that is on the stack. The area where the characters are placed is not initialized, although **WORD** will insert one trailing blank after the string.

The differences between **WORD** and **PARSE** are:

- **WORD** *skips any leading occurrences* of this character, searching for a non-delimiter character. If one is found, it is placed in a temporary storage area. Succeeding characters are then moved into this area until a delimiter character is encountered or until the specified end of the string is reached, terminating the operation. It returns the address of the string as a *counted string* (Section 3.1.3), that is, its first byte contains the length of the string. Therefore, the maximum length of a string that can be parsed by **WORD** is 255 characters.

  WORD is frequently followed by **COUNT** (Section 3.1.3) to convert a counted string to a plain character string, returning its address and length on the stack.

- **PARSE** does *not* skip leading delimiters. If it encounters a leading delimiter, it will simply report having found a zero-length string. And **PARSE** returns the address and length of the actual found string, which may be of any length.

The maximum length of a string to be parsed depends on the input source. If the source is the keyboard, the maximum length is set by the size of the terminal input buffer. If the source is a block, the maximum length is 1024. If the source is a file, the string expires at the end of the file.

The storage space used by these parsing words may also be used by other Forth functions, such as output number conversion words. As a result, when you use a parsing word to pick up a string from the input stream, you should finish working with it or promptly move it to another area (such as **PAD**) to avoid data corruption.

As an example of the use of these words, consider the following simple **TEST** examples:

```
: TEST1 ( -- )   32 WORD  COUNT TYPE ;
: TEST2 ( -- )   32 PARSE  TYPE ;
```

Both words would be used in the following way:

```
TESTn ABC      (cr)      ABC ok
```

Results from **TEST1** and **TEST2** will be identical providing there are no leading spaces; if there are leading spaces, however, **TEST2** will find an empty string and the interpreter will abort when it encounters the string **ABC** (presumably an undefined word).

Because using a space for a delimiter is so common, the word **BL** (for *blank*) is provided to return the ASCII value for the space character. Thus, phrases such as **32 WORD** can be replaced by **BL WORD**, which many find to be more readable.

COUNT may also be used with strings other than counted strings. The behavior of **COUNT** is to fetch the byte at the current address and return both the byte and the address incremented by one. Thus, successive calls to **COUNT** "walk" through the string, returning each character and incrementing the address.

Glossary

BL (– char) Core

Return *char*, the ASCII character value for a space (20_H). "B-L"

PARSE <text> (char – c-addr n) Core Ext

Parse *text* to the first instance of *char*, returning the address and length of a temporary location containing the parsed text.

WORD <text> (char – c-addr) Core

Skip any leading occurrences of the delimiter *char*. Parse *text* delimited by *char*. Return *c-addr*, the address of a temporary location containing the parsed text as a counted string. If the parse area is empty or contains only the delimiter(s), the resulting string length is zero.

References

Current input stream, Section 6.1.2
Fetching input characters to **PAD**, Section 5.4.1
>NUMBER, Section 3.6.1
Text interpreter, Section 1.1.5
Character string output (**TYPE**), Section 5.4.2

6.1.4 Dictionary Searches

It must be possible to look up words and their definitions in the dictionary. Forth provides several words to do this; each performs a search and returns information about a word, typically its *execution token*. Such searches are used by the text interpreter and colon compiler.

The word **'** ("tick") performs a dictionary search for the word that immediately follows it in the current input stream.

The phrase:

```
' <name>
```

...when typed at a terminal or executed interpretively in source text, pushes onto the stack the execution token of *name* if *name* can be found in the dictionary. If *name* cannot be found, an abort will occur with an error message such as:

<name> **?**

The precise definition of the "execution token" returned from dictionary searches varies, depending on the implementation, so the standard word **>BODY** is provided. Given an execution token, it will always return a parameter field (content) address. On many systems **>BODY** is a no-op.

The most common uses of **'** for dictionary searches are:

- To learn whether a word has been defined.
- To find the location of a word, using **>BODY** (for example, to **DUMP** its contents).
- To obtain the location of a data object (again, using **>BODY**) whose run-time behavior is other than returning its address.

Note that **'** (tick) reads forward in the input stream when it's executed. Like most other Forth words, if you use it inside a definition it will be executed when the definition is executed. If you want to compile the execution token of a word as a literal inside a definition, you should use the related word **[']**. Because **[']** is a compiler directive, it is inappropriate to use it interpretively (outside a colon definition).

The following are dictionary search words:

Glossary

' <name> (– xt) Core

Search the dictionary for *name*. If *name* is found, return its execution token; otherwise, abort. "tick"

['] <name> (– xt) Core

Similar to **'** but must be used in a colon definition. **[']** finds *name* in the dictionary and compiles its execution token as a literal. If *name* is not in the dictionary, **[']** aborts. **[']** is an **IMMEDIATE** word (executed, rather than compiled by the colon compiler; see the references section). The stack behavior shown is for the run-time code, which is that of a literal. "bracket-tick"

>BODY (xt – a-addr) Core

Given a word's execution token, return the address of the start of that word's parameter field. "to-body"

FIND (c-addr — c-addr 0 | xt 1 | xt -1)Core, Search

Attempt to find a definition whose name is in a counted string at *c-addr*. If the definition is not found, return the address and zero; if the definition is found, return its execution token. If the definition is immediate, also return +1; otherwise, return -1.

References

Execution tokens, Section 5.1.1
['], Section 6.3.3
IMMEDIATE words, Section 6.4.1
Word lists, Section 6.6
WORD, Section 6.1.3

6.1.5 Text Interpreter Conditionals

It is useful to control the logical flow when compiling an application. You may wish, for example, to load a certain source code file only if a flag indicates the need for that file. A number of Forth words provide this kind of control. These words are almost always used outside of definitions, but they all are **IMMEDIATE** (i.e., they execute when encountered during compilation) and so may be used in definitions, too, if needed.

Here are two examples:

Example 1:

```
<flag> [IF]  INCLUDE <file1>  [THEN]
```

This will load the file *file1* if the *flag* is *true* (non-zero). This can be used to manage various options at compile time.

Example 2:

```
[DEFINED] <word in file1> [IF]  INCLUDE <file2>
[ELSE] INCLUDE <file3> [THEN]
```

Depending on the presence or absence of a particular word, *file2* or *file3* may be loaded. This is useful when managing source files that may contain or need optional features.

Glossary

[DEFINED] <name> (– flag) Common usage

Search the dictionary for *name*. If *name* is found, return *true*; otherwise, return *false*. "bracket-defined"

[UNDEFINED] <name> (– flag) Common usage

Search the dictionary for *name*. If the word is found, return *false*; otherwise, return *true*. "bracket-undefined"

[IF] (flag –) Tools Ext

Begin an interpretive branch. If the *flag* is *true*, do nothing—i.e., continue interpretation. If the *flag* is *false*, parse and discard words from the parse area[1] (including nested occurrences of **[IF]** ... **[THEN]** clauses) until either the word **[ELSE]** or the word **[THEN]** has been parsed and discarded. Because **[IF]** discards **[ELSE]** (if the latter is present) when *flag* is *false*, interpretation will continue after **[ELSE]** with the contents of the **[ELSE]** clause. "bracket-if"

[ELSE] (–) Tools Ext

Parse and discard words from the parse area[1] (including nested occurrences of **[IF]** ... **[THEN]** clauses) until the word **[THEN]** has been parsed and discarded. **[ELSE]** is only executed if the *flag* for the associated **[IF]** was *true*; therefore, it always discards the words between **[ELSE]** and **[THEN]**. "bracket-else"

[THEN] (–) Tools Ext

Take no action. **[THEN]** performs no function but must exist in the source code in order to mark the end of parsing for an **[IF]** or **[ELSE]**. "bracket-then"

References

REFILL, Section 5.5.3

6.2 Defining Words

Forth provides a basic set of words used to define objects of various kinds. As with other features of Forth, this set of commands may be expanded. Some defining words that are standard in all Forth systems are introduced in Section 2, such as **:** (colon), **CONSTANT**, **VARIABLE**,

1. If the parse area becomes exhausted, it is refilled as with **REFILL**.

VALUE, and others. In this section, we discuss basic principles of defining words and how you can create custom defining words.

6.2.1 Creating a Dictionary Entry

A word is defined when an entry is created in the dictionary. **CREATE** is the basic word that does this; it (or its components) may be used by **:**, **CODE**, **VARIABLE**, **CONSTANT**, and other defining words to perform the initial functions of setting up a dictionary entry. **CREATE** behaves roughly as follows:

1. Memory is checked to see if a minimum amount remains. If not, there may be an abort. At the same time, the data-space pointer is aligned to an even cell address, if the platform the system is running on requires it.
2. **WORD** fetches the next word in the input stream. A dictionary entry is created for this word, including a pointer to the previous entry in this word list.
3. The code field of the new word is set to point to the run-time code of **CREATE**, which will push the address of this word's parameter field onto the stack when the word is executed. However, no data space is allocated by **CREATE**.

Other defining words that use **CREATE** may reset the new word's code field to define different run-time behavior by using the words **;CODE** or **DOES>**. Figure 18 shows a dictionary entry built by **CREATE**.

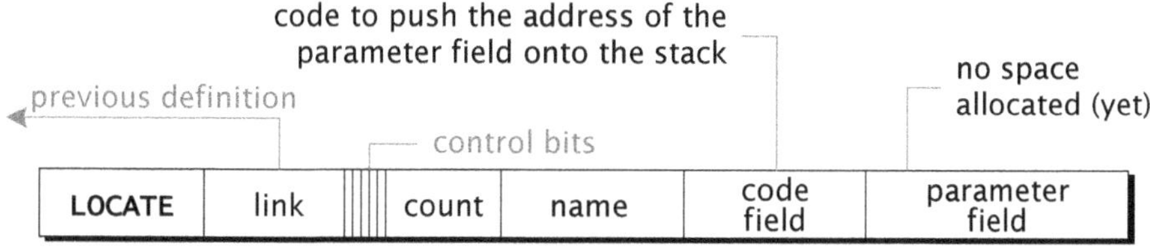

Figure 18. Dictionary entry built by CREATE

The word **UNUSED** places on the stack the number of bytes left in the memory area where dictionary entries are constructed. On some systems, this region of memory is also used for other purposes: the dictionary may start at the bottom and grow towards high memory, with something else starting at the top of this region and growing towards low memory. On such systems, **UNUSED** may give different answers at different times, even though the dictionary pointer is unchanged.

Glossary

ALLOT (u –) Core

If *n* is greater than zero, reserve *n* address units of data space. If *n* is less than zero, release |*n*| address units of data space. If *n* is zero, leave the data-space pointer unchanged

If the data-space pointer is initially aligned and *n* is a multiple of the cell size, the data space pointer will remain aligned after the **ALLOT**.

CREATE <name> (–) Core

Construct a dictionary entry for *name*. Execution of *name* will return the address of its data space. But no data space is allocated for *name*, that must be done by subsequent actions such as **ALLOT**.

UNUSED (– u) Core Ext

Return *u*, the number of bytes remaining in the memory area where dictionary entries are constructed.

References

:, Section 6.2.2

CODE, Section 6.2.3

CONSTANT, Section 2.3.2.2

ERASE, **BLANK**, **FILL**, Section 3.4

VARIABLE, Section 2.3.2.1

6.2.2 Colon Definitions

The defining word **:** (colon) is discussed briefly in Section 1.1.7, and examples appear in other sections. In this section, we describe the use and behavior of this important defining word in more detail.

The basic form of a **:** definition is:

```
: <name>   <action> ;
```

When the colon is executed, the system enters a compilation state. A dictionary entry is created for the word *name*. *action* represents a list of previously defined words that will be executed in sequence whenever *name* is invoked. The ; terminates the definition and returns the system to interpretation state.

The variable **STATE** contains the compilation-state flag. The value of **STATE** is *true* (non-zero) when compiling (e.g., between : and ;), and is *false* (zero) when interpreting. **STATE** is only changed by the following seven standard words: :, ;, **ABORT**, **QUIT**, **:NONAME**, [, and]. Programs that comply with Standard Forth may not modify **STATE** directly.

Like other defining words, : has two types of behavior—one for compile time (its defining behavior) and another for run time (the instance behavior of words it is used to define):

- The defining behavior of : constructs a dictionary entry (e.g., by using **CREATE**) and begins compiling. It also *smudges* the name so the word will not inadvertently compile a reference to itself. (The word **RECURSE** may be used if the definition of a word must call itself.)
- The instance behavior of a word defined by : is to execute the words that form the body of the word's definition.

The ; ends compilation and compiles a reference to the word **EXIT** (on most indirect-threaded implementations), or a return instruction or equivalent, depending on the implementation. The effect is to return to the calling environment.

Most of the words that make up the content of a definition are not executed during compilation; instead, references to them are compiled in the parameter field of the definition. The exception to this are *compiler directives* or *literals*. These generally have both compile-time and run-time behaviors, just as : and ; do.

Every colon definition requires a minimum of three components: a colon, a name, and a semicolon. Such a minimum definition (commonly called a *null definition*) executes properly but does no real work. But it has useful purposes; for example, to provide *placeholder* definitions for routines to be written later, or to mark a location in the dictionary as the beginning of an overlay area.

It is possible to create colon-type definitions *without* associated names. This is an advanced technique not commonly used in a Forth application but, on rare occasions, it can be useful. The word that makes nameless definitions is **:NONAME** and the syntax is simply:

```
:NONAME    <action> ;
```

A piece of code created this way is an isolated fragment; it cannot be found in the dictionary and has no referenceable name to cause it to execute. A **:NONAME** definition returns the execution token of the compiled code that is on the stack at the time the nameless definition is created. You must take action *at that time* to store the execution token in a useful place, such as in a variable or other data structure. **:NONAME** is mainly used to build definitions attached via their execution tokens to mechanisms such as execution vectors or push buttons.

The execution token may be placed on the stack as soon as **:NONAME** starts compiling. This can lead to subtle errors. For example:

```
35 :NONAME    LITERAL . ;
.  35
```

The result is not the *xt* of the nameless definition but the number you intended to compile as the literal—because **:NONAME** left the *xt* on the stack above the 35. Because of details like this, even many experienced Forth programmers avoid using **:NONAME**.

Glossary

: <name> (–) Core

Create a definition for *name*, called a *colon definition*. Enter compilation state and start compiling the definition. The run-time behavior of *name* will be determined by the previously defined words that follow—those are compiled into the body of the definition. *name* cannot be found in the dictionary until the definition is ended. At run time, the stack effects of *name* depend on its behavior. "colon"

:NONAME (– xt) Core Ext

Create an execution token *xt* and place it on the stack. Enter compilation state and start compiling the definition. The execution behavior of *xt* will be determined by the words compiled into the body of its definition. This definition may be executed by the phrase *xt* **EXECUTE**. "colon-no-name"

; (–) Core

End the current definition, allow it to be found in the dictionary and enter interpretation state. If the data-space pointer is not aligned, reserve enough data space to align it. "semi-colon"

RECURSE (–) Core
Append the execution behavior of the current definition to the current definition, so that it calls itself recursively.

References
Forth virtual machine, Section 1.1.7
Alignment, Section 2.3.3
Compiler directives, Section 6.4
Execution tokens, Section 5.1.1
EXIT, Section 4.9
EXECUTE, Section 5.1.1
Overlays, Section 6.5
Program structures, Section 4
STATE, Section 6.3.1

6.2.3 Code Definitions

The form of a **CODE** definition is:

```
CODE <name>  <assembler instructions>  <code-ending>
```

The word **CODE** performs the following functions at assembly time:

1. Construct a standard dictionary entry for *name*.
2. Set the execution token for *name* to point to *name*'s parameter field.
3. Select the **ASSEMBLER** word list.

The words used inside a **CODE** definition are executed directly. This has the effect of assembling machine instructions into the parameter field of the word being defined. There is nothing analogous to the compilation state that exists between **:** and **;**. When high-level Forth words are encountered, they are executed directly as well. Thus, when used in a **CODE** definition, words such as **SWAP** and **DUP** manipulate the stack during assembly.

Macros can be defined as colon definitions containing assembler words, provided you first select the **ASSEMBLER** word list. This works because of the normal consequence of putting executable words in a colon definition: they will be executed when the definition is executed. Thus, one 8051 assembler defines:

```
\ Subtract without borrow
: SUB ( r1 r2 -- )    C CLRB    SUBB ;
```

The new "mnemonic," used in the form:

```
<r1> <r2> SUB
```

...will assemble instructions that clear the carry bit before subtracting r_2 from r_1.

Assembler mnemonics, addressing modes, and conventions are covered in the documentation for your Forth system.

6.2.4 Custom Defining Words

One of the most powerful capabilities in Forth is the ability to define new defining words. Thus, the programmer may create new data types with characteristics peculiar to the application, new generic types of words, and even new classes of words with specified behaviors common to each class.

The programmer must specify two separate behaviors when creating a custom defining word:

- The defining behavior of the defining word (creating the dictionary entry, allocating memory, storing parameters, etc.).
- The instance behavior (the action to be performed by words created by the new defining word).

In cases discussed in following sections, defining behavior is described in high-level Forth. Several methods for specifying run-time behavior are also discussed.

6.2.4.1 Basic Principles of Defining Words

In Forth, a *defining word* will create a new dictionary entry when executed. All words defined by the same defining word share a common defining and instance behavior.

For example, **VARIABLE** is a defining word. All words defined by **VARIABLE** (*instances* of **VARIABLE**) share two common characteristics:

- *Defining behavior:* Each has one cell allotted in which a value may be stored. (Some systems may initialize this cell to zero.)
- *Instance behavior:* When executed, each of these words pushes onto the stack the address of its one-cell area.

On the other hand, all words defined by **CONSTANT**—which is another defining word—share two other behaviors:

- *Defining behavior:* Each is associated with the single-precision value that was on the stack when **CONSTANT** executed.
- *Instance behavior:* When a word defined by **CONSTANT** executes, it pushes its value on the stack.

All defining words must have a defining behavior and an instance behavior. In the examples above, the defining behavior relates to the physical construction of the word and is determined when the word is compiled. The instance behavior describes what all defined words of that type do when executed.

6.2.4.2 Constructing Custom Defining Words

There are two ways to create new defining words in Forth. When using **DOES>**, the defining behavior is described in high-level Forth. When using **;CODE**, the run-time behavior is described in assembler code. The basic principles are the same.

The general definition of a defining word looks like:

```
: <name>   <defining behavior>   <transition word>
   <instance behavior> <ending>
```

The *transition word* ends the specification of compile-time behavior and begins the specification of run-time behavior. There are two such transition words: **;CODE** begins run-time behavior described in code (assembler), whereas **DOES>** begins run-time behavior described in high-level Forth. Each of these transition words requires a different ending; in the case of **DOES>**, it is **;** (semi-colon); in the case of **;CODE**, it is an implementation-defined code ending followed by **END-CODE**.

The exact behavior of these two words is discussed in the following sections. The description of compile-time behavior is the same, regardless of which transition word is used. In fact, if you change the transition word and run-time behavior from **DOES>** plus high-level to **;CODE** plus equivalent code, no change to the compile-time behavior is necessary.

The compile-time portion of a defining word must contain **CREATE** (or a defining word that calls **CREATE**) to create the dictionary entry. If one or more parameters are to be compiled, or if space for variable data is to be allocated, it is convenient to use a previously defined defining word to handle that.

Every defining word must provide space for data or code belonging to each instance of the new class of words it is used to define. For example, when a variable is defined, a cell is allocated for its data space. If more space is needed, the usual approach is to use **CREATE** followed by **ALLOT**.

After a new defining word has been created, it can be used to create specific instances of its class, with the syntax:

```
<parameters> <defining word> <instance1>
<parameters> <defining word> <instance2>
```

...and so forth. The *instance1* and *instance2* are names that would be specified in an application. Any *parameters* depend on the defining word's requirements and they are specific to each instance.

When a defining word is executed, it may be followed by any number of words, such as **,** (to compile a single-precision value) or **C,** (to compile an eight-bit value) to fill the allotted storage area with explicit values.

Glossary

;CODE (–) Tools Ext

Begin run-time behavior, specified in assembly code. "semi-colon-code"

DOES> (–) Core

Begin run-time behavior, specified in high-level Forth. At run time, the address of the parameter field of the instance of the defining word is pushed onto the stack before the run-time words are executed. "does"

References

, and **C,**, Section 2.3.3
ALLOT, Section 2.3.3
CONSTANT, Section 2.3.2
CREATE, Section 2.3.2
DOES>, Section 6.2.4.3
VARIABLE, Section 2.3.2.1

6.2.4.3 High-level Defining Words

New defining words whose instance behavior is specified in high-level Forth may be created by a technique similar to that used for **;CODE**. For these definitions, the word **DOES>** terminates the defining behavior portion of the definition and introduces the instance behavior portion. The form of a **DOES>** definition is:

```
: <name>   <defining behavior words>
   DOES> <instance behavior words> ;
```

After such a definition is compiled, *name* can be used to define a new instance of this class of words. Here the run-time behavior is described in high-level Forth.

At run time, the address of *name*'s parameter field is pushed onto the stack before the *run-time words* are executed. This provides easy access to the parameter field.

An example of a **DOES>** definition is the word **MSG**, which might be used to type short character sequences:

```
: MSG   ( -- ) CREATE
   DOES>  ( -- ) COUNT TYPE ;
```

Here is an example of how **MSG** would be used (assuming **HEX** base):

```
MSG (CR)   2 C, 0D C, 0A C,
```

(CR) is a specific instance of the **MSG** class: it uses the same code—the **DOES>** phrase—as other words defined by **MSG**, but uses that code to emit its own unique character string.

The values that comprise the string are kept in the parameter field of the word—in this case, **(CR)**—that was defined by **MSG**. At execution time, the defining word's **DOES>** puts the address of the instance's parameter field (used here to store the string) on the stack to serve as the parameter for **COUNT**, which returns the string's length and byte address as arguments for **TYPE**.

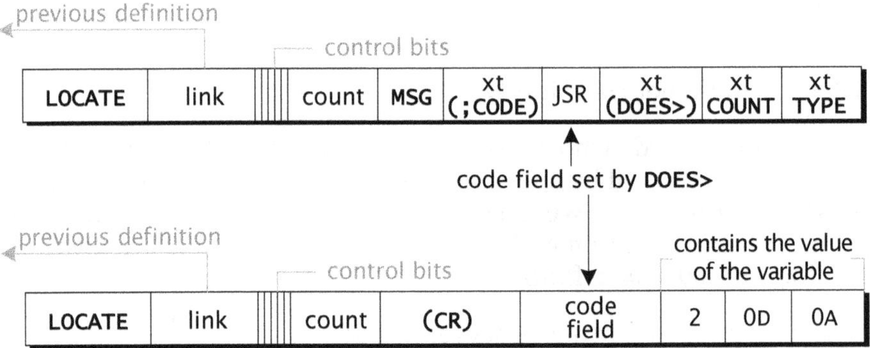

Figure 19. Structures defined by using DOES>

Figure 19 shows a possible implementation of **DOES>** that works like this:

1. The **:** compiler executes **DOES>**. The compile-time behavior of **DOES>** is to compile code that resets the code field of the new word being defined (the instance of the defining word containing **DOES>**) to point to the cell following the compiled address of **(;CODE)**.
2. After the address of **(;CODE)**, **DOES>** compiles a subroutine call to the run-time code for **DOES>**. The compiler then proceeds to finish compiling addresses in the new defining word. (The use of a subroutine call in the defining word is system dependent. However, all implementations of **DOES>** compile something in the defining word to allow the run-time code for **DOES>** to find the defining word's high-level code without losing the defined word's data space address.) When the new defining word is executed, its last step will be to change the execution token of the entry it creates to point to the jump-to-subroutine created by **DOES>** in the defining word.
3. When one of the instances created by the new defining word is executed, the virtual machine jumps to the subroutine call in the

defining word. Then the subroutine call saves the address of the cell following itself, in some CPU-dependent way, and jumps to the run-time code for **DOES>**. That code uses the address from the subroutine linkage to find the execution token for the defining word. The run-time code for **DOES>** also pushes the address of the defined word's parameter field onto the data stack.

References

, and **C,**, Section 2.3.3
CONSTANT, Section 2.3.2.2
CREATE, Section 2.3.3
TYPE, Section 5.4.2

6.3 Compiling Words and Literals

A compiling word stores addresses or values into the dictionary and allots space for definitions and data.

A literal is a number compiled directly into a definition or in some other unnamed form. Covered in this section are several Forth words for compiling literals, including **LITERAL** and **[']**.

References

CODE, Section 6.2.3
CONSTANT, Section 2.3.2.2
CREATE, Section 2.3.3
LITERAL, Section 6.3.2

6.3.1 The Forth Compiler

When a high-level definition is created in the dictionary for a given *name*, it is the task of the Forth compiler to produce a series of executable references, one for each of the previously compiled words that appears in the body of *name*'s definition. The word **COMPILE,** ("compile-comma") is a generic word used by the compiler to create those executable references. **COMPILE,** is usually invoked after the compiler finds a word in the dictionary. It expects the execution token of a word to be on the stack and it adds the behavior of that word to the definition currently being compiled. But the compiler must also handle two special cases that differ from references to previously compiled words.

The first case occurs when numbers are included in a high-level definition. The compiler handles numbers much like the standard Forth text interpreter does. When a dictionary search fails, the compiler attempts to convert the ASCII string into a number. When conversion succeeds, the number is compiled in-line with a reference to code that pushes the number's binary value onto the stack at run time. When the numeric conversion fails, the conversion word aborts and prints an error message.

The second special case occurs with words that must be executed at compile time by the compiler. Such words are called *compiler directives*. **IF**, **DO**, and **UNTIL** are examples of compiler directives. After the word is found in the dictionary, the compiler checks the precedence bit in the header of the word's dictionary entry. If the precedence bit is set (i.e., 1), the word is executed. If the precedence bit is reset (i.e., 0), a reference to the word is compiled. The precedence bit of any word may be set by placing **IMMEDIATE** directly after the word's definition.

Additionally, sometimes it is necessary to explicitly force the system into interpretation or compilation state. This is done by the words **[** (enter interpretation state, pronounced "left-bracket") and **]** (enter compilation state, pronounced "right-bracket"). These words set the value of a system variable called **STATE**. **STATE** is *true* (non-zero) when in compilation state and is *false* (zero) otherwise. The only other words that modify **STATE** are **:** (colon), **;** (semicolon), **ABORT**, **QUIT**, and **:NONAME**. It is a violation of Standard Forth to modify the value of **STATE** directly.

The most common use of **[** and **]** is to leave compile mode temporarily to perform some run-time operation at compile time. For example, in a definition containing numbers most naturally thought of in decimal, suppose you wish to refer to an ASCII code in hex:

```
: GAP ( n)   10 0 DO  [ HEX ] 0A [ DECIMAL ]
   EMIT  LOOP ;
```

Because the words that control **BASE** aren't **IMMEDIATE**, it is necessary to leave compile mode and execute **HEX** before compiling the hex code. **[** is an **IMMEDIATE** word which leaves the compiler and resumes interpretation.] returns to compile mode.

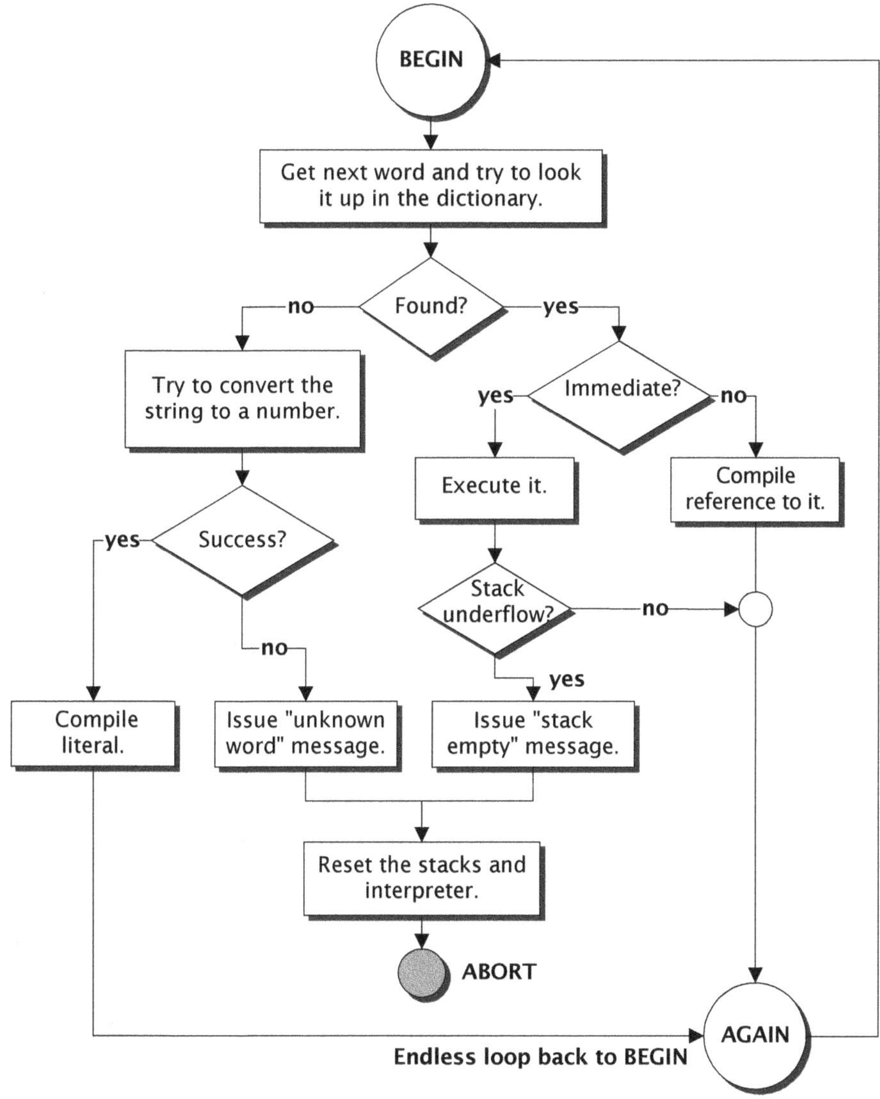

Figure 20. Action of the Forth compiler

Glossary

COMPILE, (xt –) Core Ext

Append the execution behavior of the definition represented by the execution token *xt* to the execution behavior of the current definition. "compile-comma"

STATE (– a-addr) Core, Tools Ext

Return *a-addr*, the address of a cell containing the compilation-state flag: a non-zero value (interpreted as *true*) when in compilation state, *false* (zero) otherwise.

[(–) Core

Enter interpretation state. **[** is an immediate word. "left-bracket"

] (–) Core

Enter compilation state. "right-bracket"

References

ABORT, Section 5.3
Forth virtual machine, indirect-threaded implementations, Section 1.1.7
Colon definitions, Section 6.2.2
Compiler directives, Section 6.4
Dictionary searches, Section 6.1.4
IMMEDIATE, Section 6.4.1
Input number conversion, Section 3.6.1

6.3.2 Literals and Constants

When the Forth compiler encounters a number in a **:** definition, the number is converted to binary and is compiled as a literal. The compiled form of a literal in a **:** definition has two parts: the number itself and a reference to code which, when executed, will push the number onto the stack. When Forth is compiling a definition and a number is encountered, this form is automatically compiled. Other ways in which a literal in a definition may be generated are discussed in the following section, but this is the most common situation.

On many systems, the size of a literal is optimized by the compiler; for example, a literal less than 256 will be compiled as a byte. Some optimizing compilers are able to incorporate short literals into instructions, thereby avoiding the need to push them on the stack.

A literal, which requires both an in-line number and a reference to run-time code for it, it may be larger than a constant, which needs only the reference. Therefore, a generic number that is used frequently (e.g., more than six times) should be defined as a constant to save space. There is not much difference in the times required to execute a constant and a literal. Numbers with specific meanings (e.g., **86400 CONSTANT SECONDS/DAY**) should always be defined as constants for program readability.

The word **LITERAL** compiles into a definition the value that was on the stack at compile time. When the definition is executed, that value will be pushed onto the stack. The compiled result of **LITERAL** is identical to that of a literal number, described in the previous section. **LITERAL** is useful for compiling a reference to an address or number that is computed at compile time.

A common use of **[** and **]** (leaving and entering compiling state) combined with **LITERAL** is to compile the results of complex calculations that only need to be performed once. As a trivial example, disk status information might be stored in the third cell of an array of disk data named **DISK**. A word to retrieve that information could be:

```
: STATUS   [ DISK 2 CELLS + ]  LITERAL  @ ;
```

The **[** stops compilation, and **]** restarts compilation. During this hiatus, the words **DISK 2 CELLS +** are interpreted and executed, leaving on the stack the address of the status cell, which after compilation resumes is compiled into the definition by **LITERAL**. If the calculations are in an inner loop, the time savings can be large compared to performing them at run time.

The word **2LITERAL** functions exactly the same as **LITERAL** but requires two values on the stack at compile time and will return those values, in the same order on the stack, at execution time.

SLITERAL is for use with strings. This word requires an address and length of a string on the stack at compile time. The string is compiled into the definition and, at execution time, **SLITERAL** returns the address where the string was compiled and its length. See Section 6.3.4 for a fuller description.

Glossary

LITERAL (– x) Core

At compile time, remove the top number on the stack and compile it into the current definition. At run time, return the number to the stack.

2LITERAL (– x_1 x_2) Double

At compile time, remove the top two items on the stack and compile them into the current definition. At run time, return the items to the stack in the same order. "two-literal"

References

[and], Section 6.3.1

6.3.3 Compiling Execution Tokens

The word **[']** ("bracket-tick") is used inside a definition to compile as a literal the execution token of the word that follows it at compile time. The most common use of **[']** is to obtain an execution token that will be stored in a **DEFER** (described in Section 5.1.2). Consider the following example:

```
DEFER TYPE
: PRINTER ( -- )    ['] (PRINTER) IS TYPE ;
: DISPLAY ( -- )    ['] (DISPLAY) IS TYPE ;
```

...where the words **(PRINTER)** and **(DISPLAY)** are driver-level words that route strings to a printer or display, respectively. Given these definitions, typing **PRINTER** or **DISPLAY** routes the output from **TYPE** to the appropriate device.

References

['], Section 5.1.2

6.3.4 Compiling Strings

SLITERAL is the low-level compiling word used by **S"**, **C"**, and similar string-handling words. Just as **LITERAL** compiles into a definition the number found on the stack at compile time and returns that number at execution time, **SLITERAL** compiles into a definition a string characterized by an address and length on the stack at compile time and returns the string's address and length at execution time. The address at compile time is not the same as the address at execution time—the former typically is an address in the input source being interpreted (e.g., a source file), and the latter is an address connected with the definition using **SLITERAL**.

Consider how you might define the word **S"** to begin compiling a string, terminated by a second quote, which will leave the string's address and count on the stack at execution time. It could be used as follows:

```
: ALARM-MESSAGE   S" Too Hot!" TYPE ;
```

A possible definition for **S"** would be:

```
: S"   [CHAR] " WORD  COUNT  POSTPONE SLITERAL ;
IMMEDIATE
```

When **S"** executes (at compile time, as it is marked **IMMEDIATE**), the phrase **[CHAR] "** returns the ASCII value for the quote character, which is passed to **WORD** for use as the delimiter. **WORD** parses the input stream and returns the address of a counted string in the input buffer consisting of all the characters between the **S"** (the name of the executing word) and the delimiting **"**. All spaces are included, even leading spaces, because a space is not the delimiter in this case. **COUNT** converts the counted string address to a character string address and length; these two parameters are passed to **SLITERAL**, which compiles the string into the definition. The **POSTPONE** command preceding **SLITERAL** causes **SLITERAL**'s compilation behavior to occur rather than its execution behavior. When **ALARM-MESSAGE** executes, the run-time behavior of **SLITERAL** returns the address and count of the stored message **Too Hot!** for **TYPE** to display.

Glossary

SLITERAL (– c-addr u) String

Compile into a definition a string characterized by the starting address and length on the stack at compile time. At run time, return the string's address and length to the stack. In general, the run-time address will not be the same as the compile-time address. "S-literal"

References

Defining words, Section 6.2
String comparisons, Section 3.5
POSTPONE, Section 6.4.1
Strings in data structures, Section 3.3

6.4 Compiler Directives

A *compiler directive* in Forth is a word that is *executed* at compile time, i.e., during a **:** compilation. Many such words exist: **DO**; **LOOP** and **+LOOP**; **BEGIN** and **UNTIL**; **IF**, **ELSE**, and **THEN**; literals; and others. It is rare that a user needs to add compiler directives; it is not difficult, but requires mastery of **IMMEDIATE** and **POSTPONE**.

Some compiler directives have only compile-time behavior (such as **BEGIN**). Other directives need to perform some actions at compile time and other actions at run time. For example, at compile time **DO** must mark the position to which **LOOP** or **+LOOP** will return; at run time, it must push the index and limit for the loop onto the return stack.

These functions are managed by defining (usually with **CODE**) the run-time activity as a separate word and having the compile-time definition, which is **IMMEDIATE**, compile the address of the run-time code (in addition to its other activities).

6.4.1 Making Compiler Directives

IMMEDIATE is used directly after a definition. It signals the compiler that this definition is to be *executed* at compile time (when all non-immediate words are being *compiled*). This is done by setting the new word's precedence bit (usually the high-order bit in the count field).

POSTPONE is used inside **IMMEDIATE** definitions. It has the opposite function from **IMMEDIATE**. Used in the form **POSTPONE** <name>, it causes the *compilation* behavior of *name*, rather than the *execution* behavior, to be added to the current definition. **POSTPONE** can be used with **IMMEDIATE** words (such as compiler directives) and with non-immediate words, as shown in the following examples.

Consider a common definition of **BEGIN**:

```
: BEGIN   HERE ;  IMMEDIATE
```

This definition of **BEGIN** is simply an **IMMEDIATE** version of **HERE**. The difference is that, when **HERE** appears in a normal definition, its address is compiled; it will push the value of the dictionary pointer[1] onto the stack when the word that contains **HERE** is executed. **BEGIN**, on the other hand, compiles nothing; it pushes the dictionary pointer onto the stack at compile time to serve as the address needed by **UNTIL** (or a similar structure word) to compile a conditional return to that location.

Structure words such as **IF** provide classic examples of the use of **POSTPONE**. Most of these words have a *run-time behavior* we usually think of. For example, **IF** checks the truth of the top stack item and conditionally branches. But there is also a *compile-time behavior* for **IF**, which is to compile a reference to its run-time behavior and to provide for the branching associated with the structure.

If the run-time behavior is defined as a word called **(IF)**, we could define the compiler directive **IF** this way:

```
: IF   ( -- addr )
   POSTPONE (IF)  HERE 0 , ;
IMMEDIATE
```

When executed during compilation of a word, this **IF** will compile the reference to **(IF)** and leave a one-cell space in the definition, placing the address of that cell on the stack as shown in Figure 21. Subsequent execution of **ELSE** or **THEN** will resolve the branch by storing an appropriate offset in that space.

1. Strictly speaking, **HERE** pushes on the stack the address of the next available location in data space. For implementations that intermingle dictionary entries and data space (a common strategy), it's also the next location in the dictionary. If data space is separate, **BEGIN** is defined differently.

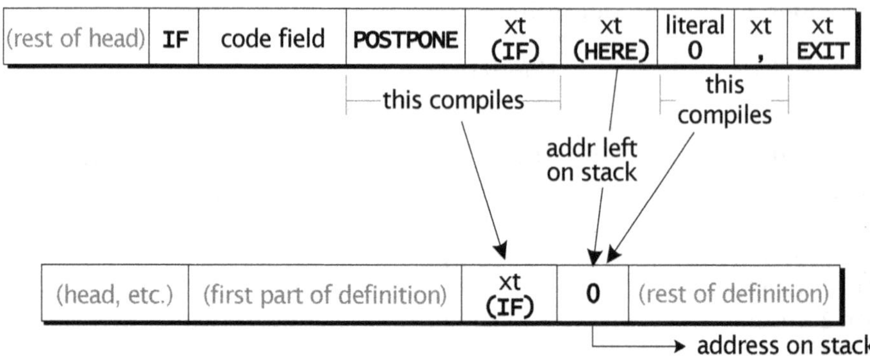

Figure 21. Compile-time action of IF

As a second example, suppose you often use the phrase ... `?DUP IF` ... in definitions and you want to create a word `?IF` that performs both functions. Here is how `?IF` would need to be defined:

```
: ?IF   POSTPONE ?DUP  POSTPONE IF ; IMMEDIATE
```

`?IF` is an `IMMEDIATE` word because it needs to set up a conditional branch at compile time. However, we do not want the run-time behavior for `?DUP` and `IF` to execute at compile time; instead, we want these words' compilation behaviors to occur. Hence, each must be preceded by `POSTPONE`. `?DUP` is non-immediate, and `IF` is `IMMEDIATE`, but the syntax for `POSTPONE` is identical.

`POSTPONE` is very similar to `[']` except, whereas `[']` compiles as a literal the execution token of the word that follows so the address will be pushed onto the stack at run time, `POSTPONE` lays down a pointer to the execution token so the word can be executed by the Forth virtual machine.

The glossary below describes the principal compiler directives. They are discussed elsewhere, but here we describe their behavior as compiler directives rather than as programming elements.

Glossary

AGAIN (–) Core Ext

At compile time, compile an unconditional backward branch to the location on the control-flow stack (usually left there by `BEGIN`; see Section 6.4.2). At run time, execute the branch.

ELSE (–) Core
At compile time, originate the true clause branch and resolve the false clause branch. It is assumed there is a branch origin on the control stack, usually left there by **IF**. Provide the location following **ELSE** as the destination address for the forward conditional branch originated by **IF**. Place a new forward reference origin on the control stack, marking the beginning of an unconditional branch at the end of the true clause (this will later be resolved by **THEN**). At run time, execute the unconditional branch to skip the false clause.

IF (x –) Core
At compile time, place a forward reference origin on the control stack, marking the beginning of a conditional branch. At run time, if *x* is zero take the forward branch to the destination that will have been supplied (e.g., by **ELSE** or **THEN**); otherwise, continue execution beyond the **IF**.

THEN (–) Core
At compile time, provide the location beyond **THEN** as the destination address for the forward branch origin found on the control stack. This origin normally will have been placed there by **ELSE** if there was a *false* clause or by **IF** if there was no *false* clause. At run time, simply continue execution.

REPEAT (–) Core
At compile time, resolve two branches, usually set up by **BEGIN** and **WHILE**. In the most common usage, **BEGIN** leaves a destination on the control-flow stack and **WHILE** places an origin under **BEGIN**'s destination. Then **REPEAT** compiles an unconditional backward branch to the destination location following **BEGIN** and provides the location following **REPEAT** to serve as the destination address for the forward conditional branch originated by **WHILE**.

At run time, execute the unconditional backward branch to the location following **BEGIN**.

UNTIL (x –) Core
At compile time, compile a conditional backward branch to the location on the control-flow stack, usually left there by **BEGIN**. At run time, if *x* is zero, take the backwards branch; otherwise, continue execution beyond the **UNTIL**.

WHILE (x –) Core
At compile time, place a new unresolved forward reference origin on the control stack under the topmost item, which is usually a destination left by **BEGIN**. At run time, if *x* is zero, take the forward branch to the destination that will have been supplied (e.g., by **REPEAT**) to resolve **WHILE**'s origin; otherwise, continue execution beyond the **WHILE**.

IMMEDIATE (–) Core
Make the most recent definition an immediate word. When the compiler encounters an immediate word, it causes it to execute at that time rather than compiling a reference to it.

POSTPONE <name> (–) Core
At compile time, add the *compilation* behavior of *name*—rather than its execution behavior—to the current definition. Usually used in **IMMEDIATE** definitions.

References

Colon definitions, Section 6.2.2
DO ... **LOOP**, program structure words, Section 4.5
Literals, Section 6.3.2
The Forth compiler, Section 6.3.1
Use of **BEGIN**, Section 4.4
Word lists, Section 6.6
['], Section 6.3.3
Compiler directives, Section 6.4

6.4.2 The Control-flow Stack and Custom Compiling Structures

The standard branching constructs in Forth (**IF** ... **ELSE** ... **THEN**, **BEGIN** ... **UNTIL**, **BEGIN** ... **AGAIN**, and **DO** ... **LOOP**) are examples of *control-flow words*. In direct management of control flow, every branch must terminate at some destination. An *origin* (abbreviated *orig* in Table 12) is the location of the branch itself; a *destination* (*dest* in Table 12) is where control will continue if the branch is taken. A natural implementation to manage control flow uses a stack to remember the origin of forward branches and the destination of backward branches. This is the *control-flow stack* in Forth. How it is implemented is system dependent, and generally is not of concern to the user; in virtually all implementations, it is the data stack at compile time.

This section describes additional primitive words which directly access the control-flow stack. With them, a programmer can create branching structures of any degree of complexity. The abilities required are compilation of forward and backward conditional and unconditional branches, and compile-time management of branch origins and destinations. These are provided by just three words: **AHEAD**, **CS-PICK**, and **CS-ROLL**. Table 12 summarizes the compilation behavior of these and of other basic Forth words that affect control flow.

Table 12: Summary of compile-time branch words

Word	Control-flow stack	Function
IF	(– orig)	Marks the origin of a forward conditional branch.
THEN	(orig –)	Resolves the branch originated by **IF** or **AHEAD**.
BEGIN	(– dest)	Marks the destination of a backward branch.
AGAIN	(dest –)	Resolves a backward unconditional branch.
UNTIL	(dest –)	Resolves a backward conditional branch.
AHEAD	(– orig)	Marks the origin of a forward unconditional branch.
CS-PICK	(i*x u – i*x x_u)	Copies item on control-flow stack.
CS-ROLL	(i*x u – (i-1)*x x_u)	Reorders items on control-flow stack.

All other branching words—such as **WHILE**, **REPEAT**, and **ELSE**—can be defined in terms of the primitive words in Table 12. For example:

```
: ELSE ( addr1 -- addr2 ) \ Resolve IF, set up for THEN
    POSTPONE AHEAD         \ Set up forward branch
    1 CS-ROLL              \ Get addr of IF's branch
    POSTPONE THEN ;        \ Resolve IF's branch
IMMEDIATE
```

In this definition, the phrase **POSTPONE AHEAD** marks the origin of an unconditional branch (around the "false clause") to be taken at the end of the "true clause." This will be resolved later by the **THEN** at the end of the **IF** statement. Because **POSTPONE AHEAD** places one item on the control-flow stack, the phrase **1 CS-ROLL** (the equivalent of **SWAP**) is needed to restore the previous origin placed there by the **IF**. Next, **POSTPONE THEN** compiles the branch resolution for this origin, providing entry to the "false clause" following **ELSE** if the conditional branch at **IF** was taken.

Glossary

AHEAD (– orig) Tools Ext

At compile time, begin an unconditional forward branch by placing *orig* (the location of the unresolved branch) on the control-flow stack. The behavior is incomplete until the *orig* is resolved, e.g., by **THEN**. At run time, resume execution at the location provided by the resolution of this *orig*.

CS-PICK (i*x u – i*x x_u) Tools Ext

Place a copy of the *u*th control-stack entry on the top of the control stack. The *zero*th item is on top of the control stack; i.e., **0 CS-PICK** is equivalent to **DUP** and **1 CS-PICK** is equivalent to **OVER**. "C-S-pick"

CS-ROLL (i*x u – (i-1)*x x_u) Tools Ext

Move the *n*th control-stack entry to the top of the stack, pushing down all the control-stack entries in between. The *zero*th item is on top of the stack; i.e., **0 CS-ROLL** does nothing, **1 CS-ROLL** is equivalent to **SWAP**, and **2 CS-ROLL** is equivalent to **ROT**. "C-S-roll"

References

Indefinite loops, Section 4.4

DO ... **LOOP**s, Section 4.5

IF ... **ELSE** ... **THEN**, Section 4.3

6.5 Overlays

Because of Forth's compilation speed, there is rarely need for a dynamic run-time overlay capability. Many resident applications have several functionally independent subsets, however, and it is conventional to organize these as mutually exclusive overlays, any one of which may be loaded into each terminal's private dictionary. This is done by explicit command. Once loaded, an overlay remains resident until replaced by another.

Examples of such overlay categories in a business environment might include order entry, payroll, and general ledger. In a scientific laboratory, there may be several data acquisition and analysis modes.

Overlays are enabled with **MARKER**. The phrase **MARKER** <name> creates a dictionary entry for *name*. When *name* is executed, it will discard the definition *name* and all words defined after *name* in a user's partition. The user's dictionary pointer will be reset to the last definition in the vocabulary before *name*. Because the dictionary pointer is reset, the dictionary is truncated spatially as well as logically. Other system-dependent actions may be taken as well, such as restoration of interrupt vectors (see your product documentation).

MARKER has two uses:

- To discard only part of your definitions. For example, when testing, you may wish to reload only the last block, not your entire application.
- To create additional levels of overlays.

Suppose your application includes an overlay called **GRAPHICS**. After **GRAPHICS** is loaded, you want to be able to load one of two additional overlays, called **COLOR** and **B&W**, creating a second level of overlay. Here is the procedure to follow:

1. Define a marker as the final definition of **GRAPHICS**, using any word you want as a dictionary marker. For example:

   ```
   MARKER OVERLAY
   ```

   Preferably, such a definition would be placed at the bottom of the **GRAPHICS** load block.
2. Execute **OVERLAY** and then redefine it (as it forgets itself) on the first line of the source code of each level-two overlay. For instance,

   ```
   ( COLOR)    OVERLAY    MARKER OVERLAY
   ```

Thus, when you execute the phrase:

```
INCLUDE COLOR
```

...the system will *forget* any definitions which may have been compiled after **GRAPHICS** and will restore the marker definition of **OVERLAY** in the event you want to load an alternate level-two definition, such as **B&W**.

By using different names for your markers, you may create any number of overlay levels.

Glossary

MARKER <name> (–) Core Ext

Create a dictionary definition for *name*, to be used as a deletion boundary. When *name* is executed, remove the definition of *name* and all subsequent definitions from the dictionary. Restore all dictionary allocation and search order pointers to the state they had just prior to the definition of *name*.

6.6 Word Lists

In general, we speak of the dictionary as a single searchable list of definitions. However, in many systems several such lists can be searched independently. These are called "word lists." Word lists have three principal uses:

- In the resident system, to segregate special-purpose words such as those in the **ASSEMBLER** to allow them to have the same names as standard Forth words.
- In a target compiler environment where two types of CPU exist, to segregate target versions of **FORTH** and **ASSEMBLER** words from the host versions.
- In applications running in the host system, to isolate particular groups of words for security or other purposes.

ANS Forth guarantees there will be at least eight word lists available to the user. Dictionary searches proceed from one word list to another in a specified sequence. This mechanism allows you to control which list or lists are searched. Within a word list, the search is from newest to oldest.

6.6.1 Basic Principles

The standard word lists provided by typical Forth systems are:

FORTH

ASSEMBLER (on most systems)
EDITOR (on systems with an internal editor)

Other lists may be created, as described below. The **FORTH** word list contains most familiar words such as **DUP**, **SWAP**, **DO**, etc. Another word list on most systems, **ASSEMBLER**, contains words used to assemble machine code. **EDITOR** contains the commands for editing source text.

The use of separate word lists makes it possible, for instance, for the word **I** to supply a loop index in one context (**FORTH**), to insert a string in another context (**EDITOR**), or to name a register in yet another (**ASSEMBLER**).

When the Forth interpreter receives a word, whether it is one you type at the keyboard or one it gets from a file, it looks for that word in an ordered sequence of word lists. That sequence is called the *search order.* A word will not be found unless it is contained in a word list in the search order. The search order may be changed at any time.

A pointer to the first word list in the search order is kept in the variable **CONTEXT**. To display the search order, use **ORDER**.

When a Forth word is compiled, it will be placed in the current *compilation word list.* That word list is not necessarily first in the interpretation search order. A pointer to the current compilation word list is kept in the variable **CURRENT**. Words are provided, as described below, to manipulate both the interpretation search order and the compilation word list.

You may change the contents of **CONTEXT** (i.e., select the word list to search first) simply by naming the desired word list. For example, the word:

```
ASSEMBLER
```

...changes **CONTEXT** so future searches will begin with the **ASSEMBLER** word list. (**CONTEXT** is set to **ASSEMBLER** by the defining words **CODE** and **;CODE**.)

Similarly, you may employ the word:

```
EDITOR
```

...to set **CONTEXT** to begin by searching the **EDITOR** word list. In many cases, **EDITOR** commands are found in **FORTH** and automatically set **CONTEXT** to the **EDITOR** word list.

The contents of **CURRENT**, which selects the compilation word list, may also be changed. The word **DEFINITIONS** sets **CURRENT** to the word list indicated by **CONTEXT**. For example, in the phrase:

```
EDITOR DEFINITIONS
```

...**EDITOR** sets the value in **CONTEXT** to be the **EDITOR** word list. **DEFINITIONS** then sets **CURRENT** also to **EDITOR**. Thereafter, any future definitions will be linked according to the **EDITOR** word list. Subsequent changes in the search order will change **CONTEXT**, but **CURRENT** remains as set until explicitly changed. When the system starts, or following an **EMPTY**, the default word list for both **CONTEXT** and **CURRENT** is **FORTH**.

Invoking the name of a word list always *replaces* the word list previously at the head of the search order. To add a word list to the head of the search order and still retain the previous word list in the search order, use **ALSO** (see below) followed by the name of the word list you want to add.

6.6.2 Managing Word Lists

Here are some words for manipulating word lists:

Glossary

ALSO (–) Search Ext
Duplicate the first word list in the search order, increasing the number of word lists in the search order by one. Commonly used in the phrase **ALSO** *name*, which has the effect of adding *name* to the top of the search order.

ASSEMBLER (–) Tools Ext
Set future dictionary searches to begin with the **ASSEMBLER** word list (available on most systems).

CONTEXT (– a-addr) Core
Return *a-addr*, the address of a cell that contains a pointer to the first word list in the search order.

CURRENT (– a-addr) Common usage
Return *a-addr*, the address of a cell that contains a pointer to the current compilation word list.

DEFINITIONS (–) Search
Change the compilation word list to be the same as the current first word list in the search order. Set a pointer to this word list in the variable **CURRENT**. Subsequent changes to the interpretation search order will not affect the compilation word list; this word list remains in effect until explicitly changed.

EDITOR (–) Tools Ext
Set future dictionary searches to begin with the **EDITOR** word list.

FORTH (–) Search Ext
Set future dictionary searches to begin with the **FORTH** word list (which contains all standard words provided by the system implementation).

ONLY (–) Search Ext
Reduce the search order to the minimum word list(s), usually just **FORTH**.

ORDER (–) Search Ext
Display the names of all word lists in the search order, in their present search order sequence. Also display the word list into which new definitions will be placed (the **CURRENT** word list).

PREVIOUS (–) Search Ext
Remove the first word list (the one in the **CONTEXT** position) from the search order. This may be used to undo the effect of an **ALSO**.

VOCABULARY <name> (–) Common usage
Create a word list *name*. Subsequent execution of *name* replaces the first word list in the search order with *name*. When *name* becomes the compilation word list, new definitions will be appended to *name*'s list.

WORDS (–) Tools
Display the names of all words in the first word list of the search order.

6.6.3 Sealed Word Lists

The word list mechanism offers an exceptionally powerful security technique. You can implement this by setting up a special application word list consisting of a limited number of commands guaranteed to be safe for users. You then ensure that no application word can change **CONTEXT**, and that **CONTEXT** is set so the text interpreter will only search the application word list.

7. Forth Cross compilers

Early Forth systems were completely self-contained: the Forth on the computer provided all OS functions, a compiler, an assembler, and programming environment as well as supporting the application. In the late 1970s, the advent of small microprocessors and their use on devices without disks, keyboards, and displays challenged this system organization, as did the widespread use of commercial host operating systems on PCs in the 1980s. In response, Forth providers developed cross compilers which ran on PCs but generated code and provided testing facilities for embedded microprocessors.

One of the agenda items for further Forth standards development is addressing issues raised by embedded systems and cross compilers. This is important, as such systems have always represented a large body of Forth use. In 1996, FORTH, Inc. and Microprocessor Engineering Ltd. (MPE) jointly developed a draft standard for such systems and both companies developed cross compilers based on it. The draft standard has been through several public review periods and may be adopted in a future standards process.

Cross compilers following the proposed standard have now been used for over ten years, by a large number of programmers for widely varying projects. Cross compilers utilizing the principles discussed in this section are available from FORTH, Inc. and support a wide range of microprocessors and microcontrollers.

Many Forth systems are written entirely in Forth (and Forth assemblers). *Metacompilers* are used to generate new kernels for resident Forths; they use many of the same strategies discussed here.

This section is intended for programmers who wish to learn more about Forth for embedded systems and about cross compiler or metacompiler strategies.

7.1 Issues in Cross Development

The following issues are peculiar to cross-development systems:

- What needs to be in the target? On many embedded systems it's inappropriate to have a full dictionary, heads, compiler, interpreter, etc., resident in the target, as memory may be extremely limited and the device may have no physical user interface. Exactly what features are required to support a reasonable development cycle?
- What about managing memory spaces? Where does the dictionary reside, and how do you manage data space? Developers of embedded systems must concern themselves with ROM or flash, RAM, on-chip and external memory, etc.
- How do you manage name-space issues? If the cross compiler itself is written in Forth, as most are, how do you distinguish the underlying system's Forth words from the versions that construct the target or that are only executable in the target?
- How can you run and test code on the target system? One of the key advantages of Forth programming is its interactive style. How can this be preserved in the face of the limited facilities provided by many targets?

All these issues have been addressed satisfactorily. The balance of this section provides a general overview of the result. Further details about specific products may be obtained from FORTH, Inc. and MPE, or from other providers of similar systems.

7.2 Host and Target Roles and Functions

Cross development in Forth is best understood by first recognizing that Forth is composed of:

- words that build and manage definitions and data structures, and
- all other executable words.

In a cross-development environment, the first set may be confined to the host, so they are called *host functions*. The second set, normally built by the first set, are referred to as *target functions*.

Host functions include all defining words, "syntactic elements" such as **IF** and **DO**, words such as **,** (comma), and **DOES>** that put things in data structures. Target functions include normally executable words like **+** and **DUP**.

A conventional Forth integrates these two. A cross-development system segregates them and manages them quite distinctly. There may be versions of target words that execute on the host as well as the target.

Host functions are defined using the resident Forth on the host computer, usually a PC running Forth under an OS. Host functions include special versions of the normal defining words and memory management facilities—they are used to construct and manage a target dictionary. A specific subset of these is specifically directed at processing the source for the purpose of building a program to run in the target.

The target is not required to provide host-type functionality, such as a text interpreter and compiler, although it may do so.

7.3 Managing Scopes

A *scope* is defined as the logical space in which a word is visible or can operate. In this context, the host and target systems require separate scopes, to distinguish (for example) the **DUP** used in the host computer's underlying Forth from the one that executes only on the target, and the **:** used to build cross-compiler functions from the one that builds target definitions.

Cross compilers define the following scopes:

- **HOST**: This scope provides access to the underlying system's Forth, and is used to construct the cross compiler. It's rarely used explicitly in programs built for the target, but is available for special needs.
- **INTERPRETER**: These words are executed on the host to construct and manage target definitions and data structures. They include all defining words plus words such as **,** (comma). New application-specific defining words are also in **INTERPRETER** scope.
- **COMPILER**: This is used to make words executed inside **TARGET** colon definitions, e.g., to construct flow-of-control structures.
- **TARGET**: This is the default scope. It contains all words that exe-

cute in the target. They are not guaranteed to be executable on the host.

By default, new commands belong to the **TARGET** scope; i.e., they are compiled onto the target. But after the **INTERPRETER** command, new words are added to the host that will be found when the host is interpreting on behalf of the target.

If you use any of these selectors to change the default scope, we recommend that you later use **TARGET** so subsequent words will again be compiled to the target.

The compiler directive in force at the time you create a new colon definition is the scope in which the new word will be found. As a trivial example:

```
TARGET ok
: Test1 1 . ; ok
Test1 1 ok

INTERPRETER ok
Test1
Error 0 TEST1 is undefined
ok
```

Table 13 summarizes the availability of words defined in various scopes.

Table 13: Availability of words defined in various scopes

If defined in:	Available in these scopes while interpreting:	compiling:
COMPILER	Not allowed	TARGET
HOST	HOST, INTERPRETER, COMPILER	HOST, INTERPRETER, COMPILER
INTERPRETER	TARGET	INTERPRETER
TARGET	Not allowed	TARGET

Scopes are usually defined by using wordlists and search orders.

7.4 Data Space Management

Target memory space can be divided into multiple sections of three types, shown in Table 14. Managing these spaces separately provides an extra measure of flexibility and control, even when the target processor does not distinguish code space from data space.

At least one instance of each section must be defined, including its upper and lower address boundaries, before it is used. Address ranges for instances of the same section type may not overlap. The syntax for defining a memory section is:

```
<low address> <high address> <type> SECTION <name>
```

An instance becomes the current section of its type when its name is invoked. The compiler will work with that section as long as it is current, maintaining a set of allocation pointers for each section of each type. Only one section of each type is current at any time.

Table 14: Types of memory space in cross compilers

Type	Description
CDATA	Code space; includes all code plus initialization tables. May be in PROM or flash. CDATA may not be accessed directly by standard programs.
IDATA	Initialized data space; contains preset values specified at compile time and instantiated in the target automatically as part of power-up initialization. It is writable at run time, so it must be in RAM.
UDATA	Uninitialized RAM data space, allocated at compile time. Its contents cannot be specified at compile time.

Multiple sections of a given type enable you to specify on-chip and external RAM or to handle non-contiguous memory maps. For example, you may wish to have a CDATA section in flash containing a kernel and another in RAM where you can download definitions for testing. When the new definitions are stable, they can be added to the kernel. Similarly, you might define a small section of UDATA in internal RAM (perhaps for stacks and system variables) and a larger section in external RAM.

As an example, consider this report showing the memory allocation for a SwiftX system on an 8051 (a Harvard architecture part with segregated code and data space). It includes code space sections in PROM and RAM (the latter for testing), as well as internal and external UDATA sections. The "used" column reports how much of each section is occupied by the SwiftX kernel; the remainder is available to the application.

Start	End	Size	Used	Unused	Type	Name
8000	BFFF	16384	0	16384	CDATA	PRAM
0000	7FFF	32768	6868	25900	CDATA	PROM
F000	FF7F	3968	47	3921	IDATA	EXT-IDATA
C000	EFFF	12288	1672	10616	UDATA	EXT-UDATA
0040	007F	64	15	49	UDATA	INT-UDATA

7.4.1 Vectored Words

The words used to allocate and access memory are vectored to operate on the current section of the current type. Using a section-type selectors—**CDATA**, **IDATA**, or **UDATA**—sets the vectors for those words. If you only have one section of each type, the section names are rarely used; but, for example, if you have multiple **IDATA** sections, using the name specifies where the next data object to be defined will go.

The vectored words are given in the glossary below.

Glossary

ORG (addr –) Cross[1]
Set the address of the next available location in the current section of the current section type.

HERE (– addr) Cross
Return the address of the next available location in the current section of the current section type.

ALLOT (n –) Cross
Allocate *n* bytes at the next available location in the current section of the current section type.

1. "Cross" refers to the draft Cross-compiler wordset which is not part of the ANS Forth standard.

ALIGN (–) Cross
Adjust the space allocation pointer for the current section of the current section type to be cell-aligned.

C, (b –) Cross
Compile *b* at next available location (**CDATA** and **IDATA** only).

, (x –) Cross
Compile *x* at the next available location (**CDATA** and **IDATA** only).

7.4.2 Data Types

Target defining words may place their executable components in code space. Data-defining words such as **CREATE**—and custom defining words based on **CREATE**—make definitions that reference the section that is current when **CREATE** is executed.

Because **UDATA** is only allocated at compile time, there is no compiler access to it. UDATA is allocated by the defining words themselves; a summary of defining words is given below. At power-up, **UDATA** is uninitialized.

VALUEs must be in **IDATA** or **CDATA**, because they are initialized. **IDATA** is the normal place; **CDATA** works only if code space is writable. **VARIABLE**s are switch selectable: they are usually in **UDATA** but can be configured to be in **IDATA** and initialized to zero. We don't specify where **CONSTANT**s go because some compilers compile references to **CONSTANT**s as literals; for that reason, we follow the rule that they cannot be changed and do not specify where they go.

The **@** and **!** words, as well as the string-initialization words **FILL**, etc., may be used at compile time if the destination address is in **IDATA**. It's an ambiguous condition (FORTH, Inc. compilers will abort) to attempt to access **UDATA** other than from code executing in the target. If you have an active cross-target link (XTL), you can read and write target RAM—but that is achieved by using the host to send commands to the target.

References

Cross-target links, Section 7.5.

7.4.3 Effects of Scoping on Data Object Defining Words

Defining words other than **:** (colon) are used to build data structures with characteristic behaviors. Normally, an application programmer is primarily concerned with building data structures for the target system; therefore, the dominant use of defining words is in the **TARGET** scope while in interpreting state. You may also build data objects in **HOST** that may be used in all scopes except **TARGET**; such objects might, for example, be used to control the compiling process.

Data objects fall into three classes:

- Objects in initialized data memory—e.g., words defined by **CREATE**, **VALUE**, etc., including most user-defined words made with **CREATE ... DOES>**.
- Objects in uninitialized data memory—e.g., words defined by the use of **VARIABLE**, **BUFFER:**, etc.
- Constants—words defined by **CONSTANT** or **2CONSTANT**.

Unlike target colon definitions, target data objects may be invoked in interpreting state. However, they may not exhibit their defined target behavior because that is available only in the target or when you're connected to a target by a cross-target link, as described in Section 7.5.

Constants will always return their value; other words will return the address of their target data space address. **IDATA** objects may be given compiled, initial values with **,** (comma) and **C,** (c-comma), and you may also use **@** and **!** with them at compile time. However, there is no way to initialize **UDATA** objects at compile time.

Some special issues arise when creating custom data objects in a cross-compiled environment: defining words are executed on the host to create new definitions that can be executed on the target. Therefore, you must be in the **INTERPRETER** scope when you create a custom defining word, and you must be aware of what data space you are accessing in the new data object.

Consider this example:

```
INTERPRETER
\ ARRAY is an array of specified size in UDATA.
: ARRAY ( n -- )
   IDATA CREATE                   \ New definition
   UDATA HERE OVER ALLOT          \ Get addr, allocate space
   IDATA ( Loc ) , ( Size) ,      \ Save size & address
DOES> ( i -- addr )               \ Take index, return addr
   2@ ROT MIN +                   \ Compute indexed address
   ;

TARGET
100 ARRAY STUFF
```

You must specify **INTERPRETER** before you make the new defining word, then return to **TARGET** to use this word to add definitions to the target. The **INTERPRETER** version of **DOES>** allows you to reference **TARGET** words in the execution behavior of the word, as that will be executed only on the target.

When **CREATE** (as well as the memory allocation words listed above) is executed to create the new data object, it uses the current section type. The default in our practice is **IDATA**. Defining words that explicitly use **UDATA** (**VARIABLE**, etc.) do not affect the current section type. If you wish to force a different section type, you may do so by invoking one of the selector words (**CDATA**, **IDATA**, or **UDATA**) inside the defining portion or before the defining word is used. If you do this, you must assume responsibility for reasserting the default section.

You can control where individual instances of **CREATE** definitions go, like this:

```
IDATA
CREATE BYTES 1 C, 2 C,
UDATA
CREATE STUFF 100 ALLOT
```

In this case, the data space for **BYTES** is in initialized data space, but the data space for **STUFF** is in uninitialized data space.

CDATA CREATE (followed by data compiled by words such as **,** and **,"**) is useful for defining data structures such as messages or fonts that won't be modified at run time.

7.5 Interactive Programming

The most important facility a Forth cross compiler can provide is the ability to program and test your target interactively. The objective is always to reproduce as nearly as possible the intimate environment presented by a resident Forth.

This is done in Forth cross compilers by a facility called a *cross-target link* or XTL. This involves a connection with the target, which may be any available technology: serial line, parallel line, USB, JTAG, etc. It also requires a tiny amount of code on the target to receive commands from the host and execute them, and to send requests to the host.

The target needs to be able to:

- Receive a byte from the host and store it at a specified address.
- Interrogate a specified address and send its contents to the host.
- Commence executing at a specified address.

Given these facilities, the host can download either a package of pre-compiled code or a small set of instructions (such as a single definition), execute them, and communicate results to the host. The required footprint for these facilities can be quite small.

Typically, the host compiles a kernel consisting of the facilities listed above plus a basic set of Forth primitives. This may reside in EEPROM or flash. Based on this, a link is established with the host, and thereafter the host can incrementally compile and download individual definitions, execute definitions, and report results.

The heads of compiled definitions are retained in the host, along with an image of the target's **CDATA** and **IDATA**. Thus, the host can "know" at all times what the target's code and initialized data space contains.

The target may also send commands to the host. Commands such as **KEY**, **EMIT**, **ACCEPT**, and **TYPE** can be defined in the target to send a command byte plus other parameters to the host, requesting the host to provide appropriate services (e.g., return keyboard data or display a character string).

Once a kernel has been installed on the target and an XTL link established, the programmer has a relationship with the target that's almost as intimate and effortless as with a resident Forth. A representative procedure will flow like this:

- The user types commands, such as **FOO 100 DUMP** (desiring to display 100 bytes starting at the address returned by **FOO**).
- The host's stack, which contains the specified address and length, is downloaded to the target.
- The address of the target's **DUMP** is found in the host's image of the target dictionary.
- The target is requested to begin execution at this address.
- Because the target's **TYPE** is programmed to request the host to display the string, the resulting output appears on the host's screen.
- The target's stack is uploaded to the host.

The result is operationally indistinguishable from interactive debugging on a resident Forth.

A typical cross-development cycle starts with downloading (flashing, burning, etc.) a basic kernel consisting of support for the XTL and a representative set of primitives. Thereafter, the programmer can download and test definitions individually and, as they achieve stability, add them to the kernel image. When all application definitions have been tested, the kernel image includes the entire application.

When debugging of this complete program is finished, it should be possible to remove the target's code that supports the XTL and permanently install the final code.

7.6 I/O Drivers for Embedded Systems

One of the major differences between programming for an embedded system and for a resident Forth is that embedded systems typically run stand-alone with no host OS. Therefore, the programmer is responsible for writing drivers for any devices attached to the system. Often these consist of devices designed and developed specifically for the project, with no prior use or support software. Forth is an ideal tool in such situations, because its inherently interactive nature plus an active cross-target link (Section 7.5) make it easy for the programmer to debug new hardware.

The general approach to writing drivers in Forth is not significantly different from writing drivers in assembly language or C: you must study the documentation for the device in question, determine how to control the device, decide how you want to use the device for your application, and then write the code.

A few suggestions may help you take advantage of Forth's interactivity and ease of interfacing to various devices. Here we offer some general guidelines to make writing and testing drivers easier.

1. *Name your device registers*, usually by defining them as constants. This will help make your code more readable. It will also help "parameterize" your driver: for example, if you have several devices that are similar except for their hardware addresses, you can write the common control code and pass to it a port or register address to indicate the specific device, efficiently reusing the common code.

   Special registers associated with other devices may be named at the beginning of the file containing the driver. For example, the file containing code for the 68332 Periodic Interval Timer (PIT) contains:

   ```
   \ Periodic interrupt control register:
   $FFFFFA22 CONSTANT PICR
   \ Periodic interrupt timing register:
   $FFFFFA24 CONSTANT PITR
   ```

2. *Test the device* before writing a lot of code for it. It may not work, it may not be connected properly, and it may not work exactly as the documentation says it should. It's best to discover these things before you've written a lot of code based on incorrect information, or have gotten frustrated because your code isn't behaving as you believe it should.

   If you've named your registers and have your target board connected, you can use the XTL to test your device. Memory-mapped registers can be read or written using **C@**, **C!**, **@**, **!**, etc. (depending on the width of the register), and the **.** ("dot") command can be used to display the results. (Usually you want the numeric base set to **HEX** when doing this!) For example, to look at the Port A data register, you could type:

   ```
   PORTA C@ .
   ```

   Try reading and writing registers; send some commands and see if you get the results you expect. In this way, you can explore the device until you really understand it and have verified that it is at least minimally functional.

3. *Design your basic strategy for the device.* For example, if it's an input device, will you need a buffer or are you only reading single, occasional values? Will you be using it in a multitasked application? If so, will more than one task be using this device? In a multitasked environment, it's often advisable to use interrupt-driven drivers so I/O can proceed while the task awaiting it is asleep and other tasks can run. An interrupt (or expiration of a count of values read, etc.) can wake the task. Multitasking facilities are very implementation-dependent; see your product documentation for a discussion of these features.
4. *Keep your interrupt handlers simple!* If you're using interrupts, the recommended strategy is to do only the most time-critical functions (e.g., reading an incoming value and storing it in a buffer or temporary location), then wake the task responsible for the device so that task can handle any high-level processing.

8. Programming Style and Editing Standards

In this section, we explore some of the issues that make Forth code easier to read and to maintain, notably formatting standards and naming conventions. In addition, we are reprinting a set of "rules for readable Forth," published by Leo Wong on the Internet newsgroup comp.lang.forth.

Successful Forth programming groups generally acknowledge the importance of agreeing within the group on a single set of coding standards. This contributes significantly to long-term code maintainability and facilitates code-sharing within the group, because all group members become comfortable reading the group's code.

Two sets of source guidelines are provided: one is used by FORTH, Inc. for file-based source and one is recommended by the Open Firmware working group for use with Open Firmware. Open Firmware (IEEE Std. 1275-1994) is a Forth-based system for use in boot firmware used on SPARC systems, PowerPC PCI bus systems, and others. You will notice that, in Section 8.2, Forth words are spelled in lower case. This is conventional in Open Firmware and some Forth systems, although traditionally (and elsewhere in this book) upper case has been used for standard Forth words. This issue should be addressed in your group's coding standards. Additional guidelines for **BLOCK**-based source are given in Section C.4.

Style and readability are highly subjective matters. We encourage you to modify the guidelines in this section to suit your own taste and the consensus of your group. The important thing is to have *some* set of standards and follow it consistently!

8.1 FORTH, Inc. Editing Standards

This section describes the source code editing standards used at FORTH, Inc. to ensure readability and notational consistency across all Forth systems.

8.1.1 Stack Effects

1. All colon or code definitions must include a comment identifying stack parameters on entry and exit. If no stack parameters are used, an "empty" stack comment is still required.
2. The format of the comment is: `( input -- output )` with the rightmost item in each list representing the top of the stack.

   Example 1, input only
   ```
   : TYPE ( addr n -- )
   ```
   Example 2, output only
   ```
   : -FOUND ( -- addr addr' flag )
   ```
   Example 3, both input and output
   ```
   CODE @ ( addr -- n )
   ```
   Example 4, no arguments
   ```
   : NO-OP ( -- )
   ```
3. The stack comment begins one space after the name of the word. Remember to leave one space after the opening `(`. The last character of the comment should be followed by one space and the terminating parenthesis. Exactly three spaces follow the right parenthesis before the code begins.
4. The specific description of a stack item should follow these conventions:

`addr`	address
`b`	8-bit byte
`char`	ASCII character
`n`	single-length number, usually signed
`u`	single-length unsigned number
`d`	double-length signed number
`ud`	double-length unsigned number
`flag`	Boolean truth flag (0=false)

   These special cases should be used when appropriate:

`c l`	screen position, in columns and lines
`s d n`	source, destination, count (in that order)
`y x`	2-vector (for graphics, etc.; single-precision unless otherwise noted)
`f l`	First, last limits; inclusive
`f l+1`	First, last limits; exclusive at end

   Other special situations may be dealt with similarly if necessary to improve clarity, but use single characters where possible. Remember to describe any special stack notation in the source comments!

5. Where there are several arguments of the same type and if clarity demands that they be distinguished, use ' (prime) or suffix numerals. For example:

```
CODE RSWAP ( n addr addr' -- n addr )
```

...shows that the address returned is the same as the first one input.

8.1.2 General Comments

1. All source files should begin with a comment that succinctly describes the contents of the file. This should be followed by any discussion that applies to the file as a whole, a list of required support features (over and above ANS Forth), and a list of words in this file that are intended for "public" use (as opposed to words intended for use only within the file as support words).
2. Use a *block comment* before each closely related group of definitions. It should describe the group as a whole (e.g., assumptions or rules of usage) and the individual words in the group. A block comment begins with:

```
{ ---------------------------------------------
```

and ends with:

```
---------------------------------------------- }
```

3. Comments within definitions (other than stack effects) should help a reader understand what the code is doing from the application perspective, or elucidate any possibly obscure strategy.

good:

```
177566 ( SEND +2) ,  177562 ( RCV+2) ,
```

redundant:

```
DUP 0= ABORT" Value is zero" \ Aborts if zero
```

not helpful:

```
TEMP @   ( Fetch content of TEMP)
```

In general, discussions of usage should go in block comments. Comments should begin with a capital letter and otherwise be lower case except as standard usage indicates, e.g.,

```
( Defining words )
( DLL interface )
```

8.1.3 Spacing Within Files

1. Blank lines are valuable. Use them to separate definitions or groups of definitions. Avoid a dense clump of lines with a lot of blank lines below, unless the clump is a single definition. A blank line inside a definition is usually not helpful and should be avoided. Try to leave at least one blank line at the end.
2. Definitions should begin in the left-most column of a line, with the following exceptions:
   - If the definition is prefaced by a bar (|) to make it headless, the bar should go in the first column followed by one space. The definition should begin immediately thereafter.
   - Two or three related variables, constants, or other data items may share a line if there is room for three spaces between them.
   - Very short colon definitions may share a line provided they are closely related, spaced properly internally, and separated from each other by at least three spaces.
3. The name of a definition must be separated from its defining word by only one space. If it is a **CONSTANT** or other object with a specified value, the value must be separated from the defining word by only one space.
4. Individual instructions in a **CODE** definition must be separated by three spaces. Components of each instruction must be separated by only one space. For example:

   ```
   R0 POPR   1 R0 R0 ADDS   R0 PUSHR
   ```
   [1]

   This makes it easy for a person to identify individual instructions.
5. Second and subsequent lines of colon and **CODE** definitions must be indented by multiples of three spaces (e.g., 3, 6, 9). Indentation beyond one set of three spaces is used to indicate nested structures.

1. From SwiftX™ for the ARM microcontroller family.

6. Forth examples in documentation also should conform to these rules.

8.2 Open Firmware Coding Style

This section describes the coding style in some Open Firmware implementations. These guidelines are a "living" document that came into existence in 1985. By following these guidelines, you will produce code similar in style to a large body of existing Open Firmware work. This will make your code more easily understood by others within the Open Firmware community.

8.2.1 Typographic Conventions

The following typographic conventions are used in this document:

- The underscore symbol _ is used to represent space characters (i.e., ASCII 0x20).
- The ellipsis symbol ... is used to represent an arbitrary amount of Forth code.
- Within prose descriptions, Forth words are shown in **this** font.

8.2.2 Use of Spaces

Because Forth code can be very terse, the judicious use of spaces can increase the readability of your code.

Two consecutive spaces are used to separate a definition's name from the beginning of the stack diagram, another two consecutive spaces (or a new line) are used to separate the stack diagram from the word's definition, and two consecutive spaces (or a new line) separate the last word of a definition from the closing semi-colon. For example:

```
: new-name__(_stack-before_--_stack-after_)__foo__bar__;
: new-name__(_stack-before_--_stack-after_)
___foo_bar_framus_dup_widget_foozle_ribbit_grindle
;
```

Forth words are usually separated by one space. If a phrase consisting of several words performs some function, that phrase should be separated from other words/phrases by two consecutive spaces or a new line.

```
: name__(_stack before_--_stack
after_)__xxx_xxx__xxx_xxx__;
```

When creating multiple-line definitions, all lines except the first and last should be indented by three spaces. If additional indentation is needed with control structures, the left indent for each nesting level should be three spaces to the right of the preceding level's indent.

```
: name__(_stack before_--_stack after_)
___xxx...
______xxx...
______xxx...
___xxx
;
```

8.2.3 Conditional Structures

In `if…then` or `if…else…then` control structures that occupy no more than one line, two spaces should be used both before and after each `if`, `else`, or `then`.

```
__if__xxx__then__
__if__xxx__else__xxx__then__
```

Longer constructs should be structured like this:

```
<code to generate flag>__if
___<true clause>
then
<code to generate flag>__if
___<true clause>
else
___<false clause>
then
```

8.2.4 Finite Loop Structures

In **do…loop** constructs that occupy no more than one line, two spaces should be used both before and after each **do** or **loop**.

```
<code to calculate limits>__do__xxx__loop__
```

Longer constructs should be structured like this:

```
<code to calculate limits>__do
___<body>
loop
```

The longer **+loop** constructs should be structured like this:

```
<code to calculate limits>__do
___<body>
<incremental value>_+loop
```

8.2.5 Indefinite Pre-testing Loop Structures

In **begin…while…repeat** constructs that occupy no more than one line, two spaces should be used both before and after each **begin**, **while**, or **repeat**.

```
__begin__<flag code>__while__<body>__repeat__
```

Longer constructs:

```
begin__<short flag code>__while
___<body>
repeat
begin
___<long flag code>
while
___<body>
repeat
```

8.2.6 Indefinite Post-testing Loop Structures

In **begin…until** and **begin…again** constructs that occupy no more than one line, two spaces should be used both before and after each **begin**, **until**, or **again**.

```
__begin__<body>__until
__begin__<body>__again
```

Longer constructs:

```
begin
___<body>
until
begin
___<body>
again
```

8.2.7 Block Comments

Block comments begin with _. All text after the space is ignored until after the next new line. It would be possible to delimit block comments with parentheses, but the use of parentheses is reserved by convention for stack comments.

Precede each non-trivial definition with a block comment giving a clear and concise explanation of what the word does. Put more comments at the very beginning of the file to describe external words which could be used from the User Interface.

8.2.8 Stack Comments

Stack comments begin with **(_** and end with **)**. Use stack comments liberally within definitions. Try to structure each definition so that, when you put stack comments at the end of each line, the stack picture makes a nice pattern.

```
: name (stack before -- stack after)
___xxx xxx bar ( stack condition after the execution of bar)
___xxx xxx foo ( stack condition after the execution of foo)
___xxx xxx dup ( stack condition after the execution of dup)
```

8.2.9 Return Stack Comments

Return stack comments are also delimited with parentheses. In addition, the notation **r:** is used at the beginning of the return stack comment to differentiate it from a data stack comment.

Place return stack comments on any line that contains one or more words that cause the return stack to change. (This limitation is a practical one; it is often difficult to do otherwise due to lack of space.) The words **>r** and **r>** must be paired inside colon definitions and inside **do...loop** constructs.

```
: name ( stack before -- stack after )
___xxx >r  ( r:addr )
___xxx r> ( r: )
```

8.2.10 Numbers

Hexadecimal numbers should be typed in lower case. If a given number contains more than four digits, the number may be broken into groups of four digits with periods. For example:

```
dead.beef
```

All literal numbers should have a preceding h# (for hex) or d# (for decimal). The only exception is in tables, where the number base is explicitly specified. For example:

```
hex
create foo
   1234 ,  abcd ,  56ab ,  8765 ,
   0023 ,  ...
```

8.3 Wong's Rules for Readable Forth

This set of rules for readable Forth was posted in comp.lang.forth by:

Leo Wong
New York State Department of Civil Service
Albany, NY 12239

...with additional commentary by Wil Baden and including quotes from Leo Brodie (author of the popular tutorial *Starting Forth;* see Appendix A, *Bibliography).* These rules are not provided here as definitive guidelines—they are presented to provoke thought about which approaches may be most useful in your own programming practice.

1. Use the word that fits the data.
2. Do not use ASCII codes (or other "magic numbers") in colon definitions.
3. Do not factor just to factor.
4. Get all three right: code, comment, and name.
5. Do not use syntactic sugar.
6. Eschew sophistication.
7. Test it, even if it's obvious.
8. Do not shun Scylla by falling into Charybdis.[1]
9. Feature the stack machine.
10. Pattern names after other names.

These rules are not for beginners learning their Forth ABCs, but might be helpful to a person who has written a program and wants to make it clearer.

8.3.1 Example: Magic Numbers

Here are some examples:

1. In the *Odyssey*, the mighty Ulysses was required, at one point, to sail through a strait that was guarded on one side by the many-headed monster Scylla, and on the other by Charybdis, the whirlpool of oblivion. Many sailors tried so hard to avoid the one that they succumbed to the other.

```
: STAR   42 EMIT ;
: STAR   ." *" ;
: STAR   [CHAR] * EMIT ;
```

Each of these definitions has a fault:

- The first forces the reader to know that ASCII 42 means * (although this could be remedied by a comment).
- The second uses a word intended for strings.
- The third is wordy in the source, although it compiles the same result as the first.

I don't consider the lack of a stack comment in these definitions a fault. I find the third **STAR** to be the most readable and, hence, preferable.

Two rules:

1. Use the word that fits the data.
2. Do not use ASCII codes or other unidentified numbers in colon definitions.

8.3.2 Example: Factoring

From the first edition of *Starting Forth* (p. 43):

```
: QUARTERS   4 /MOD  . ." ONES AND "  . ." QUARTERS " ;
```

From the second edition (p. 40):

```
: $>QUARTERS  ( dollars -- quarters dollars)  4 /MOD ;
: .DOLLARS  ( dollars -- )  .  ." dollar bills" ;
: .QUARTERS  ( quarters -- )  .  ." quarters " ;
: QUARTERS  ( dollars -- )
   $>QUARTERS  ." Gives " .DOLLARS  ." and " .QUARTERS
;
```

In the second edition, a name and two stack comments are wrong (as is the output, not shown here). In addition, this approach is both larger and slower without contributing significantly to readability or functionality.

Rules:

3. Do not factor just to factor.
4. Get all three right: code, comment, and name.

8.3.3 Example: Simplicity

Two solutions adapted from *Starting Forth*, 2nd edition (pp. 277-278):

(1)

```
: bdot"   BRIGHT  R>  COUNT  2DUP + >R  TYPE  -BRIGHT ;
: B."   POSTPONE bdot"  [CHAR] " WORD  C@ 1+ ALLOT ;
IMMEDIATE
```

Brodie: "The foregoing solution is messy and probably not transportable."

[Note: transportability is limited by the assumptions this approach makes about the implementation.]

(2)

```
: B."  POSTPONE BRIGHT  POSTPONE ."  POSTPONE -BRIGHT ;
IMMEDIATE
```

Brodie: "The disadvantage of this solution over the previous one is that every invocation of **B."** compiles two extra addresses. The first solution is more efficient and therefore preferable if you have the system source listing and lots of invocations of **B."**. The second solution is simpler to implement, and adequate for a small number of invocations.

"Other languages may be easier to learn; but what other languages let you extend the compiler like this?"

An alternative that doesn't include the compilation features might be:

```
: .BRIGHT  ( a u)  BRIGHT TYPE -BRIGHT ;
```

Rules:

5. Do not use syntactic sugar.
6. Eschew sophistication.

8.3.4 Example: Testing Assumptions

In *Thinking Forth* (reprint edition, p. 219), Brodie quotes Moore:

"In books you often see a lot of piece-wise linear approximations that fail to express things clearly. For instance the expression

x = 0 for t < 0

x = 1 for t ≥ 0

"This would be equivalent to:

```
t 0< 1 AND
```

"...as a single expression, not a piece-wise expression."

Rule:

7. Test it even if it's obvious.

8.3.5 Example: IF Avoidance

Forth programmers strive to avoid **IF**, some going so far as to use **CASE** whenever possible. Here are two examples, from *Starting Forth,* of **IF**-avoidance:

First the **IF** versions (second edition, p. 183):

```
: CATEGORY  ( weight-per-dozen -- category#)
   DUP 18 < IF  0  ELSE
   DUP 21 < IF  1  ELSE
   DUP 24 < IF  2  ELSE
   DUP 27 < IF  3  ELSE
   DUP 30 < IF  4  ELSE
                5
   THEN THEN THEN THEN THEN  SWAP DROP ;
```

(Note: the "official table" on which **CATEGORY** is based is ambiguous. See p. 85.)

```
: LABEL   ( category# -- )
   DUP  0= IF  ." Reject "        ELSE
   DUP 1 = IF  ." Small "         ELSE
   DUP 2 = IF  ." Medium "        ELSE
   DUP 3 = IF  ." Large "         ELSE
   DUP 4 = IF  ." Extra Large "   ELSE
                  ." Error "
   THEN THEN THEN THEN THEN  DROP ;
```

Now the "simple and elegant for experts" versions (pp. 189 and 253):

```
CREATE SIZES  18 C,  21 C,  24 C,  27 C,  30 C,  255 C,
: CATEGORY  ( weight-per-dozen -- category# )
   6 0 DO  DUP  SIZES I + C@
   < IF  DROP  I LEAVE  THEN  LOOP ;

CREATE "LABEL"
ASCII " STRING Reject  Small   Medium  Large   Xtra
LrgError  "
: LABEL  (  category# -- )
   8 *  "LABEL"  +  8 TYPE SPACE ;
: LABEL   0 MAX  5 MIN  LABEL ;
```

It may seem unfair of me to give the code without the explanations, but:

- Experts wouldn't need the explanations.
- I would have to mention the bugs in the elegant **LABEL**.

Which versions would you rather maintain?

Rule:

8. Do not shun Scylla by falling into Charybdis.

8.3.6 Example: Stack Music

What is stack noise to you and me is music to a stack machine. It is time to face the music.

In *Thinking Forth*, Brodie gives a solution (reprint edition, p. 222) to a phone-rate problem posed and analyzed earlier in the book (pp. 45–51):

```
\ Telephone rates                                03/30/84
CREATE FULL      30 ,  20 ,  12 ,
CREATE LOWER     22 ,  15 ,  10 ,
CREATE LOWEST    12 ,   9 ,   6 ,
VARIABLE RATE      \ Points to FULL, LOWER or LOWEST
                 \ depending on time of day
FULL RATE !      \  For instance
: CHARGE   ( o -- )  CREATE ,
   DOES>   ( -- rate )  @  RATE @ +  @ ;
0 CHARGE 1MINUTE     \ Rate for first minute
2 CHARGE +MINUTES    \ Rate for each additional minute
4 CHARGE /MILES      \ Rate per each 100 miles

\ Telephone rates                                03/30/84
VARIABLE OPERATOR?   \ 90 if operator assisted; else 0
VARIABLE #MILES      \ Hundreds of miles
: ?ASSISTANCE  ( Direct-dial charge -- total charge)
   OPERATOR? @ + ;
: MILEAGE  ( -- charge )  #MILES @  /MILES * ;
: FIRST  ( -- charge )  1MINUTE  ?ASSISTANCE  MILEAGE +
;
: ADDITIONAL  ( -- charge)  +MINUTES  MILEAGE + ;
: TOTAL  ( #minutes -- total charge)
   1- ADDITIONAL *  FIRST + ;
```

No stack noise. Readable?

Here's a try at a solution that requires stack manipulations:

```
\ Phone-rate table from Brodie, Thinking Forth,
\ reprint edition, p. 51
\ Rates are used as offsets into arrays
0 CELLS CONSTANT FULL
1 CELLS CONSTANT LOWER
2 CELLS CONSTANT LOWEST
\ Array-defining word
: FOR   CREATE  DOES>  ( rate - charge-per-minute)  + @ ;
\ Table comprises three arrays
\ Charge-per-minute at FULL  LOWER LOWEST  rate
    FOR FIRST           30 ,  22 ,  12 ,
    FOR +MINUTES        20 ,  15 ,   9 ,
    FOR DISTANCE        12 ,  10 ,   6 ,
```

```
90 CONSTANT ASSISTANCE   \ Charge for operator assistance
: ?ASSISTANCE   ( flag - charge)   ASSISTANCE AND ;
: ADDITIONAL   ( #minutes-1 rate - charge)   +MINUTES * ;
: MINUTES   ( #minutes rate - charge)
   DUP FIRST   ROT 1- ROT   ADDITIONAL + ;
: MILES   ( distance #minutes rate - charge)   DISTANCE * *
;
: TOTAL   ( distance #minutes rate assistance-flag - charge)
   ?ASSISTANCE >R   2DUP MINUTES >R   MILES   2R> + + ;
```

Stack music. Unreadable?

Rule:

9. Feature the stack machine.

8.3.7 Summary

How do we feel about these rules? Are any of them helpful? Hurtful? Are there better rules? Do we want rules anyway? These are questions for you to answer, should you so choose.

8.4 Naming Conventions

Table 15 presents some naming conventions that have been widely used in Forth for many years. These take advantage of Forth's flexible naming rules to use special characters to convey additional meaning.

In this table, the word *name* refers to some word the programmer has chosen to represent a Forth routine.

Where possible, a prefix before a name indicates the type or precision of the value being operated on, whereas a suffix after a name indicates what the value is or where it is stored.

Table 15: Naming conventions

Format	Meaning	Examples
!name	Store into name	!DATA
#name	Size or quantity	#PIXELS
	Output numeric operator	#S
	Buffer name	#I
'name	Address of name	'S
	Address of pointer to name	'TYPE
(name)	Internal component of name, not normally user-accessible	(IF) (FIND)
	Run-time procedure of name	(:)
	File index	(PEOPLE)
*name	Multiplication	*DIGIT
	Takes scaled input parameter	*DRAW
+name	Addition	+LOOP
	Advance	+BUF
	Enable	+CLOCK
	More powerful	+INITIALIZE
	Takes relative input parameters	+DRAW
-name	Subtract, remove	-TRAILING
	Disable	-CLOCK
	not name (opposite of name)	-DONE
	Returns reversed truth flag (1 is *false*, 0 is *true*)	-MATCH
	Pointers, especially in files	-JOB
.name	Print named item	.S
	Print from stack in named format	.R .$
	Print following string	." string"
	May be further prefixed with data type	D. U. U.R
/name	Division	/DIGIT
	Initialize routine or device	/COUNTER
	"per"	/SIDE

Table 15: Naming conventions *(continued)*

Format	Meaning	Examples
1name	First item of a group	1SWITCH
	Integer 1	1+
	One-byte size	1@
2name	Second item of a group	2SWITCH
	Integer 2	2/
	Two-cell size	2@
;name	End of something	;S
	End of something, start of something else	;CODE
<name	Less than	<LIMIT
	Open bracket	<#
	From device name	<TAPE
<name>	Name of an internal part of a device driver routine	<TYPE>
>name	Towards name	>R, >TAPE
	Index pointer	>IN
	Exchange, especially bytes	>< (swap bytes)
		>MOVE< (move, swapping bytes)
?name	Check condition, return *true* if yes	?TERMINAL
	Conditional operator	?DUP
	Check condition, abort if bad	?STACK
	Fetch contents of name and display	?N
@name	Fetch from name	@INDEX
Cname	One-byte character size, integer	C@
Dname	Double-cell integer	D+
Mname	Mixed single and double operator	M*
Tname	Three-cell size	T*
Uname	Unsigned encoding	U.
[name]	Executes at compile time	[']
\name	Unsigned subtraction (ramp-down)	\LOOP

Table 15: Naming conventions *(continued)*

Format	Meaning	Examples
`name!`	Store into name	`B!`
`name"`	String follows, delimited by "	`ABORT" xxx"`
`name,`	Put something into dictionary	`C,`
`name:`	Start definition	`CASE:`
`name>`	Close bracket	`#>`
	Away from name	`R>`
`name?`	Same as `?name`	`B?`
`name@`	Fetch from name	`B@`

APPENDIX A: BIBLIOGRAPHY

American National Standard For Information Systems: Programming Languages - Forth (ANSI X3.215-1994). American National Standards Institute, 11 W. 42nd St., New York, NY 10036, (212) 642-4900.

This is the official reference for Standard Forth. It includes definitions for all Standard words as well as specific rules of usage and an explanatory appendix. The last draft of this document is available on the Internet.

Bailey, G., Sanderson, D., Rather, E. "clusterFORTH, A High-Level Network Protocol" *Proceedings of the 1984 FORTH Conference.* Rochester, NY: The Institute for Applied Forth Research, 1984.

This is difficult to find, but describes an interesting and complex protocol developed for a challenging application at the airport at Riyadh, Saudi Arabia.

Brodie, L. *Starting FORTH*, Englewood Cliffs, NJ: Prentice-Hall, 1981, 2nd ed. 1987. Contact: Forth Interest Group, 100 Dolores St., Suite 183, Carmel, California 93923.

This book was written for readers who are not necessarily computer-knowledgeable, and is both accessible and entertaining. Unfortunately, it is also very dated with respect to contemporary practice. Partially updated versions are available on the Internet.

Brodie, L. *Thinking FORTH*, Englewood Cliffs, NJ: Prentice-Hall, 1984; reprinted by the Forth Interest Group, 100 Dolores St., Suite 183, Carmel, California 93923, 1994.

This book is also rather dated, but is very valuable for understanding good Forth style.

FORTH, Inc. *SwiftForth Reference Manual.* Hawthorne, CA: FORTH, Inc., 1998-2006. This proprietary document is included as a PDF with all SwiftForth systems (including the evaluation versions) and describes FORTH, Inc.'s Windows Forth in detail.

FORTH, Inc. *SwiftX Reference Manual.* Hawthorne, CA: FORTH, Inc., 1998-2006. This proprietary document is included as a PDF with all SwiftX cross-compilers (including the evaluation versions) and describes FORTH, Inc.'s Forth cross-compilers in detail. Separate documents cover processor-specific topics.

ISO/IEC 15145:1997: *Information technology—Programming languages—FORTH.* This is the International Standard equivalent of ANS Forth. In the U.S., it is available through the American National Standards Institute, 11 W. 42nd St., New York, NY 10036, (212) 642-4900. For sources in other countries or on-line ordering, see http://www.iso.ch.

This document is technically identical to the ANSI document referenced above.

Koopman, P. *Stack Computers, The New Wave.* Chichester, West Sussex, England. Ellis Horwood Ltd., 1989.

Koopman addresses hardware implementations of the Forth virtual machine.

Moore, C.W. "The Evolution of Forth — An Unusual Language" *Byte*, August 1980.

Primarily of historical interest, this article was the cover article in an issue devoted to Forth. It was the first widely circulated publication on Forth.

Noble, J.V. *Scientific Forth.* Charlottesville, VA: Mechum Banks Publishing, 1992.

Dr. Noble describes uses of Forth in mathematics and other scientific applications.

Pountain, R. *Object Oriented Forth.* New York: Academic Press, 1987.

Many OOP extensions to Forth have been developed. This book describes one of the early ones.

Pelc, Stephen. *Programming Forth.* Southampton, England: Microprocessor Engineering Ltd., 2005.

A good modern text by the Managing Director of one of the leading Forth vendors. Downloadable from www.mpeforth.com.

Rather, E.D. *Forth Application Techniques.* Hawthorne, CA: FORTH, Inc., 2003.

An introductory text on Forth used for courses at FORTH, Inc. Includes many examples and problem sets. An ideal workbook for the beginning Forth programmer.

Rather, E.D. "Forth Programming Language" *Encyclopedia of Physical Science & Technology* (V. 5) Academic Press, Inc., 1987, 1992.

This is an overview of Forth for a technical audience.

Rather, E.D. "Fifteen Programmers, 400 Computers, 36,000 Sensors and

Forth" *Journal of Forth Application and Research* (V. 3, #2, 1985), P.O. Box 27686, Rochester, NY 14627.

This paper describes the overall project for which the protocol in the Bailey paper referenced above was used.

Rather, E.D., Colburn, D.R., and Moore, C.H. "The Evolution of Forth" *ACM SIGPLAN Notices*, Vol. 28, No. 3, March 1993.

This paper presents a detailed history of the development of Forth, from the early 1970s through the early 1990s. It is available at www.forth.com.

Appendix B: Glossary & Notation

This section describes technical terms and notational conventions used in this manual. Additional notation specific to certain sections is described in those sections.

In this manual, the words "shall" and "must" indicate mandatory behavior. The word "will" indicates predicted or consequential behavior. The word "may" indicates permitted or desirable, but not mandatory, behavior. The phrase "may not" indicates prohibited behavior.

Abbreviations

ALU	Arithmetic Logic Unit
ANS	American National Standard
ASCII	American Standard Code for Information Interchange
CPU	Central Processing Unit
H	Hexadecimal (base 16), when used as a subscript
I/O	Input/Output
IEC	International Electrotechnical Commission
IEEE	Institute of Electrical and Electronics Engineers
ISO	International Organization for Standardization
JTAG	Joint Test Action Group (IEEE 1249.1 standard)
OS	Operating System
PC	Personal Computer
PCI	Peripheral Component Interconnect, a common PC bus
PROM	Programmable Read-Only Memory
RAM	Random-Access Memory
ROM	Read-Only Memory
USB	Universal Serial Bus
VM	Virtual Machine

B.1 Glossary

address unit — In Standard Forth, the units in which the length of a region of memory is expressed, or the units into which the region is divided for the purpose of locating data objects. These are nearly always bytes, and are referred to in this manual simply as bytes.

aligned address — The address of a memory location at which a character, cell, cell pair, or double-cell integer can be accessed. For cell-aligned addresses, the address is evenly divisible by the cell size in bytes.

ANS Forth — The Forth programming language as defined by the American National Standard X3.215, 1994.

ASCII string — A string whose data contains one ASCII character per byte. An ASCII string is specified by a cell pair representing its starting address and its length in bytes.

big-endian — Describes a CPU's byte-ordering system in which the highest-order byte of a cell is at the lowest address (i.e., appears first in a data stream). *Little-endian* is the converse of this. Motorola processors are big-endian and Intel processors are little-endian.

body — The portion of a definition that contains its executable code and/or data. See also *head*.

cell — The primary unit of information storage in the architecture of a Forth system. The word length of the processor is always referred to as a cell. This is also the size of an address, and is the size of a single item on Forth's stacks.

cell pair — Two cells that are treated as a single unit. The cells may contain a double-length number, two related single-length numbers (such as a 2-vector), or two entirely unrelated values. *A cell pair in memory* is contiguous: the cell at the lower address is "first" and its address identifies the pair. Unless otherwise specified, *a cell pair on the stack* has the first cell immediately above the second cell.

character — In Standard Forth, one meaning of this word is the number of address units needed to store a character. In this manual, characters are assumed to occupy one byte each. The length of a character string in bytes is, therefore, equal to the number of characters in it (plus one if it is a *counted string*—see below).

character-aligned address — In Standard Forth, the address of a memory location at which a character can be accessed. In nearly all implementations, a character occupies a single byte and this is an arbitrary byte address.

code space — The logical area of the dictionary in which word definitions are implemented.

compile — Transform source code into dictionary definitions.

compilation behavior — The behavior of a Forth definition when its name is encountered by the text interpreter in compilation state.

counted string — A data structure consisting of one character containing the length followed by 0–255 data characters. A counted string in memory is identified by the address of its length character.

cross-compilation — Generation on a host system of an executable program for a target CPU that may be different from the host's CPU.

data field — The data space associated with a word defined via CREATE.

data space — The logical area of the dictionary in which data can be accessed.

data space pointer — The address of the next available data space location. The Forth word HERE returns this address. On implementations where data space is intermingled with dictionary definitions, it is the same as the dictionary pointer.

data stack — A stack that may be used for passing parameters between procedures. When there is no possibility of confusion, the data stack is referred to simply as "the stack." See also *return stack*.

defining word — A Forth word that creates a new definition when executed.

definition — A Forth execution procedure compiled into the dictionary.

dictionary — An extensible structure containing definitions and associated data space.

dictionary pointer — The address of the next available location in the dictionary. On implementations where data space is intermingled with dictionary definitions, it is the same as the data space pointer (above).

double-cell integer — A double-precision integer, signed or unsigned, occupying two cells. *On the stack*, the most-significant cell is above the least-significant cell. *In memory*, the most-significant cell is normally at the lower address, independent of processor type (see *big-endian*). Placing a single-cell integer zero on the stack above a single-cell unsigned integer produces a double-cell unsigned integer with the same value.

exception frame — The implementation-dependent set of information recording the current execution state, necessary for exception processing using the Forth words **CATCH** and **THROW**.

exception stack — A stack used for nesting exception frames. It may be, but need not be, implemented using the return stack.

execution behavior — The behavior of a Forth definition when it is executed.

execution token — A single-cell value that identifies the execution behavior of a procedure. Multiple definitions may have the same execution token if their definitions have equivalent execution behaviors.

flag — A single-cell Boolean true/false value. A word using a flag as input treats zero as *false*, and any non-zero value as *true*. A word returning a flag returns either all bits zero (*false*) or all bits one (*true*).

head — The portion of a dictionary entry containing the word's name, length, and other identifying information. See also *body*.

headless — In some systems, especially metacompilers and cross-compilers, it is possible to make definitions whose heads are kept only on the host. The target versions of these definitions do not have heads and cannot be referenced by name internally. Definitions made with **:NONAME** are also headless.

immediate word — A Forth word whose compiling behavior is to perform its execution behavior. Commonly used to compile program-flow structures.

input stream — ASCII string data input to the host interpreter. It may come from an input device (such as a keyboard) or from a file. The input stream is the vehicle by which user commands, program source, and other data are provided to the host system.

interpretation behavior — The behavior of a Forth definition when its name is encountered by the text interpreter in interpretation state.

keyboard event — A value received by a Forth system as a result of a user action at the user input device. This manual's use of the word *keyboard* does not exclude other types of user input devices.

metacompiler — Most Forth systems are written in Forth. A metacompiler is used to generate a new Forth system, for the same or a different target.

name space — The logical area of the dictionary in which definition names are stored during compilation and testing in the host computer.

number — In this manual, *number* used without qualification means "integer." *Double number* or *double-precision number* means "double-cell integer."

parse — To select and exclude a character string from the parse area using a specified set of delimiting characters, called delimiters.

parse area — The portion of the input stream that has not yet been processed by the host interpreter and is, therefore, available for processing by the host interpreter and other parsing operations.

return stack — A stack that may be used for program execution nesting, DO loop execution, temporary storage, and other purposes.

stack — An area in memory containing a last in, first out list of items. See also *data stack* and *return stack*.

Standard Forth — This refers to a Forth system that complies with the *ISO/IEC 15145:1997* and ANSI X3.215:1994 standards for the Forth programming language.

variable — A named region of data space, located and accessed by its memory address.

whitespace character — A blank or non-graphic character encountered by the Forth interpreter while processing source in a text file. Definitions of whitespace vary; in ANS Forth it includes all control characters.

word — The name of a Forth definition. In the text interpreter, *word* can also refer to a sequence of non-space characters to be processed.

word list — A list of related Forth definition names that may be examined during a dictionary search. A word list is a subset of the entire Forth dictionary.

B.2 Data Types in Stack Notation

Table 16 gives a description of the Standard Forth notation used to refer to the different data types that may appear in stack notation or descriptions in this manual. Some items are implementation-dependent; their stack size is noted as "impl." Additional tables in this section describe other notational conventions.

Table 16: Notation for the data type of stack arguments

Symbol	Data type	Size on stack
a-addr	A byte address that is cell-aligned (the address is evenly divisible by the cell size in bytes).	1 cell
addr	Address.	1 cell
b	A byte, stored as the least-significant eight bits of a stack entry. The remaining bits of the stack entry are zero in results, and are ignored in arguments.	1 cell
c or *char*	An ASCII character, stored as a byte (see above) with the parity bit reset to zero.	1 cell
c-addr	A byte address that is character-aligned (on current systems a character is always one byte, so this amounts to an arbitrary byte address).	1 cell
d	A double-precision, signed, two's complement integer, stored as two stack entries (least-significant cell underneath the most-significant cell). On 16-bit machines the range is from -2**31 through +2**31-1. On 32-bit machines, the range is from -2**63 through +2**63-1.	2 cells
+d	A double-precision integer which is guaranteed to be >0.	2 cells
dest	Control-flow destination.	impl.

Table 16: Notation for the data type of stack arguments *(continued)*

Symbol	Data type	Size on stack
echar	Extended character (occupying the two low-order bytes of a stack item).	1 cell
flag	A single-precision, Boolean truth flag (zero means *false*, non-zero means *true*). See Section B.3 for details.	1 cell
*i*x*, *j*x*, etc.	Zero or more cells of unspecified data type; normally used to indicate that the state of the stack is preserved during, or is restored after, an operation.	Varies
ior	Result of an I/O operation. See Section 5.5.1 for use of *iors* in the file access words.	1 cell
len	Length of a string or buffer.	1 cell
loop-sys	Loop-control parameters. These include implementation-dependent representations of the current value of the loop index, its upper limit, and a pointer to a *termination location* where execution continues following an exit from the loop.	impl.
nest-sys	Implementation-dependent information for procedure calls. It may be kept on the return stack.	impl.
n	A signed, single-precision, two's complement number. On 16-bit machines, the range is -2**15 through +2**15-1. On 32-bit machines, the range is -2**31 through +2**31-1. If a stack comment is shown as *n*, *u* is implied, unless specifically stated otherwise (e.g., **+** may be used to add signed or unsigned numbers). If there is more than one input argument, signed and unsigned types may not be mixed.	1 cell
+n	A single-precision number that may not be negative and has the same positive upper limit as *n*, above.	1 cell
orig	Control-flow origin.	impl.
u	An unsigned, single-precision integer, with the range 0 to 2**16-1 on 16-bit machines, or 0 through 2**32-1 on 32-bit machines.	1 cell

Table 16: Notation for the data type of stack arguments *(continued)*

Symbol	Data type	Size on stack
ud	An unsigned, double-precision integer, with the range 0 to 2**32-1 on 16-bit machines, or 0 through 2**64-1 on 32-bit machines.	2 cells
x	A cell (single stack item), otherwise unspecified.	1 cell
xt	Execution token. This value identifies the execution behavior of a definition. When this value is passed to **EXECUTE**, the definition's execution behavior is performed.	1 cell

Some data types are sub-types of other data types. Figure 22 shows the hierarchy for single-cell and double-cell types. Any Forth definition that accepts an argument of a type shown in the figure must also accept all the subtypes below it. For example, a word with an input stack argument of type *n* also accepts arguments of type *+n* and *char*.

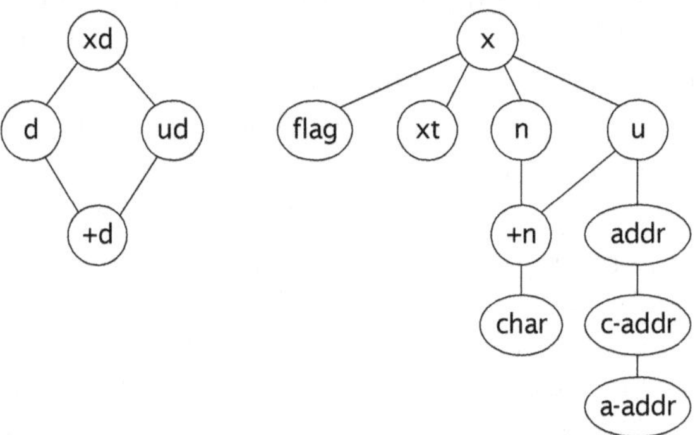

Figure 22. Hierarchy of data types

Standard Forth does not require data-type checking, and most implementations do not include it among their standard functions. Also, most implementations do not include arithmetic error checking on standard math functions (such as overflow on a multiply operation). The reason for both of these restrictions is that error checking and data-type checking on low-level functions could be prohibitively costly in execution time. Most Forth implementations do support whatever hardware error-detection functions exist, such as a trap for divide by zero, or the various exceptions signaled by the 80387/80486 floating-point processor. An application may, of course, build in error checking and/or type checking at any level deemed necessary, simply by redefining the words in question and adding an outer layer of protection.

B.3 Flags and IOR Codes

Procedures that accept flags as input arguments shall treat zero as *false*, and any non-zero value as *true*. A flag returned as an argument is a *well-formed* flag if all bits are zero (*false*), or all bits are one (*true*).

Certain device control and other functions return an *ior* (I/O Result) to report the results of an operation. An *ior* may be treated as a flag, in the sense that a non-zero value is *true*; however, it is not necessarily a well-formed flag, because its specific value often is used to convey additional information. A returned value of zero for an *ior* shall mean successful completion (i.e., no error); non-zero values may indicate an error condition or other abnormal status, and are device dependent.

B.4 Forth Glossary Notation

Words described in this manual are grouped functionally. An alphabetical list of all words is given in Appendix D.

Each entry consists of two parts: an index line and a semantic (behavioral) description of the word. The index line is a single-line entry containing, from left to right:

- Definition name in upper-case, monospaced, boldface letters;
- Stack behavior (the notation follows the conventions described in Sections B.2 and B.3, above).

The first paragraph of the behavioral description concludes with the natural-language pronunciation of the word (shown in distinctive type), if it is not obvious.

A word's behavior may be context dependent. The behavior(s) for each such word are described, as applicable, for:

- **Compiling**
  An action taken by the system when adding to the Forth dictionary.

- *name* **Execution**
  The behavior of *name* when executed, where *name* is an instance of a class of words created by a defining word (see Section 6.2).
- **Interpreting**
  An action taken by the system when the name of a word is encountered by the text interpreter in interpretation state.
- **Run-time**
  The behavior executed by the system.

While many words—such as defining words and compiler directives—possess specific compiling behaviors, the default compilation behavior of a word is to append its *execution behavior* to the current definition. Behaviors in different modes will be shown if they differ.

Some words will be executed (i.e., will perform their behavior) when encountered in compiling mode. In Forth, these are known as *immediate* words. If execution of such a word will cause some run-time action in the word being compiled, this is shown as a separate run-time behavior.

Appendix C: Blocks for Disk Storage

Early Forth implementations ran standalone on various minicomputers and microprocessors, with no other operating system. They organized disk into 1024-byte "blocks," mapping blocks to physical disk sectors. This method was extremely fast, significantly faster than any OS. It was also highly reliable, in that there was no disk directory which could become damaged leading to loss of data.

In the 1980s, many Forth systems were adapted to run under a host OS, such as MS-DOS, MacOS, Windows, or Unix. Those requiring compatibility with block-based Forths retained the block organization, mapping Forth blocks to host OS files. This approach facilitated a migration path from the purely native systems, and also helped those attempting to port complex applications to more modern platforms.

By the late 1990s, the number of active block-based Forths had become very small, and an increasing number of implementors simply used OS-based text files for program source. As that is now the prevailing mode of operation, we have moved this discussion of disk block management to an appendix, in order to keep it available for those who may encounter block-based systems.

This section discusses the words used to access and manage disk blocks and block buffers in Forth. If you have a block-based Forth, refer to your system documentation for additional instruction on implementation-specific features.

C.1 Overview

The block-based disk access method is intended to be simple and to require minimum effort. The disk driver makes data on disk directly accessible to other Forth words by copying disk data into a buffer in memory, and placing the buffer's address on the stack. Thus, Forth routines access disk data using the same techniques as for other kinds of memory access. Because disk data always appears to be in memory, this scheme is a form of *virtual memory* for program source and data storage.

Another consideration in the design of the disk driver is to make disk access as fast as possible. Because disk operations are very slow compared to memory operations, data is read from disk or written to disk only when necessary.

The disk is partitioned into 1024-byte data areas called *blocks*. This standard unit has proven to be a useful increment of mass storage. Used for source text, for example, it contains an amount of source that fits comfortably on a modest display. As the basis for a database system, 1024 is a common multiple of typical record sizes.

Each block is addressed by a block number. On native Forth systems, the block number is a fixed function of the block's physical position on the disk. Absolute addressing of the disk both speeds the driver's execution and eliminates most of the need for disk directories and indexes. On OS-hosted Forth systems, the blocks may be located in one or more files, each an integral multiple of the block size; an internal table maps OS files to block space.

C.1.1 Block-Management Fundamentals

A program ensures that a block in memory is in a *block buffer* by executing the word **BLOCK**. **BLOCK** uses a block number from the stack and returns the address in memory of that block's first byte. For example:

```
9 BLOCK U.
```

...will return an address such as:

```
46844 ok
```

...where 46844 is the address of the first byte of the buffer containing block 9. If a block is already in memory, **BLOCK** will not re-read it from disk.

Although **BLOCK** uses a disk read to get data if it is not already in memory, **BLOCK** is not merely a read command. If **BLOCK** must read a requested block from disk, it uses **BUFFER** to select a buffer to hold the block's contents. **BUFFER** frees a block buffer, writing the buffer's previous contents to disk if it is marked (by **UPDATE**, see below) as having been changed since it was read into memory.

BUFFER expects a block number on the stack and returns the address of the first byte of the buffer it assigns to this block. For example:

```
127 BUFFER U.
```

...will get a block buffer, assign block number **127** to the buffer, and then type the address of the buffer's first byte:

```
36084 ok
```

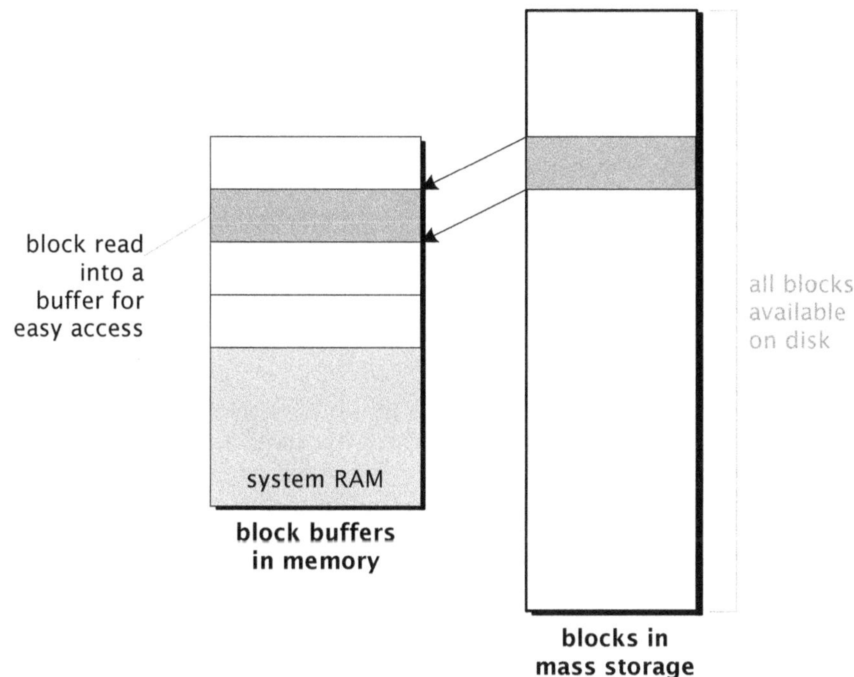

Figure 23. Relationship between blocks and block buffers

Although **BUFFER** may write a block, if necessary, it will *not* read data from disk. When **BUFFER** is called by **BLOCK** to assign a buffer, **BLOCK** follows by reading the requested disk block into the buffer.

The following example displays an array of the first 100 cells in block 1000, shown with five numbers per line:

```
: SHOW ( -- )          \ Display array contents
   100 0 DO
      I 5 MOD 0= IF CR THEN    \ Allow 5 per line
      1000 BLOCK I CELLS + ?   \ Show Ith value in block
   LOOP ;
```

The phrase **I CELLS +** converts the loop counter from cells to bytes (because internal addresses are always byte addresses) and adds the resulting byte offset to the address of the block buffer returned by **BLOCK**. The word **?** fetches and types the cell at that address.

BUFFER may be used directly (i.e., without being called by **BLOCK**) in situations where no data needs to be read from the disk. Examples include initializing a region of disk to a default value such as zero, and a high-speed data acquisition routine writing incoming values 1024 bytes at a time from a memory array directly to disk.

Forth systems have at least one, and usually many, block buffers. The number of buffers may be changed easily. Applications with several users accessing disk heavily may run slightly faster with more buffers. Your product documentation will give details on changing the size of the buffer pool.

The command **UPDATE** marks the data in a buffer as changed, so it will be saved to disk when that buffer must be used for another block. **UPDATE** works on the most recently referenced buffer, so it must be used immediately after any operation that modifies the buffer's data.

The following example uses **BUFFER** to clear a range of blocks to zero:

```
: ZEROS ( first last -- )
   1+ SWAP DO
      I BUFFER 1024 ERASE  UPDATE
   LOOP ;
```

As another example, assume that an application has defined **A/D** to read a value from an A/D converter. To record up to 512 samples in block 700, use:

```
: SAMPLES ( n -- )          \ Record n samples
   512 MIN 0 DO             \ Clip n at 512
      A/D                                \ Read one sample
      700 BLOCK I CELLS + ! UPDATE  \ Record it
   LOOP ;
```

In this example, the phrase **512 MIN** "clips" the specified number of samples at 512. As in the example of **SHOW** above, the phrase **I CELLS** converts the loop counter (in samples) into a byte offset to be added to the address of the start of the block. **BUFFER** cannot be used in this case, because we are adding samples one at a time and must preserve previous samples written in the block.

Because **BLOCK** maps disk contents into memory, *virtual memory* applications are simple. The first step is to write a word to transform an application address into a physical address consisting of a block number and an offset within that block. For a virtual byte array, such a definition is:

```
: VIRTUAL ( i -- a )        \ Return the addr of the ith byte
   1024 /MOD                \ Q=blk offset, R=byte in block
     250 +                  \ Add starting blk#=250
   BLOCK + ;                \ Fetch block, add byte offset
```

Here, 1024 is the number of bytes per disk block and 250 is the block number where the virtual array starts. The array may occupy any number of blocks, limited only by physical mass storage constraints.

Fetch and store operations for this virtual memory scheme are defined as:

```
: V@ ( i -- n )     \ Return ith byte in the array
    VIRTUAL C@ ;

: V! ( b i -- )     \ Store b in ith byte
    VIRTUAL C!  UPDATE ;
```

BLOCK does not normally perform any error checking or retries at the primitive level, because an appropriate error response is fundamentally application-dependent. Some applications processing critical data in non-real-time (e.g., accounting applications) should attempt retries[1] and, if these fail, stop with an error message identifying bad data. But applications running continuously at a constant sampling rate (e.g., data loggers) cannot afford to wait and should simply log errors.

1. Most disk controllers and all OSs perform retries automatically. On these, there is nothing to be gained by attempting retries from within a Forth application.

Glossary

BLOCK (u — addr) Block

Return the address of a buffer containing a copy of the contents of block *u*, having read it from disk, if necessary. If a read occurred, the previous contents of the buffer is first written to disk, if the buffer has been marked as updated.

BUFFER (u – addr) Block

Return the address of a buffer marked to contain block *u*, having written its previous contents to disk, if necessary (does not perform any read operation).

UPDATE (–) Block

Mark the most recently referenced buffer as having been updated. The contents of a buffer that has been marked in this way will be written to disk when its buffer is needed for a different block.

FLUSH (–) Block

Ensure that all updated buffers are written to disk, and free all the buffers.

SAVE-BUFFERS (—) Block

Write all updated buffers to disk, leaving them in memory but with their **UPDATE** flags cleared.

EMPTY-BUFFERS (–) Block Ext

Erase all block buffers without saving them. **EMPTY-BUFFERS** works by clearing the update bits in all buffers and performing a **FLUSH** to free the buffers.

C.2 Loading Forth Source Blocks

Most compiled languages require a three-step process to construct executable programs:

1. Compile the program to an object file on disk.
2. Link this program to other previously compiled and/or assembled routines.
3. Load the result into memory.

This often-lengthy procedure hampers programmer effectiveness. Forth supports fully interactive programming by shortening this cycle to a single, fast operation: it compiles from source code to executable form in memory. This process is accomplished by the word **LOAD**.

C.2.1 The LOAD Operation

LOAD specifies interpretation of source text from a disk block. It expects on top of the stack the block number of the Forth block to be loaded:

```
<number> LOAD
```

This block number is also stored in the variable **BLK**, used by Forth's text interpreter. If **BLK** contains zero, the source is not a block and usually is the terminal. When **BLK** is zero, the word **SOURCE-ID** returns a value indicating the input source (zero if it is the user input device or terminal, -1 if it is a character string passed by **EVALUATE**, and optionally a file-identifier if the input is a text file—see Section 5.5). A consequence of this convention is that Block 0 cannot be used for source text.

When **LOAD** is encountered, interpretation of text from the current input source is suspended and input is taken from the specified disk block. The text interpreter starts at the beginning and processes each word until it reaches the end of the block (after 1024 characters). On some systems, if the word **EXIT** is encountered interpretively in the block, it will cause processing to terminate at once.

When all processing specified by the disk block is complete—assuming no errors were encountered while processing the block—execution resumes with input from the source that was in control when the **LOAD** was encountered.

If a block contains definitions, the result of a **LOAD** operation will be to process them via the text interpreter and compile them into the dictionary. The process of **LOAD**ing disk blocks is identical to processing the same information entered at the terminal or loaded from a text file, but all information in a single disk block is processed as a single string (i.e., there will be no embedded carriage returns).

The block to be loaded may itself contain a **LOAD** command, at which point the loading of the first block is suspended. When this occurs, the current block number and text interpreter pointers are saved on the return stack, pending loading of the requested block. This nested loading process may continue indefinitely, subject to return stack size.

A group of blocks to be loaded should be specified by **LOAD** commands contained in a single block, called a *load block*, as opposed to serial nesting (i.e., having each block load the next block in sequence). From a management viewpoint, loading groups of related blocks from a single load block aids readability and maintainability.

The command **THRU** can load a group of sequential blocks. For example, if blocks 260 through 270 need to be loaded:

```
260 270 THRU
```

A **LOAD** operation may also be compiled in a definition, in which case the requested **LOAD** is done when the definition is executed. Following the **LOAD**, execution will resume at the word immediately after **LOAD**.

If an error is detected during the loading process, an error message is produced and all loading ceases. Both the return stack and the data stack are cleared, and Forth reverts to terminal input.

During loading, all text interpreter input is taken from the specified disk block. All output, however, proceeds to its normal destination. Thus, **.** ("dot") or other output commands will send output to the terminal of the task executing the **LOAD**.

Glossary

BLK `( – a-addr )` Block

Return *a-addr*, the address of a cell containing the number of the mass-storage block being interpreted, or zero if the current input source is not a block. "B-L-K"

LOAD `( i*x u – j*x )` Block

Save the current input source specification in a system-specific manner. Store *u* in the variable **BLK**, thus making block *u* the input source. Set the input buffer to contain the contents of block *u*. Set the buffer pointer **>IN** to zero and interpret the buffer contents. When the parse area is exhausted, restore the prior input specification. Any other stack effects are due to the words executed as a result of the **LOAD**.

THRU `( i*x u1 u2 – j*x )` Block Ext

Execute **LOAD** in sequence for each of the blocks numbered u_1 through u_2. Any other stack effects are due to the words executed as a result of the **LOAD**s.

References

EXIT, Section 4.9
Input source identification, Section 6.1.1
Text file identifiers, Section 5.5.1

C.2.2 Named Program Blocks

The defining word **CONSTANT** may be used to give names to important blocks, such as load blocks, which load other blocks to form a utility or application. For example, define:

```
120 CONSTANT OBSERVING
```

...which will be used as:

```
OBSERVING LOAD
```

The above has the effect of loading block 120 and executing any other **LOAD** instructions specified in that block.

CONSTANT is particularly appropriate when you want to use the name in additional ways, such as:

```
OBSERVING LIST
```

We recommend the use of a *key block* for each major section of an application. The key block should primarily load other associated blocks, specified numerically or through constants; it may also contain other brief, application-wide definitions. Then you can see at a glance which of your application blocks are loaded, and in what order.

This technique is much safer than *chaining* blocks (i.e., serial nesting), which can cause return-stack overflow. Generally, a single block naming all key blocks in the system is loaded immediately after booting.

A convenient side effect of named blocks is that they can be successfully **LOAD**ed regardless of the current number conversion base. But, for this reason, named key blocks should have a **DECIMAL** command in the first line to guard against incorrect loading of subsidiary blocks due to an unexpected current base.

References

CONSTANT, Section 2.3.2.2
LOAD and the return stack, Section C.2.1
LIST, Section C.3

C.3 Block-based Programmer Aids and Utilities

As a consequence of its standalone heritage, Forth has traditionally accompanied its block-based systems with a rich portfolio of programmer aids and utilities. These will vary depending upon the implementation, but a fully supported block system will normally include:

- **An editor.** Traditional Forth block editors format a block in 16 lines of 64 characters each, a convenient size on most displays. By convention, the first line of each block includes a comment summarizing the contents of that block. The balance of the block should contain a few simple definitions related to its stated objective. Most block editors provide a command line and are string oriented. Some are quite powerful; all include the basic command **LIST** to display a block, and the variable **SCR** which contains the number of the block most recently **LIST**ed.
- **Shadow-block, on-line documentation.** Space within a block is limited, so comments are conventionally kept in a separate block and the system pairs each source block with its "shadow." From a keyboard, you should be able to toggle between a source block and its shadow. Shadow blocks are not compiled or executed.
- **Program-listing utilities.** Typical systems include a utility to print indexes (the first, or comment, line from each of a range of blocks) and lists of blocks. Depending on the printer, normally it is possible to print a source and shadow block pair side-by-side, with three pairs on a page.
- **Disk-management utilities.** These include simple functions for moving blocks and their associated shadows, initializing regions of disk, browsing a disk (displaying the first-line comments), etc.
- **Source-block comparison utilities.** Comparison utilities that highlight differences between ranges of similar blocks are extremely helpful on multi-programmer projects when work has to be merged from several sources.
- **Programmer aids.** The words described in Section 1.4 (page 38)

are normally available on block-based systems. **LOCATE**, for example, will show the block from which a word was compiled; with one keystroke, you can display its associated shadow block.

Consult your product documentation for further details regarding your system's features.

Glossary

LIST (u –) Block Ext
Display block *u* in a system-dependent format (usually 16 lines of 64 characters each). Store *u* in the variable **SCR**.

SCR (– a-addr) Block Ext
Return *a-addr*, the address of a cell containing the block number of the most recently **LIST**ed block. "S-C-R"

C.4 Style Guidelines for Block-based Source

The purpose of this section is to describe a set of editing standards used to ensure the readability and notational consistency of block-based Forth source code.

C.4.1 Stack Effects

1. Any colon or code definition which expects or leaves data stack arguments must include a comment identifying them.
2. The format of the comment is:

   ```
   ( input -- output )
   ```

   ...with the rightmost item on each side of the dash representing the top item on the stack. If there is input but no output, you may omit the dash.

   Example 1, input only:
   ```
   : TYPE ( addr n -- )
   ```
   Example 2, output only:
   ```
   : -FOUND ( -- addr addr' flag )
   ```
   Example 3, input and output:
   ```
   CODE @ ( addr -- n )
   ```
3. The stack comment begins one space after the name of the word.

Remember to leave one space after the opening `(`. The terminating parenthesis should follow the last character without an intervening space. Exactly three spaces follow the right parenthesis before the code begins, if it begins on the same line.

4. The specific notation used to represent each stack item should follow these conventions:

`addr`	address
`b`	eight-bit byte
`c`	ASCII character
`n`	single-precision number, usually signed
`u`	single-precision unsigned number
`flag`	Boolean truth flag (0=*false*)

The following special cases should be used when appropriate:

`l c`	screen position, in lines and columns (in that order)
`s d n`	source, destination, count (in that order)
`y x`	2-vector (*x,y* coordinate pairs, e.g., for graphics)
`f l`	first, last limits; inclusive
`f l+1`	first, last limits; exclusive at end
`c t`	cylinder, track (for disk drivers)

Other special situations may be dealt with similarly, if necessary to improve clarity, but use single characters where possible.

5. Where several arguments are of the same type and clarity demands that they be distinguished, use `'` (prime) or suffix numerals. For example:

```
CODE RSWAP ( n addr addr' -- n addr )
CODE RSWAP ( n addr1 addr2 -- n addr1)
```

...both show that the address returned is the same as the first one input.

C.4.2 General Comments

1. All source files must start with a comment succinctly describing their contents. Examples of good and bad style follow:

good:
```
( Double-precision arithmetic)
```
wordy:
```
( This code contains double-precision operators)
```
useless:
```
( Misc. OPS)
```

2. Comments within source (other than stack effects) should be restricted to situations in which a serious ambiguity needs to be resolved.

   good:

   177566 `( Send +2)` *and* **177562** `( RCV+2)`

   redundant:

   DUP 0= ABORT" Value is zero" `( Aborts if zero)`

   not helpful:

   S) 0 MOV `( Move top of stack to R0)`

3. Comments should begin with a capital letter and otherwise be lower case, except as standard usage indicates, e.g.,

```
( Defining words)
( RX01 Bootstrap)
```

C.4.3 Spacing Within Source

1. Blank lines within source are valuable. Use them to separate definitions or groups of definitions. Avoid a dense clump of lines at the top of a file with a lot of blank lines below, unless the clump is a single definition. Never have two blank lines together except at the end.
2. Definitions should begin in the left-most column of a line, except that two or three related **VARIABLE**s, **CONSTANT**s, or other data items may share a line if there is room for three spaces between them.
3. The name of a definition must be separated from its defining word by only one space. If it is a **CONSTANT** or other data item with a specified value, the value must be separated from the defining word by only one space.
4. Within a colon definition, three spaces are required after the stack comment. Thereafter, words are separated by one space, except when a second space is added between groups of closely related words.
5. Second and subsequent lines of colon and **CODE** definitions must be indented by multiples of three spaces (e.g., 3, 6, 9). Indentation beyond one set of three spaces indicates nested structures.

Examples of Forth in documentation should conform to these rules.

APPENDIX D: INDEX TO FORTH WORDS

This section provides an alphabetical index to the Forth words in the glossaries of this book. Each is shown with its stack arguments and a page reference where you may find more information.

Stack operations are described in Section 2.1. The stack-argument notation is described in Appendix B, Table 16. Where several arguments are of the same type, and clarity demands that they be distinguished, numeric subscripts are used.

On the following pages, the "Wordset" column identifies the Standard Forth word list in which each word appears. "Core" words are required in all Standard Forth systems. Words marked "Common usage" are not mentioned in Standard Forth but may be found in many Forth systems. All other designations represent optional Standard Forth wordsets (groupings by logical function) that may be present in some systems. You may use **ENVIRONMENT?** (Section 5.2) to determine whether a particular optional wordset is present.

Word	Stack	Wordset	Pg
(	(–)	Core, File	40
.(	(–)	Core Ext	40
+	(n1 n2 – n3)	Core	55
-	(n1 n2 – n3)	Core	56
,	(x –)	Core	68
.	(n –)	Core	88
,	(x –)	Cross	201
1+	(n1 – n2)	Core	56
1-	(n1 – n2)	Core	56
2+	(n1 – n2)	Common usage	56
2-	(n1 – n2)	Common usage	56
' <name>	(– xt)	Core	116
' <name>	(– xt)	Core	162
!	(x a-addr –)	Core	70
#	(ud1 – ud2)	Core	92

Word	Stack	Wordset	Pg
#>	(ud – c-addr u)	Core	92
#S	(ud1 – ud2)	Core	92
*****	(n1 n2 – n3)	Core	55
***/**	(n1 n2 n3 – n4)	Core	55
***/MOD**	(n1 n2 n3 – n4 n5)	Core	55
," <string>"	(–)	Common usage	79
.'	(addr –)	Common usage	43
." <string>"	(–)	Core	78
.R	(n1 +n2 –)	Core Ext	89
.S	(–)	Tools	53
/	(n1 n2 – n3)	Core	56
/MOD	(n1 n2 – n3 n4)	Core	56
/STRING	(c-addr1 u1 n – c-addr2 u2)	String	81
: <name>	(–)	Core	168
:NONAME	(– xt)	Core Ext	168
;	(–)	Core	168
;CODE	(–)	Tools Ext	172
?	(a-addr –)	Tools	53
?	(a-addr –)	Tools	89
?DO	(n1 n2 –)	Core Ext	108
?DUP	(x – 0 | x x)	Core	49
@	(a-addr – x)	Core	70
@EXECUTE	(i*x addr – j*x)	Common usage	116
[	(–)	Core	178
['] <name>	(– xt)	Core	116
['] <name>	(– xt)	Core	162
[CHAR] <c>	(– char)	Core	74
[DEFINED] <name>	(– flag)	Common usage	163
[ELSE]	(–)	Tools Ext	164
[IF]	(flag –)	Tools Ext	164
[THEN]	(–)	Tools Ext	164

Word	Stack	Wordset	Pg
[UNDEFINED] <name>	(– flag)	Common usage	164
****	(–)	Block Ext, Core Ext	40
]	(–)	Core	178
+!	(n a-addr –)	Core	70
+LOOP	(n –)	Core	108
<	(n1 n2 – flag)	Core	98
<#	(ud – ud) *or* (n ud – n ud)	Core	92
<>	(n1 n2 – flag)	Core Ext	98
=	(n1 n2 – flag)	Core	98
>	(n1 n2 – flag)	Core	98
>BODY	(xt – a-addr)	Core	162
>FLOAT	(c-addr u – true | false); (F: – r |)	Floating	153
>IN	(– a-addr)	Core	157
>NUMBER	(ud1 c-addr1 u1 – ud2 c-addr2 u2)	Core	86
>R	(S: x –) (R: – x)	Core	52
0<	(n – flag)	Core	98
0<>	(n – flag)	Core Ext	98
0=	(n – flag)	Core	98
0>	(n – flag)	Core Ext	98
2!	(x1 x2 a-addr –)	Core	70
2*	(x1 – x2)	Core	56
2/	(x1 – x2)	Core	56
2@	(a-addr – x1 x2)	Core	70
2>R	(S: x1 x2 –) (R: – x1 x2)	Core Ext	52
2CONSTANT <name>	(x1 x2 –)	Double	65
2DROP	(x1 x2 –)	Core	51

Word	Stack	Wordset	Pg
2DUP	(x1 x2 – x1 x2 x1 x2)	Core	51
2LITERAL	(– x1 x2)	Double	180
2OVER	(x1 x2 x3 x4 – x1 x2 x3 x4 x1 x2)	Core	51
2R@	(S: – x1 x2) (R: x1 x2 – x1 x2)	Core Ext	52
2R>	(S: – x1 x2) (R: x1 x2 –)	Core Ext	52
2ROT	(x1 x2 x3 x4 x5 x6 – x3 x4 x5 x6 x1 x2)	Double ext	51
2SWAP	(x1 x2 x3 x4 – x3 x4 x1 x2)	Core	51
2VARIABLE <name>	(–)	Double	63
ABORT	(i*x –); (R: j*x –)	Core, Exception Ext	127
ABORT" <text>"	(i*x flag –); (R: j*x –)	Core, Exception Ext	127
ABS	(n — +n)	Core	59
ACCEPT	(c-addr +n1 – +n2)	Core	129
AGAIN	(–)	Core Ext	105
AGAIN	(–)	Core Ext	184
AHEAD	(– orig)	Tools Ext	188
ALIGN	(–)	Core	68
ALIGN	(–)	Cross	201
ALIGNED	(addr – a-addr)	Core	68
ALLOCATE	(u – a-addr ior)	Memory	139
ALLOT	(u –)	Core	68
ALLOT	(u –)	Core	166
ALLOT	(n –)	Cross	200
ALSO	(–)	Search Ext	192
AND	(x1 x2 – x3)	Core	59
ASSEMBLER	(–)	Tools Ext	192
AT-XY	(u1 u2 –)	Facility	132
BASE	(– a-addr)	Core	30

Word	Stack	Wordset	Pg
BEGIN	(–)	Core	105
BIN	(fam1 – fam2)	File	137
BL	(– char)	Core	74
BL	(– char)	Core	161
BLANK	(c-addr u –)	Core	70
BLK	(– a-addr)	Block	156
BLK	(– a-addr)	Block	254
BLOCK	(u — addr)	Block	252
BUFFER	(u – addr)	Block	252
BUFFER: <name>	(n –)	Common usage	68
C!	(c c-addr –)	Core	71
C" <string>"	(– c-addr)	Core Ext	78
C,	(char –)	Core	69
C,	(b –)	Cross	201
C@	(c-addr – c)	Core	71
C+!	(c c-addr –)	Common usage	71
CASE	(–)	Core Ext	111
CATCH	(i*x xt – j*x 0 | i*x n)	Exception	127
CELL+	(a-addr1 – a-addr2)	Core	69
CELLS	(n1 – n2)	Core	69
CHAR <c>	(– char)	Core	74
CHAR+	(c-addr1 – c-addr2)	Core	69
CHARS	(n1 – n2)	Core	69
CLOSE-FILE	(fileid – ior)	File	134
CMOVE	(c-addr1 c-addr2 u –)	String	82
CMOVE>	(c-addr1 c-addr2 u –)	String	82
COMPARE	(c-addr1 u1 c-addr2 u2 – n)	String	84
COMPILE,	(xt –)	Core Ext	178
CONSTANT <name>	(x –)	Core	65
CONTEXT	(– a-addr)	Core	192
COUNT	(c-addr1 – c-addr2 u)	Core	76

Word	Stack	Wordset	Pg
CR	(–)	Core	133
CREATE <name>	(–)	Core	69
CREATE <name>	(–)	Core	166
CREATE-FILE	(c-addr u fam – fileid ior)	Core	134
CS-PICK	(i*x u – i*x xu)	Tools Ext	188
CS-ROLL	(i*x u – (i-1)*x xu)	Tools Ext	188
CURRENT	(– a-addr)	Common usage	192
CVARIABLE <name>	(–)	Common usage	63
D-	(d1 d2 – d3)	Double	57
D.	(d –)	Double	89
D.R	(d +n –)	Double	89
D+	(d1 d2 – d3)	Double	57
D<	(d1 d2 – flag)	Double	99
D=	(d1 d2 – flag)	Double	99
D>F	(d –); (F: – r)	Floating	146
D>S	(d – n)	Double	57
D0<	(d – flag)	Double	99
D0=	(d – flag)	Double	99
D2*	(d1 – d2)	Double	57
D2/	(d1 – d2)	Double	57
DABS	(d – +d)	Double	60
DASM	(addr –)	Common usage	43
DECIMAL	(–)	Core	31
DEFER <name>	(–)	Common usage	118
DEFINITIONS	(–)	Search	193
DELETE-FILE	(c-addr u – ior)	File	135
DEPTH	(– +n)	Core	49
DF!	(df-addr –); (F: r –)	Floating Ext	145
DF@	(df-addr –); (F: – r)	Floating Ext	145
DFALIGN	(–)	Floating Ext	152

Word	Stack	Wordset	Pg
DFALIGNED	(addr — df-addr)	Floating Ext	152
DFLOAT+	(df-addr1 – df-addr2)	Floating Ext	152
DFLOATS	(n1 – n2)	Floating Ext	152
DMAX	(d1 d2 – d3)	Double	60
DMIN	(d1 d2 – d3)	Double	60
DNEGATE	(d – -d)	Double	60
DO	(n1 n2 –)	Core	108
DOES>	(–)	Core	172
DROP	(x –)	Core	50
DU<	(ud1 ud2 – flag)	Double Ext	99
DUMP	(addr +n –)	Tools	53
DUP	(x – x x)	Core	50
EDITOR	(–)	Tools Ext	193
EKEY	(– u)	Facility Ext	130
EKEY?	(– flag)	Facility Ext	130
EKEY>CHAR	(u – u 0 | char -1)	Facility Ext	130
ELSE	(–)	Core	101
ELSE	(–)	Core	185
EMIT	(b –)	Core	132
EMIT?	(– flag)	Facility Ext	132
EMPTY-BUFFERS	(–)	Block Ext	252
ENDCASE	(x –)	Core Ext	111
ENDOF	(–)	Core Ext	111
ENVIRONMENT?	(c-addr u – false | i*x true)	Core	53
ENVIRONMENT?	(c-addr u – false | i*x true)	Core	123
ERASE	(c-addr u –)	Core Ext	71
EVALUATE	(i*x c-addr u – j*x)	Core, Block	157
EXECUTE	(i*x xt – j*x)	Core	116
EXIT	(–); (R: nest-sys –)	Core	113
F-	(F: r1 r2 – r3)	Floating	147

Word	Stack	Wordset	Pg
F!	(f-addr –); (F: r –)	Floating	145
F*	(F: r1 r2 – r3)	Floating	147
F**	(F: r1 r2 – r3)	Floating Ext	147
F.	(F: r –)	Floating Ext	143
F/	(F: r1 r2 – r3)	Floating	147
F@	(f-addr –); (F: – r)	Floating	145
F~	(– flag); (F: r1 r2 r3 –)	Floating Ext	148
F+	(F: r1 r2 – r3)	Floating	147
F<	(– flag); (F: r1 r2 –)	Floating	148
F>D	(– d); (F: r –)	Floating	146
F0<	(– flag); (F: r –)	Floating	148
F0=	(– flag); (F: r –)	Floating	148
FABS	(F: r1 – r2)	Floating Ext	147
FACOS	(F: r1 – r2)	Floating Ext	149
FACOSH	(F: r1 – r2)	Floating Ext	149
FALIGN	(–)	Floating	152
FALIGNED	(addr – f-addr)	Floating	152
FALOG	(F: r1 – r2)	Floating Ext	149
FALSE	(– flag)	Core Ext	99
FASIN	(F: r1 – r2)	Floating Ext	149
FASINH	(F: r1 – r2)	Floating Ext	149
FATAN	(F: r1 – r2)	Floating Ext	149
FATAN2	(F: r1 r2 – r3)	Floating Ext	150
FATANH	(F: r1 – r2)	Floating Ext	150
FCONSTANT <name>	(F: r –)	Floating	144
FCOS	(F: r1 – r2)	Floating Ext	150
FCOSH	(F: r1 – r2)	Floating Ext	150
FDEPTH	(– +n)	Floating	146
FDROP	(F: r –)	Floating	146

Word	Stack	Wordset	Pg
FDUP	(F: r – r r)	Floating	146
FE.	(F: r –)	Floating Ext	143
FEXP	(F: r1 – r2)	Floating Ext	150
FEXPM1	(F: r1 – r2)	Floating Ext	150
FILE-POSITION	(fileid – ud ior)	File	137
FILE-SIZE	(fileid – ud ior)	File	137
FILE-STATUS	(c-addr u – x ior)	File Ext	137
FILL	(c-addr u b –)	Core	71
FIND	(c-addr — c-addr 0 | xt 1 | xt -1)	Core, Search	162
FLITERAL	(F: r –)	Floating	144
FLN	(F: r1 – r2)	Floating Ext	150
FLNP1	(F: r1 – r2)	Floating Ext	150
FLOAT+	(f-addr1 – f-addr2)	Floating	152
FLOATS	(n1 – n2)	Floating	152
FLOG	(F: r1 – r2)	Floating Ext	150
FLOOR	(F: r1 – r2)	Floating Ext	147
FLUSH	(–)	Block	252
FLUSH-FILE	(fileid – ior)	File Ext	135
FM/MOD	(d n1 – n2 n3)	Core	57
FMAX	(F: r1 r2 – r3)	Floating	147
FMIN	(F: r1 r2 – r3)	Floating	147
FNEGATE	(F: r1 – r2)	Floating	148
FORTH	(–)	Search Ext	193
FOVER	(F: r1 r2 – r1 r2 r1)	Floating	146
FREE	(a-addr – ior)	Memory	139
FROT	(F: r1 r2 r3 – r2 r3 r1)	Floating	147
FROUND	(F: r1 – r2)	Floating	148
FS.	(F: r –)	Floating Ext	143
FSIN	(F: r1 – r2)	Floating Ext	150
FSINCOS	(F: r1 – r2 r3)	Floating Ext	150
FSINH	(F: r1 – r2)	Floating Ext	151

Word	Stack	Wordset	Pg
FSQRT	(F: r1 – r2)	Floating Ext	148
FSWAP	(F: r1 r2 – r2 r1)	Floating	147
FTAN	(F: r1 – r2)	Floating Ext	151
FTANH	(F: r1 – r2)	Floating Ext	151
FVARIABLE <name>	(–)	Floating	144
GET-XY	(– u1 u2)	Common usage	133
HERE	(– addr)	Core	82
HERE	(– addr)	Cross	200
HEX	(–)	Core Ext	31
HOLD	(char –)	Core	94
I	(– n)	Core	108
IF	(x –)	Core	101
IF	(x –)	Core	185
IMMEDIATE	(–)	Core	186
INCLUDE <filename>	(–)	Common usage	136
INCLUDED	(c-addr u –)	File	136
INCLUDE-FILE	(fileid –)	File	135
INVERT	(x1 – x2)	Core	59
IS <defer-name>	(xt –)	Common usage	118
J	(– n)	Core	109
KEY	(– b)	Core	130
KEY?	(– flag)	Facility	130
LEAVE	(–)	Core	109
LIST	(u –)	Block Ext	257
LITERAL	(– x)	Core	180
LOAD	(i*x u – j*x)	Block	254
LOCATE <name>	(–)	Common usage	41
LOOP	(–)	Core	108
LSHIFT	(x1 u – x2)	Core	56
M-	(d1 n – d2)	Common usage	58
M*	(n1 n2 – d)	Core	57
M*/	(d1 n1 +n2 – d2)	Double	58

<table>
<tr><th>Word</th><th>Stack</th><th>Wordset</th><th>Pg</th></tr>
<tr><td>M/</td><td>(d n1 – n2)</td><td>Common usage</td><td>58</td></tr>
<tr><td>M+</td><td>(d1 n – d2)</td><td>Double</td><td>58</td></tr>
<tr><td>MARKER <name></td><td>(–)</td><td>Core Ext</td><td>190</td></tr>
<tr><td>MAX</td><td>(n1 n2 – n3)</td><td>Core</td><td>59</td></tr>
<tr><td>MIN</td><td>(n1 n2 – n3)</td><td>Core</td><td>59</td></tr>
<tr><td>MOD</td><td>(n1 n2 – n3)</td><td>Core</td><td>56</td></tr>
<tr><td>MOVE</td><td>(addr1 addr2 u –)</td><td>Core</td><td>71</td></tr>
<tr><td>MS</td><td>(u –)</td><td>Facility Ext</td><td>138</td></tr>
<tr><td>NEGATE</td><td>(n – -n)</td><td>Core</td><td>59</td></tr>
<tr><td>NIP</td><td>(x1 x2 – x2)</td><td>Core Ext</td><td>50</td></tr>
<tr><td>NOT</td><td>(x – flag)</td><td>Common usage</td><td>99</td></tr>
<tr><td>NUMBER</td><td>(c-addr u – n | d)</td><td>Common usage</td><td>87</td></tr>
<tr><td>NUMBER?</td><td>(a n - 0 | n 1 | d 2)</td><td>Common usage</td><td>87</td></tr>
<tr><td>OF</td><td>(x1 x2 – | x1)</td><td>Core Ext</td><td>111</td></tr>
<tr><td>ONLY</td><td>(–)</td><td>Search Ext</td><td>193</td></tr>
<tr><td>OPEN-FILE</td><td>(c-addr u fam –
fileid ior)</td><td>File</td><td>135</td></tr>
<tr><td>OR</td><td>(x1 x2 – x3)</td><td>Core</td><td>59</td></tr>
<tr><td>ORDER</td><td>(–)</td><td>Search Ext</td><td>193</td></tr>
<tr><td>ORG</td><td>(addr –)</td><td>Cross</td><td>200</td></tr>
<tr><td>OVER</td><td>(x1 x2 – x1 x2 x1)</td><td>Core</td><td>50</td></tr>
<tr><td>PAD</td><td>(– addr)</td><td>Core Ext</td><td>75</td></tr>
<tr><td>PAGE</td><td>(–)</td><td>Facility</td><td>133</td></tr>
<tr><td>PARSE <text></td><td>(char – c-addr n)</td><td>Core Ext</td><td>161</td></tr>
<tr><td>PICK</td><td>(+n – x)</td><td>Core Ext</td><td>50</td></tr>
<tr><td>POSTPONE <name></td><td>(–)</td><td>Core</td><td>186</td></tr>
<tr><td>PRECISION</td><td>(– u)</td><td>Floating Ext</td><td>143</td></tr>
<tr><td>PREVIOUS</td><td>(–)</td><td>Search Ext</td><td>193</td></tr>
<tr><td>QUIT</td><td>(i*x –);
(R: j*x –)</td><td>Core</td><td>158</td></tr>
<tr><td>R/O</td><td>(– fam)</td><td>File</td><td>138</td></tr>
<tr><td>R/W</td><td>(– fam)</td><td>File</td><td>138</td></tr>
<tr><td>R@</td><td>(S: – x) (R: x – x)</td><td>Core</td><td>52</td></tr>
</table>

Word	Stack	Wordset	Pg
R>	(S: – x) (R: x –)	Core	52
READ-FILE	(c-addr u1 fileid – u2 ior)	File	136
READ-LINE	(c-addr u1 fileid – u2 flag ior)	File	136
RECURSE	(–)	Core	168
REFILL	(– flag)	Block Ext, Core Ext, File Ext	136
REFILL	(– flag)	Block Ext, Core Ext, File Ext	158
RENAME-FILE	(c-addr1 u1 c-addr2 u2 – ior)	File Ext	135
REPEAT	(–)	Core	105
REPEAT	(–)	Core	185
REPOSITION-FILE	(ud fileid – ior)	File	138
REPRESENT	(c-addr u – n flag1 flag2); (F: r –)	Floating	153
RESIZE	(a-addr1 u – a-addr2 ior)	Memory	139
RESIZE-FILE	(ud fileid – ior)	File	135
RESTORE-INPUT	(xn … x1 n – flag)	Core Ext	158
ROT	(x1 x2 x3 – x2 x3 x1)	Core	50
RSHIFT	(x1 u – x2)	Core	56
S" <string>"	(– c-addr u)	Core, File	78
S" <string>"	(– c-addr u)	Core, File	138
S>D	(n – d)	Core	58
SAVE-BUFFERS	(—)	Block	252
SAVE-INPUT	(– xn … x1 n)	Core Ext	158
SCR	(– a-addr)	Block Ext	257
SEARCH	(c-addr1 u1 c-addr2 u2 – c-addr3 u3 flag)	String	84
SEE <name>	(–)	Tools	43

Word	Stack	Wordset	Pg
SET-PRECISION	(u –)	Floating Ext	143
SF!	(sf-addr –); (F: r –)	Floating Ext	145
SF@	(sf-addr –); (F: – r)	Floating Ext	146
SFALIGN	(–)	Floating Ext	152
SFALIGNED	(addr – sf-addr)	Floating Ext	152
SFLOAT+	(sf-addr1 – sf-addr2)	Floating Ext	152
SFLOATS	(n1 – n2)	Floating Ext	153
SIGN	(n –)	Core	92
SLITERAL	(– c-addr u)	String	181
SM/REM	(d n1 – n2 n3)	Core	58
SOURCE	(– c-addr u)	Core	159
SOURCE-ID	(– n)	Core Ext, File	156
SPACE	(–)	Core	133
SPACES	(u –)	Core	133
STATE	(– a-addr)	Core, Tools Ext	178
SWAP	(x1 x2 – x2 x1)	Core	50
THEN	(–)	Core	101
THEN	(–)	Core	185
THROW	(k*x n – k*x | i*x n)	Exception	127
THRU	(i*x u1 u2 – j*x)	Block Ext	254
TIME&DATE	(– u1 u2 u3 u4 u5 u6)	Facility Ext	138
TO <name>	(x –)	Core Ext	71
-TRAILING	(c-addr u1 – c-addr u2)	String	81
TRUE	(– flag)	Core Ext	99
TUCK	(x1 x2 – x2 x1 x2)	Core Ext	50
TYPE	(c-addr u –)	Core	132
U.	(u –)	Core	89
U.R	(u +n –)	Core Ext	89
U<	(u1 u2 – flag)	Core	99
U>	(u1 u2 – flag)	Core Ext	99

Word	Stack	Wordset	Pg
UM*	(u1 u2 – ud)	Core	58
UM/MOD	(ud u1 – u2 u3)	Core	58
UNLOOP	(–)	Core	109
UNTIL	(x –)	Core	105
UNTIL	(x –)	Core	185
UNUSED	(– u)	Core Ext	166
UPDATE	(–)	Block	252
VALUE <name>	(x –)	Core Ext	65
VARIABLE <name>	(–)	Core	63
VOCABULARY <name>	(–)	Common usage	193
W/O	(– fam)	File	138
WH <name>	(–)	Common usage	41
WHERE <name>	(–)	Common usage	41
WHILE	(x –)	Core	105
WHILE	(x –)	Core	186
WITHIN	(x1 x2 x3 – flag)	Core	59
WORD <text>	(char – c-addr)	Core	161
WORDS	(–)	Tools	53
WORDS	(–)	Tools	193
WRITE-FILE	(c-addr u fileid – ior)	File	137
WRITE-LINE	(c-addr u fileid – ior)	File	137
XOR	(x1 x2 – x3)	Core	59

General Index

See also *Appendix D: Index to Forth Words.*

www.ingramcontent.com/pod-product-compliance
Lightning Source LLC
Chambersburg PA
CBHW071545080326
40689CB00061B/1843
9781419675492